Unsung Heroes of
The Lord of the Rings

Unsung Heroes of
The Lord of the Rings

From the Page to the Screen

Lynnette R. Porter

PRAEGER

Westport, Connecticut
London

Library of Congress Cataloging-in-Publication Data

Porter, Lynnette R., 1957–
 Unsung heroes of the lord of the rings : from the page to the screen / Lynnette R. Porter.
  p. cm.
 Includes bibliographical references (p.) and index.
 ISBN 0-275-98521-0 (alk. paper)
  1. Tolkien, J. R. R. (John Ronald Reuel), 1892–1973. Lord of the rings. 2. Tolkien,
J. R. R. (John Ronald Reuel), 1892–1973—Film and video adaptations. 3. Tolkien, J. R. R.
(John Ronald Reuel), 1892–1973—Characters—Heroes. 4. Fantasy fiction, English—
History and criticism. 5. Lord of the Rings films—History and criticism. 6. Middle
Earth (Imaginary place) 7. Heroes in motion pictures. 8. Heroes in literature. I. Title.
PR6039.O32L6313 2005
828'.91309—dc22   2004028035

British Library Cataloguing in Publication Data is available.

Library of Congress Card Number: 2004028035

ISBN: 0-275-98521-0

First published in 2005

Praeger Publishers, 88 Post Road West, Westport, CT 06881
An imprint of Greenwood Publishing Group, Inc.
www.praeger.com

Printed in the United States of America

The paper used in this book complies with the
Permanent Paper Standard issued by the National
Information Standards Organization (Z39.48-1984).

10 9 8 7 6 5 4 3 2 1

Contents

Contents

Preface

As the news media persistently tell us, the world is a different place than it was prior to September 11, 2001. Even within our seemingly safe homes or communities, danger is more tangible, and the publics in many Western countries have drawn together, in doubt or defiance or both. Local heroes seem more important, and media outlets take more time to highlight the heroics of the "little people"—those everyday firefighters, police officers, bus drivers, train commuters, teachers, grandmothers, and so on who act bravely in moments of crisis. Many U.S. cities feature local heroes in special ceremonies to honor their deeds; they are made Grand Marshals of holiday parades, or they speak as role models before civic and school groups.

Even as communities within countries pull together, the world seems ever more divided into camps of "good" or "evil." Simplifying the world into black or white makes political rhetoric easier, but it does not explain the complex issues surrounding the widening divisions between "us" and "them." Large-scale international conflict seems inevitable under these conditions, and people living in such a world look for heroes who will do what is right, even when they face censure.

In a world that at once seems larger, fraught with potential international peril, and smaller, as communities draw closer in crisis or crisis preparation/prevention, heroes are especially important. However, the focus is not on kings, queens, presidents, prime ministers, or other national leaders. Instead the "everyperson" hero is celebrated more often, and individuals can only hope they might act as courageously or responsibly if they face an overwhelming, unexpected danger. The everyperson hero acts during a crisis, whether that be on a battlefield or in the corner convenience store. Everyperson heroes may face danger on the job, or take on a difficult task with little hope of success—all to help others. Everyperson heroes take on the jobs no one else wants to do, or they jump in to make a difference in a critical situation. These heroes are especially important when the world seems to change at a frighteningly fast pace.

J. R. R. Tolkien knew well an era of change. Throughout the twentieth century, he witnessed two destructive world wars and their aftermath, as well as an increase in global travel and trade and the further industrialization of his homeland. Although Tolkien stated that *The Lord of the Rings* was not an allegory of conflicts during his or the readers' lifetimes, nevertheless, readers in different eras have read their own fears and hopes into the works and found analogies. During the past fifty years since the first volume was published, readers have identified with certain characters or paralleled world events in their time with the events described in Middle-earth. Undoubtedly, as events unfold in the twenty-first century, new readers also will interpret the books and characters for another age.

Throughout this book, the less frequently discussed characters of Tolkien's books are given their due as heroes. They illustrate the qualities of modern (twenty-first century) popular heroes who come from the ranks of "people" like us—ordinary beings who surpass what they or others might have expected from them. They are the characters who, in common terms, might have said, "Let's roll" before taking on a heroic challenge. They are the ones who act behind the scenes and are seldom or belatedly recognized for their important actions, many of which pave the way for others' heroics or for the eventual success of a mission.

Although Tolkien's *The Lord of the Rings* and Peter Jackson's adaptation of it are full of heroes, the "unsung" heroes are the focus of this book. The following chapters highlight the heroic actions of Meriadoc Brandybuck (Merry), Peregrin Took (Pippin), Legolas Greenleaf, and Gimli of the Fellowship; the Elves Galadriel and Arwen Undómiel; and the human woman Éowyn. These characters best illustrate everyperson heroes. Although these characters live in a mythic past, they are relevant as heroes and role models in a modern world.

Conventions Used throughout the Book

The word *trilogy* may be misleading, but I use it to reference all three volumes within Tolkien's single story/book and all three films within Jackson's single adapted story. As critics and Tolkien have mentioned, the story is one long work, not three separate stories, or an original and two sequels.[1] For convenience in publishing, the long story was split into three volumes, but each is not meant to stand alone. Similarly, Jackson's trilogy breaks the story in a logical place for the structure of each film, while making the viewing experience manageable; however, the place where a film ends sometimes differs from the place where Tolkien ended a book. The extended versions of Jackson's trilogy, which include scenes not seen in the original theatrical releases and scenes that have been reinstated full length, are best suited for home viewing, when the audience can take a break when they need one. The use of *trilogy* refers to the works being considered as three subtitles within the complete story: *The Fellowship of the Ring*, *The Two Towers*, and *The Return of the King*. I distinguish where the subtitle is Tolkien's printed version or Jackson's films.

Obviously, Tolkien is the creator of the story, and his books are the original text. However, Jackson's adaptation has become so popular with audiences that it has taken on a life of its own and may be seen as a separate "text" or work that can be analyzed on its own merits. In this book, I differentiate between *Tolkien's trilogy* and *Jackson's trilogy* because the structure, plot developments, and characterizations sometimes differ. Not only is there a difference between each artist's perception of the story, Tolkien's as originator and Jackson's as interpreter, but there are also differences between the nature of books and films and the ways that people make meaning from information presented by each medium. The use of Tolkien's trilogy or Jackson's trilogy indicates in which "version" of the story the example takes place.

The cinematic adaptation involved the collaborative effort of hundreds of people from many countries. To simplify the discussion of the films, not to give Peter Jackson sole credit for the work, I refer to *Jackson's trilogy*, *Jackson's writing*, *Jackson's directing*, and so on. Fran Walsh, Philippa Boyens, and Peter Jackson wrote the screenplay. Walsh and Boyens should be equally recognized for their creativity and hard work, and I do not mean any slight when Peter Jackson's name occurs most frequently. Jackson also was not the only director; several people directed scenes at different New Zealand locations on any given day. However, again to simplify as well as to use the name listed in the film credits as director, I cite only Jackson's name as director.

Another term, *hero*, is not specific to gender. *Hero*, not *heroine*, refers to a female character.

The term *Quest* describes Frodo's mission of destroying the One Ring. Although a quest usually requires heroes to search for something, in *The Lord of the Rings*, the objective is to get ride of, to destroy, not to seek. However, *Quest* also takes on a personal meaning for each of the heroic characters described in this book as they either seek—or unexpectedly discover—important qualities within themselves.

Hobbits, *Elves*, *Men*, *Dwarves*, *Wizards*, and *Orcs* are capitalized. For simplicity, I refer to *Orcs* as one large group and do not distinguish, for example, Uruk-hai from other Orcs. *Men* refers to humans as a group, including males and females of all ages. The lowercase *men* refers to males in the discussion of gender issues.

Structure of the Book

An introduction to some important names in literary criticism and some typical definitions of *hero* are provided first. The operational definition of *everyday hero* is presented in chapter 1 and used throughout later chapters to illustrate the heroics of each character. Chapters 2 through 6 emphasize characters and their heroic development in the story. Chapter 2 is a discussion of Meriadoc (Merry) Brandybuck as a knowledgeable hero; chapter 3's focus is on Peregrin (Pippin) Took as an impulsive, youthful hero. Éowyn's emergence as an action hero and comments about gender expectations are discussed in chapter 4. The power of the Elves and the behind-the-scenes work of Galadriel and Arwen Undómiel are emphasized in chapter 5. In chapter 6, the strong friendship between opposites is analyzed in the relationship between Legolas and Gimli. Chapter 7 summarizes the importance of heroism throughout *The Lord of the Rings* and indicates ways in which the heroes may have continuing importance in popular culture.

Notes are provided at the end of the text. In addition, selected online and print sources have been annotated, and a bibliography of consulted sources is provided at the end of the book.

Introduction

Readers who enjoy J. R. R. Tolkien's *The Lord of the Rings* and filmgoers who thrill to Peter Jackson's adaptation of the books are not always the same people. Some fans of the books have been dismayed, if not downright angry, at the differences between the books and the latest nonbook version of Tolkien's epic. Fans of the films may not like the books because they are long and lack the rapid action sequences common on screen. Then there are those who enjoy both tellings of the story but appreciate the differences and similarities of the adaptations of Tolkien's text into other media, most recently as films. I am one of this latter group. I do not consider Jackson's works superior or inferior to the original books—they are simply different and will be discussed in light of their own merits.

Since 1999, when word of the filming began to spread rapidly through Internet communities, and popular fan Web sites such as TheOneRingNet became established places where production news was posted daily, Tolkien's works celebrated an unprecedented revival. Although many of his books have been extremely popular at different points throughout the latter half of the past century, for a time in the early 2000s, everything remotely related to Tolkien took on special meaning as Jackson's films moved from production to postproduction to release of each of the three films. Discussing *The Lord of the Rings* for at least the next few years probably means talking about both the books and the films. *The Lord of the Rings* may face a similar fate as *The Wizard of Oz*—to become best known on film—although the books on which the film was based remain popular.

Jackson's films came about during a pivotal period in recent history. All three movies were filmed primarily during approximately eighteen months ending in late 1999. The first film was released in December 2001, with pickups and editorial work on the second film leading to a December 2002 release. There was some concern about the title of the second film, *The Two Towers*, in light of the tragedy involving New York's Twin Towers. In an article titled "Epic Fantasy and Global Terrorism," Ken Gelder notes, "It was difficult not to notice the synchronicity between New York's destroyed two towers and the second book . . . *The Two Towers*—signposted as an already completed film-yet-to-come shortly after the 11 September attacks."[1] Some critics began to assign new, political "roles" to characters, which neither Tolkien nor Jackson could have anticipated. In a modern political twist, for example, Saruman was compared to Osama bin Laden and Sauron to Saddam Hussein. The commentary adds a note that it is "sadly simplistic" to call *The Two Towers* "brazenly pro-war" or "Western propaganda."[2]

In a 2003 interview with Charlie Rose, actor Viggo Mortensen (Aragorn in Jackson's films) commented that some countries may view the U.S. government as Saruman; however, he also cautioned against any critical comparison between the films and world politics. Mortensen emphasized that the films were not created as a political commentary, no matter which world power might be considered the good guys or bad guys.[3] Whether Westerners who ignore the rest of the larger world and pay attention only to their own society's needs are viewed as Hobbits, or whether Westerners are seen as Sauron's invaders, militarily, culturally, and/or economically, the story has taken on new dimensions in the early 2000s. It depends on readers' and film audiences' political perspective to see the tale as escapist or symbolic of current events.

Although Jackson's technically well-made films, in all likelihood, would have been widely acclaimed in a different political climate, the publics in many Western countries, especially the United States, seemed interested in a clearcut battle between good and evil. Being suddenly and unexpectedly thrust into an international battle for the survival of the cultures and places they love made the Hobbits, Elves, Dwarves, and Men of Middle-earth seem a whole lot more like the United States and coalition allies to many filmgoers.

This resonance with allies had another link, as well—England. Tolkien wrote *The Lord of the Rings* in part as a mythical history of England, and, indeed, the Hobbits and the Shire recall an idyllic England before industrialization, a fantasized genteel world of civilized beings living in relative harmony. The modern world is becoming increasingly complex; often it seems to break down because of the latest computer virus, gap in security measures, or technology failure. As well, new products and improved technologies flood the market every day. Keeping up with the latest innovations in Western societies that prize the latest gadget becomes increasingly difficult. Going back to a simpler, slower time to embrace the values of family and nature may appeal to modern audiences. In any other time, fantasy, especially an English fantasy tale, may not have been as popular for Americans in particular, but for other cultures or countries worldwide as well.

Perhaps Jackson's films have created a mythology for the twenty-first-century, Westernized world. Much of the current global emphasis is on terror and warfare, and the international community is involved. U.S. leaders have drawn a line between "allies" and "enemies," and the political distinctions portrayed in the media between the two have been more black and white than gray in the early 2000s. Jackson's cinematic world is often this clearcut between the forces of good (the peoples of Rohan and Gondor in the world of Men, Hobbits, Elves, Dwarves, and Gandalf both gray and white) and evil (Saruman and his flunkies, an assortment of Orcs, the Nazgûl, and the lead villain, Sauron).

Individuals, however, may be "saved." Although individuals may face moments of temptation and act temporarily "bad," they are redeemed through some selfless act or have a change of heart. For example, Boromir both covets the Ring and tries to take it from Frodo, but he also sacrifices himself trying to protect Merry and Pippin from Orcs. Denethor, who, while temporarily mad in his grief over the anticipated fall of Minas Tirith and the idea of losing both sons, tries to burn Faramir alive so that he and his son may die together. However, before his own death, Denethor comes to his senses, realizing his fatherly love for Faramir. Individuals can decide how they should act; they have free will. Groups, on the other hand, often seem to be mindless, especially in the case of "evil."

Another facet of the current political climate that also resonates with Jackson's mythology is the importance of close ties among friends and family. "Family values" takes on greater personal significance when daily life seems uncertain. Spending more time with loved ones, as well as coming together within a community or a country, has been a social focus especially since 2001. The close bonds among the Fellowship, the familial bonds among the Hobbits, the numerous examples of parents and children (surrogate or natural), and the close friendships developed among allies also make Jackson's films timely and probably add to their great popularity.

The emphasis on Jackson's films in this introduction and in about half of each chapter does not indicate any lessening in the importance of Tolkien's books. There is currently less cinematic criticism of Jackson's films beyond the reviews published on the release of each film, and further analysis of character, story development, and film techniques used to tell the story is warranted. Although fans compare the books and films, few authors have done so to date, and a look at the similarities and differences between Tolkien's works and Jackson's adaptations is also needed for a more thorough understanding of *The Lord of the Rings*.

Critics and fans are blessed with an abundance of materials created by Tolkien and Jackson and released in multiple media formats. Tolkien's writing process is documented through the drafts and revisions he created over the span of many years; his correspondence and interviews provide insight into Tolkien the author and the man. Fifty years of literary criticism also provides not only insight into *The Lord of the Rings*, but also into its rising and falling popularity through the years, as well as the wide range of opinions about the ultimate value of the work.

Jackson's cinematic journey, including his work as a writer of the adapted screenplay, director, and film producer, also has been documented through the series of DVDs released by New Line Cinema. The extended versions of the theatrical releases also include a variety of special materials that document the creative processes behind the final films. In addition, the amount of publicity and number of marketing ventures surrounding the creation and release of the films provide additional insights into the popular appeal—and possible longevity—of this cinematic adaptation of Tolkien's epic. The amount of material surrounding Tolkien's original creative effort and Jackson's technological and twenty-first-century-mindset adaptation provides fans and critics with plenty to analyze and evaluate for many years to come.

To me, Tolkien's epic is timeless, and Jackson's adaptation likely to become a classic. With respect to both, the following chapters highlight the heroic deeds of seven important characters and indicate the continuing relevance of *The Lord of the Rings* in modern popular culture.

1

Literary and Cinematic Heroes

The term *hero* is bandied about in many ways, especially in a chaotic world. Everyone looks for someone in whom to believe, someone with the answers, someone who makes a positive difference in a time of crisis.

Readers and filmgoers often look outward to find their heroes. They remember favorite books of childhood because of a hero who was a role model, daring to do what they only dreamed. They quote favorite lines spoken by a superhero from the movie screen, imitating the actor's inflection or accent. Books and films frequently provide the public with their ideal leaders, role models, even saviors. Those heroes of legends and myths who survive the journey into the twenty-first century do so because they still offer the qualities that the public values—whether valiant heroics, the charisma to win legions of devoted followers, or the ability not only to fight an enemy (in an internal or an external struggle), but to win.

With the growth of television and Internet news, 24/7, the ability to show real heroes in action also has influenced the public's perception of what it takes to become a hero. Such real-life heroes act forcefully for the general good. Action news segments can show crises as they happen, as well as the public servants or average citizens who take charge and save others. Local news programs frequently feature special segments to honor community heroes, from the grandmother who tutors children in reading to the firefighter who pulled a family from their burning home. The term *hero* now blurs the line between real life and fictional life.

That line becomes even fuzzier when sports figures and film/TV stars are viewed as heroes based on a specific talent, such as athleticism or the ability to act. In a similar way, the actors who portray cinematic heroes often are idolized not for their work as thespians but for the heroic characters they bring to life. Popular science fiction and fantasy films can achieve almost cult status when they tap into the public's desire for recognizable heroes. The clamor for sequels to films such as *The Matrix* or *Spider-Man* and the worldwide acclaim for the annual installments of *The Lord of the Rings* are not only for the latest in cinema technologies, the artistic qualities of the films, or the creativity of the story. Filmgoers identify with the heroes. Even if they do not want to *be* those characters (or face in real life the traumas endured by them), they value the heroes' qualities and want to believe that such heroism is possible.

The search for heroes starts as an outward search, but as acclaim and identification with characters in recent films such as *The Lord of the Rings* have shown, many fans also look inward for those qualities found in their favorite characters that might also be found in themselves. If, for example, someone as small as a Hobbit can help save the world from the domination of evil, can you or I do something just as brave, even if on a much smaller scale? The modern search for heroes takes readers or film audiences not only outside themselves to look for those role models and special characters who highlight the best the culture has to offer, but eventually it may take them inward, to find within themselves those traits valued in heroic characters.

The Need for a New Definition of *Hero*

Current ways to identify heroes have been based on specific literary devices or cultural values. What is needed is a way to evaluate (1) a character and (2) his/her actions in (3) literature, film, television and other media, and real life. This definition may be applied to the many interpretations of a character—or differing analyses of the actions emphasized in a particular version of a work. For example, director Peter Jackson's analysis of what is important at a particular point in *The Lord of the Rings* may be based on what will work on film, not how the story should be revealed across the pages of a Tolkien chapter. Jackson may have a different perspective on how a character should be portrayed, and this perspective may differ not only from Tolkien's vision but also from the actor's.

An effective definition of hero should be able to account for these variations in interpretation of the same character within the same story. The hero's actions, as well as personal characteristics, should be part of the definition, no matter which medium is used to tell the story or illustrate the character's personality. The definition of *hero* should not rely only on the structure of plot development or a character's social status, which are two areas on which many definitions of classic literary heroes are based. A hero for modern times, no matter when or where the character's actions take place (e.g., in the Middle Ages or eighty years in the future, in Middle-earth or another galaxy), *may* but is not required to meet the definitions of classic literary heroes in order to serve as a "modern" hero.

Definitions of *hero* should reflect a culture's values, even as the story-telling medium changes. King Arthur is a good example of a literary hero who has been reconstructed to fit the definition of *hero* for a specific time and place. There are many different Arthurs in books and films who are meaningful to different cultures at different times. These Arthurs reflect the changing definitions of a culture's "modern" hero—or a hero relevant for the current time. In the twentieth and early twenty-first centuries, for example, literary critics, film critics, and the reading and viewing public all have a say in determining what makes a hero relevant for the time. As a result, Arthur has been interpreted many ways at many times: a "classic literary hero" as defined by such notable literary scholars as Northrop Frye, James Campbell, and Lord Raglan (whose methods for determining a hero will be discussed later in this chapter); an animated Disney character; a song-belting monarch; a Pythonesque comic; and a dramatic warlord. Arthur represents values held dear to people at the time that his story is retold.

To capitalize on the popular myth, different ways to interpret the myth also are popular. The Arthurian legend has been "constructed, deconstructed, reconstructed, and generally tampered with in a myriad of ways, generally for some polemic purpose, including political purposes." Further, these interpretations go beyond the use of popular media; tourism, such as tours of Glastonbury, also become big business when myth takes hold of popular imagination.[1]

A similar situation is now occurring with J. R. R. Tolkien's *The Lord of the Rings*. Criticism alternately has favored and vilified Tolkien's signature work, but popular acclaim has kept the books in demand for fifty years. Periodic dramatizations help to continue the story's popularity for new audiences. BBC Radio broadcasts presented each book in the story, and Ralph Bakshi brought the story to film in the late 1970s. With Peter Jackson's cinematic trilogy (2000–2003), interest in all things Tolkien reached an unprecedented worldwide high. In May 2003, word came of a 2005 London musical to be built around the trilogy.[2] In December 2003, a Cincinnati, Ohio, theatre company staged a (presumably shortened) version of *The Return of the King*; during the previous two years, they produced stage versions of *The Fellowship of the Ring* and *The Two Towers*.[3] The characters in *The Lord of the Rings* seem to have the lasting appeal of an Arthur, or perhaps Western culture has simply embraced a new mythology of a heroic, seemingly simpler past that offers role models for a decidedly modern world.

In addition, New Zealand has become the holiday destination for fans. Although Tolkien fans still visit areas in England where he worked or lived, more people now know of the New Zealand filming locations, thanks to the Internet community of Ringers and books like Ian Brodie's popular guides to the New Zealand locales used in *The Lord of the Rings* films.[4] New Zealand, for many fans, is synonymous with Middle-earth. It is perceived as a magical realm that is yet unspoiled by humans.

The portrayals of the characters in Tolkien's books and Jackson's films probably are the most familiar versions to the majority of *Lord of the Rings* fans and therefore will be the focus of examples and comments throughout this book. Although the characters' names and backgrounds are the same in book and film, there are differences in the ways the characters are portrayed. Most notably, Arwen is primarily an invention for the films, rather than a character in the books. However, several characters' lines and scenes differ in the adaptation. Jackson's trilogy often modernizes the characters, making them especially useful as heroic role models in a twenty-first-century world.

For example, in Tolkien's *The Lord of the Rings*, Aragorn may be categorized as a literary hero, whose path in the story parallels that of an Arthur or other heroes whose story follows a specific structure and who come from a specific background that leads them to develop as heroes. Tolkien's Aragorn always knows that he will someday be king and accepts his destiny. Jackson's (and actor Viggo Mortensen's) Aragorn often doubts himself and expresses modern angst over the difficulties of leading in wartime. Aragorn is a traditional hero in both trilogies, but the ways in which his heroic traits are illustrated differ.

In a discussion of *Lord of the Rings* heroes, the characters most often listed as heroic are Aragorn, Gandalf, Frodo (although sometimes he is described as a flawed or sacrificial hero), and Sam (often noted as the true hero of the tale). The reasons why each is acclaimed as a hero by different critics vary, but these characters are the subjects of much scrutiny in determining heroes.

However, if filmgoers who have seen Peter Jackson's trilogy are asked just who are the heroes, they probably would respond with a wide range of names, depending on personal identification with one or several characters. Aragorn, Gandalf, Frodo, and Sam might still make many lists, but so might Legolas and Gimli. The "lesser characters," including Merry, Pippin, Éowyn, Galadriel, and Arwen, might receive votes as popular heroes, those characters viewers love to watch and with whom they can identify in the struggle to survive a suddenly chaotic world. These characters may not appear in as many scenes, or have so many lines, but they still play important roles in the story.

As the public looks for more heroes in what seems to be global chaos and growing uncertainty, the common, everyday, "lesser" heroes are becoming more important in Western culture, and a new definition of *hero* needs to be developed to incorporate popular values into the methods used to determine literary and cinematic heroes.

Literary Definitions of *Hero*

Definitions of *hero* change not only with the times but also with the medium. Such notable authors and critics as Lord Raglan (*The Hero*), Northrop Frye (*Anatomy of Criticism*), and Joseph Campbell (*The Hero with a Thousand Faces*) have categorized literary heroes. Recent Tolkien scholars often refer to these predecessors when discussing the many possible heroes in *The Lord of the Rings*. For example, Anne C. Petty (*Tolkien in the Land of Heroes*) includes a discussion of Frye and Campbell in her analysis of major characters as heroes. Yet these definitions lack some characteristics that current readers and film audiences use in developing their popular definitions of *hero*.

Shorter, context-specific definitions of one type of hero, such as a weaponed hero, or traits associated with the term *hero* also have been used to describe heroes in books and films. A basic understanding of the ways others have defined heroes may help modern readers and film audiences to clarify their own definition.

Lord Raglan's Classic Literary Heroes

In Lord Raglan's 1936 book, *The Hero*, a list of twenty-two characteristics describes the classic literary hero.[5] The more categories into which the character fits, the closer he comes to being a true literary hero, one along the lines of King Arthur. The way that the items are phrased, with the use of *he* and *his*, as well as the content of the items, limits the definition to male characters. For example, an item such as "he marries a princess" certainly limits the number of characters who can be defined as a hero. This classification scheme also favors those who come from the nobility or upper class of society. Raglan's measure does a good job of describing a classic hero, such as Aragorn, when the structure of a book, in addition to characterization, is being discussed. However, not all the details used in Raglan's list may be appropriate or useful in a film adaptation of a book. Would filmgoers really need to know that the hero's mother is a "royal virgin" or that eventually he has a peaceful reign? These facts may be important in a book, and be given their due explanation in the structure of the story, but they are the kinds of items that are more likely to be deleted in a film version favoring lots of action instead of explication.

Most classic heroes, including Arthur and Aragorn, are described along similar lines within epic tales. According to Raglan, the hero's development follows a traditional sequence of events. There is something strange or mysterious about the hero's birth. He is taken away from one or both parents after an attempt to murder him, and he is reared by surrogate parent(s). When the hero reaches adulthood, he returns to his rightful home, usually a kingdom. However, his life is not easy. He must overcome some difficulty and show his worth or prowess by fighting an evil king, a dragon or beast, a giant, or another enemy or obstacle. Once he emerges victorious, he settles down with a royal bride and has at least a few happy years as ruler. Later, however, he is driven out of his kingdom and dies somewhat mysteriously. He does not have a child to succeed him, and his burial also may be mysterious—such as his body is not buried—but he is remembered with monuments. Readers, more than filmgoers, can see the parallels between Raglan's definition of a classic hero and Arthur's and Aragorn's lives; some details are omitted in retellings of the tale, especially on film.

Anyone familiar with such legendary heroes as a King Arthur can see the pattern in the specific story. Raglan's scale does a fine job of pinpointing characteristics of epic or mythic heroes from literature. It ignores characters who are not high-born or who become heroes in moments of crisis, not by destiny, or the character's tendency to seek out or repeatedly perform heroic acts.

In her 2002 book *Myth and Middle-earth*, Leslie Ellen Jones uses this scale to identify heroes in many tales, including *The Lord of the Rings*. On Raglan's scale of twenty-two items, Jones gives Aragorn a score of thirteen. His score is only slightly lower than Arthur's sixteen.[6]

Several other *Lord of the Rings* characters fare about midrange on such a literary scale, even though film audiences or book readers see these characters as heroes. For example, according to events described in Tolkien's trilogy, Frodo may receive fewer points than Aragorn, but more than other characters, if the "king" and "rule" parts of the list are stretched and events reorganized. For example, Frodo is adopted (not truly spirited away, as in Raglan's sequence) at the age of twenty-one to live with Bilbo in Hobbiton, far away from Buckland, where Frodo's parents lived. On his thirty-third birthday, or coming of age, he inherits his "kingdom" (Bag End). At this point the chronology differs, because first Frodo "reigns" peacefully for seventeen years, then he attains a victory of sorts over the evil of the Ring and helps prevent the doom of Middle-earth. On returning home and receiving much less acclaim than might be expected from everyone in the Shire but his companions, Frodo renounces his role in the running of the Shire. He is driven, in part by his own demons, from the throne (Bag End) and the Shire. He has no children to succeed him. Tolkien does not explain Frodo's life, or death, past the point when he departs the Grey Havens, so Frodo's conformity to the items on Raglan's scale referring to death cannot be accurately determined.

Although an Elven prince, Legolas is even more difficult to categorize within Raglan's schema, although his heroic actions are described in print and given glorious embellishment on film. His "death" is one problem— eventually he sails to Valinor when the sea longing finally calls him home, but Tolkien does not describe this as "death" or even indicate when or how Legolas dies, much less if there are memorials built for him, which is an important point in Raglan's scale. Although Legolas is identified as a prince, Tolkien does not discuss his actions as a leader of Elves, which causes a problem if readers use a literary scale like Raglan's to determine who is the hero of the tale.

Poor Sam, for example, fares even worse on Lord Raglan's scale, simply because he is not born into royalty or an upper-class family. Nevertheless, his actions on many occasions, whether as leader or follower, can be deemed heroic.

Female characters, because they are not described in as much detail throughout the three volumes of *The Lord of the Rings*, can be scored on fewer items in Lord Raglan's literary hero scale because less is known about their complete lives. In addition, Raglan's scale does not include items specific to females, such as "she marries a prince" or "she rules her country with her consort." The fact that these characters face problems that prevent them from receiving a high score on Raglan's scale does not make them any less heroic or their actions any less important to the plot.

The definition of a literary hero works well for a major character such as Aragorn, who seems destined to be a hero and a beloved king. It does not work well for other characters who may be deemed heroic by popular standards. A different type of hero—or at least a more inclusive definition of hero—is more useful to modern readers and filmgoers.

Northrop Frye's Hierarchy of Heroes

Northrop Frye's method of determining a literary hero requires readers to consider the hero's ability to act and, thus, to further the plot.[7] According to Frye, types of heroes include the heroes of myth and of romance. (Frye does list other types of heroes, but these are two effective examples of his definitions.)

Heroes of myth are godlike, spiritual, or mystical, such as Merlin or Gandalf. They have special powers because of their special status; their

abilities surpass those of mere humans. Whereas Merlin, in most versions of
the Arthurian legend, uses his powers to assist Arthur, teach him a lesson,
or influence events, Gandalf seldom uses magical power. He prefers to
counsel leaders and to become directly involved in events as they unfold.
For example, in Peter Jackson's adaptation of *The Lord of the Rings*, film
audiences do not see Gandalf making Frodo's or Aragorn's problems disappear with a wave of his staff. In only a few scenes in the entire trilogy
does Gandalf use special powers. When he is confined to the top of Isengard's steep tower, he converses with a tiny winged creature who seems to
take this message to one of the Eagles. Gandalf is rescued from impris-
onment by leaping onto the back of an Eagle, who carries him away from
Saruman.[8] Later, when the Fellowship travels through the mines of Moria,
Gandalf lights the darkness by illuminating his staff.[9] These special powers
are used sparingly and are not the dramatic feats of magic that readers or
film audiences might expect from a "mythic hero."

Gandalf's true supernatural power is well illustrated in Jackson's trilogy
when Gandalf the Gray defeats the Balrog, appears to die, and is reborn as
Gandalf the White.[10] He returns to an astonished Fellowship, who are amazed
that he has come back to them after what they were certain was his death.

Only a few characters might be mythic heroes in Tolkien's story or
Jackson's adaptation, but even then, Saruman or Sauron, who also seem to
have supernatural powers, are much less likely to be considered as heroes by
readers or filmgoers. Even Gandalf, who is much more likely to be viewed
as a hero, does not seem to fit Frye's definition as effectively as other heroes
from literature, much less from film.

Another category in Frye's series of definitions is the romantic hero,
often found in classic literature. A romantic hero comes from a medieval
time, and Arthur again is a good example. The romantic hero is chivalric
and brave. Possibly Tolkien's Aragorn could be placed in this category,
although he certainly is not emphasized as such in the books. Certainly in
Jackson's films, Aragorn is portrayed more often as a romantic hero—
courtly in his concern for Éowyn, alternately passionate and resigned to loss
in his relationship with Arwen. During the coronation scene in Jackson's
The Return of the King, Aragorn passionately kisses a suddenly shy Arwen.[11]
The King is reunited with the future Queen, and film audiences see a
happy ending for Aragorn. It does not hurt his romantic image that in this
scene Aragorn is clean, well groomed, and dressed in regal finery. He looks
like a romantic hero. However, even in Jackson's adaptation, which enhances the possibility of Aragorn's romances with both Arwen and Éowyn,
most readers or filmgoers would not classify Aragorn solely as a romantic
hero. He fights far too often and well (and seldom looks clean enough to be
a romantic hero) for romance to be his only aim.

Once again, although Frye's categories are useful in a discussion of classic literary heroes, they do not seem to apply to all types of heroes found in *The Lord of the Rings*. They may at times pertain to a few characters, but they are more effectively used with characters in print and those who follow a more traditionally told path on the way to becoming a hero.

Joseph Campbell's Heroes on a Quest

A discussion of literary heroes cannot take place without at least a nod to Joseph Campbell's description of a Quest and the hero's path throughout the Quest: departure, initiation, and return.[12] In particular, Campbell's sequence of departure, initiation, and return is especially appropriate for a discussion of the Hobbits. For example, Pippin and Merry depart not only from the Shire but from all of their previous life experiences. They emotionally depart from their previous security and innocence, and especially in Pippin's case, from childhood. Their initiations are many—into new cultures and a violent world inhabited by much larger beings. They eventually return physically to the Shire, and they in time return to their true Hobbit natures. In fact, Merry's and Pippin's return and reintegration into Shire life are much more successful than Frodo's or Sam's. Campbell's phases of departure, initiation, and return are further discussed as part of Merry's heroic development in the next chapter.

Sometimes the hero on a Quest receives supernatural help, although Gandalf does not often use his wizardly powers in front of the Fellowship. Instead, his knowledge often guides the many heroes. He especially aids Pippin as a mentor, and he often advises Frodo and Aragorn, as well as King Théoden and Denethor, Steward of Gondor. As mentioned previously, Gandalf is unlike other spiritual or magical beings found in other stories as he seldom uses his powers directly. He does assist the heroes on their Quest, but his help is more often in the form of companionship and counsel.

Campbell also describes different transformations of the hero as specific literary types: hero as warrior, lover, tyrant, world redeemer, or saint. Merry and Éowyn most obviously are transformed into heroic characters as they became true warriors. Some readers or filmgoers may even consider Galadriel a "saintly" hero working behind the scenes for world salvation. Although not all of Campbell's types apply to Tolkien's heroes, some transformations, such as hero as warrior, may be useful to describe some characters.

Additional Ways to Identify Heroes

The previously discussed methods of identifying and categorizing literary heroes can be used in limited ways to help define Tolkien's many "unsung" heroes, who are just as worthy as more traditional heroes who are typically thought of as classic heroes. These frequently used methods to define literary heroes can be supplemented by shorter definitions provided by other critics and authors. They may become part of a larger definition of fictional heroes who can serve as role models for current readers or filmgoers.

Almira Poudrier, for example, explains that heroes bearing weapons "can embody characteristics that most humans...recognize as good qualities...[and] use their might in the service of right."[13] Swords are a better weapon for heroes than are guns, because children who may role play as their heroes probably will have a more difficult time acquiring a sword instead of a gun. Also, swords are heavier and take more skill to wield, making them less likely to be real weapons used by children. Heroes who use swords must come close to their enemies; they cannot fight from a distance or wipe out many faceless combatants at once when they use this weapon. This definition of a weaponed hero can fit many *Lord of the Rings* characters who are good with weapons and fight in the service of right, such as Aragorn (sword), Gimli (axe), and Legolas (bow). In addition, weaponed heroes who act honorably and have integrity can "teach all of these things to willing and eager minds."[14] The emphasis here is on *right action* and the *ability to act honorably*, even in combat. The focus is not on the weapons or their destructive uses.

Weaponed heroes are not the only ones applicable to an epic. The way that heroes act should be considered as well. As Patrick Curry notes, the War of the Ring is not the only story in Tolkien's *The Lord of the Rings*. The Ring's destruction is "made possible by countless acts of courage, kindness, and help, both small and great"; the cumulative effect can bring change as surely as one great act. However, the epic is not limited to heroic deeds. In fact, both before and after the War of the Ring, Tolkien includes chapters showing "an appreciation of life itself, at once natural and spiritual, as the ultimate value."[15] Such a good life, and joy in experiencing it, comes as much through the works of the "humble and ordinary as those of the mighty."[16] Heroes do not always have to fight or live in conflict. They may, as Éowyn and Sam do after the war, become healers—Éowyn of people, Sam of the natural world in the Shire.

Tolkien emphasizes the value of loyalty more than any other characteristic in his heroes, and this trait is part of his larger definition of hero. All heroes in *The Lord of the Rings*—those commonly recognized as classic heroes as well as the unsung ones discussed in this book—are loyal to their companions. Whether loyalty arises from love of family members, between master and servant, among comrades whose friendship is forged in battle, or toward a noble ruler, this theme resonates throughout both Tolkien's and Jackson's trilogies. Loyalty in *The Lord of the Rings* is "sacrifice for the sake of others as a basic principle of goodness and setting the world right."[17] This trait is typical of all heroes. It is an important theme for modern readers and film audiences, too, who see on the news the selfless heroism of public servants or know about the hero next door who takes care of an elderly neighbor. Loyalty to friends, colleagues, and family, as well as respect for others in general, is a trait commonly found in heroes.

These additional elements of a hero still may not create a complete definition of popular real-life or fictional heroes who may serve as role models or heroes relevant in a modern world. Jackson's trilogy further shifts the emphasis from a depiction of classic literary heroes to include late twentieth- to early twenty-first-century influences, which should be considered in the formation of a more practical definition of *hero* for current readers or film audiences.

Peter Jackson's Vision of Heroes

Filmgoers in the 2000s have another "text" by which to consider the heroics of lesser emphasized characters: Peter Jackson's cinematic trilogy adapted from Tolkien's books. Although Jackson often stays close to the print version of the story, he also strays in cinematically valid but character-changing ways. Character development, dialogue, and actions directed by Jackson also are modified by the actors' interpretations and physical embodiment of the roles. Tolkien's rich word descriptions enliven and further his characters' development but leave readers to picture events and characters in their own way. In contrast, because of the medium of film, Jackson and company direct viewers' attention and determine what a character should emphasize within a scene. Camera movement, lighting, music, and eventually the editing to make a final theatrical version of the film all help determine the "heroic" moments and heroes within a scene—and in the three action-packed films, there are many. The process of filmmaking allows viewers to see many characters as popular heroes.

Camera Angles, Shots, and the Final Edit

Camera angles play an important part in focusing the audience's attention or influencing the audience's perception of the action. Providing a shot looking up from a Hobbit's line of sight can play up size differences and give a different perspective to the scene. Pulling back to wider shots of a battlefield highlights the enormity of the battle. The sweeping grandeur of the lighting of the beacons in *The Return of the King*, for example, provides a visual bridge between action scenes and, accompanied by Howard Shore's grand score, indicates the importance of these beacons in furthering the action.[18] The use of miniatures, scale doubles, and computer-generated image (CGI) techniques can establish the "reality" of locations within Middle-earth and the relationships among characters from different races. Because the camera either brings the audience closer or pulls them back from the action, focuses their attention on a detail or character, and provides the window through which audiences view the story, this aspect of filmmaking both limits the audience's creativity in interpreting the story and provides a rich visual canvas to enthrall viewers.

The editing of the film, with the selection of shots and sequences of different shots within a scene, also helps focus the audience's attention and highlight heroic moments. To feel what it might be like to ride with the Rohirrim into battle, for example, involves a variety of shots and techniques. A close-up of Merry trembling as he looks across the Pelennor Fields to the waiting enemy highlights this soon-to-be-heroic Hobbit's first impression of battle.[19] It helps to emphasize Merry's ability to overcome his fear once he enters the battle. A quite different perspective is achieved with a sweeping camera movement to give film audiences a sense of riding on horseback among the enemy and between the legs of a charging mûmakil.[20] The camera movement and length of the shot allow audiences to live vicariously and get a sense of what the characters are experiencing. The ferocity as well as the speed of hand-to-hand combat is achieved through a series of intercut brief shots of beloved characters fighting one-on-one with an enemy. The action in each shot is so brief, and the number of cuts so many, that audiences get a dizzying sense of what it might feel like to fight in such an intense battle. The audience's attention is directed by the images shown on screen, and a character's heroic development may be emphasized by the way a scene is filmed and edited.

Lighting

Lighting also plays a role in setting the mood and location. Andrew Lesnie, the cinematic trilogy's director of photography, explains that lighting as well as the actors' performances can create an atmosphere that affects the audience in subtle ways. Aragorn's coronation is an emotional scene that Lesnie feels is best left to the actors, instead of lighting techniques, to set the mood: "although the scene has a vibrant look, it's the action within that drives" the multilayered emotional impact of the scene.[21]

More direct lighting techniques are used to establish the tone in other scenes. In Jackson's adaptation, when the Hobbits return to the Shire they find it untouched by Sauron's evil or Saruman's intervention, an important change from Tolkien's scenes of the scouring of the Shire. Lesnie elaborates that the look of the Shire needs to be different when the Hobbits return; it should not be the same bright, happy place they leave in the first film. To underscore that the returning travelers are now different, although the Shire is the same, Lesnie lights the Shire "to emulate the quality of late-afternoon light found in works by classic English landscape painters ... and some of New Zealand's landscape photographers."[22] Such subtle techniques in film can influence the audience's perception of the scene and support elements of an actor's performance.

The Addition of Music

Books, obviously, lack a musical score, whereas dramatic emphasis, mood, setting, and characterization can be established with the proper score. Jackson adds that the actors' performances are "immediately amplified in power ... [with] the right score behind the pictures." Howard Shore's award-winning score offers a "dark beauty" to match the films' scope and themes.[23]

Simply by hearing a CD of the score, listeners can understand what must be happening while that music is played in the film, and audiences who have seen one or more films may mentally "see" the corresponding scene. A crescendo may highlight action or emotional high point on screen; the tempo identifies what the actors are doing or the pace of the action.

For example, Shore's "Hope and Memory" from *The Return of the King* soundtrack[24] highlights on film the urgency of Gandalf's departure with Pippin from Edoras, once Pippin has gazed into the palantír.[25] The music also supports the scene's emotional center, in which Pippin is taken from Merry. At the beginning of the piece, the beat is strong, just like Gandalf's relentless footsteps from the Golden Hall to the stable where Shadowfax is waiting. Four beats per measure of music allow the strings to pound out the pace as Gandalf hurries the Hobbits along. Suddenly, the music becomes quieter, and woodwinds take the melody into a softer, gentler section, one that "sounds" like the Shire. It is well suited for Merry's reassurance to Pippin and their last brief moments together before Gandalf urges Shadow-fax to run from the barn. As Gandalf departs in haste, Shore's score increases in volume and thematic poignancy, highlighting Merry's and Pippin's al-most overwhelming emotions. The beat changes, too, into three beats per measure, more like riding Shadowfax would feel. As Gandalf and Pippin ride into the distance, their forms increasingly smaller on screen, Jackson cuts to a shot of a devastated Merry and a regretful Aragorn. The music again slows, quiets, and ends with the scene.

Even listeners who have not seen the sequence from the film can hear the different "emotions" in the music. The tempo changes, as does the melody; the music rises and falls along with the dramatic pitch. The music emphasizes the emotions captured by the camera angles and shots and shown through the actors' performances.

The score also provides a dramatic emphasis to the many moments of tragedy as well as heroism during battle scenes. It creates a different image for each character, as themes representing the Shire, Edoras, Isengard, or other locations and characters indicate who is arriving on screen and how the mood should be set. It alerts listeners to a change in direction, supports the action, and aurally creates character and setting.

In addition to the instrumental accompaniment to scenes, some actors add their voices to the music of Middle-earth. Jackson's adaptation contains a surprising number of snippets of songs that provide insight into the characters who sing them. Bilbo, for example, sings and then hums a few bars of a traveling song as he leaves Bag End in *The Fellowship of the Ring*.[26] Aragorn sings twice: once in *The Fellowship of the Ring*,[27] first when he sings part of the lay of Beren and Luthien (see chapter 5 for more details about the connection between Beren and Aragorn, Luthien and Arwen), and once during his coronation in *The Return of the King*.[28] In the extended version of *The Two Towers*,[29] Éowyn sings a lament during her cousin Théodred's burial. The Elves of Lothlorien also sing a lament, this time for Gandalf, in *The Fellowship of the Ring*.[30]

These characters' songs often underscore their vulnerability, which also makes them appealing heroes for modern times. Although Aragorn can outsmart the Ring Wraiths in Bree, lead the Hobbits toward Rivendell, and provide for their needs along the trail, he is more than an accomplished ranger. He also is a Man who knows the songs and stories of the Elves and, unknown to the Hobbits at that time, relates the sad story of Beren's and Luthien's love to his own relationship with Arwen. Even at his coronation, Aragorn/Elessar is not a cocky ruler or an overtly proud king; he is almost hesitant as he sings, again in Elvish. He seems sensitive and humble, endearing modern traits in a manly hero.

Éowyn is a strong woman who has survived many sorrows (and will survive many more). At her cousin's funeral, however, she barely contains her grief as her voice rises clearly. She honors her cousin even as she mourns him. Hers is the voice of duty, as well as love, as she leads the women who have come to mourn the king's son.

What is perhaps most surprising is Pippin's role in the musicality of the trilogy. Only he gets more songs than Aragorn. Pippin sings three times, and the choice of song and occasion for it show a great deal about his maturing character. First, as several Hobbits, including the four who will become members of the Fellowship, spend a casual evening at the Green Dragon, Pippin is shown as the center of attention.[31] While Frodo and

Sam talk with other Hobbits about mysterious visitors traveling near and through the Shire, Pippin is singing and dancing on a table. Encouraged by Merry, Pippin gleefully performs for the other patrons by singing a drinking song. Although Merry also sings, Pippin stands higher on the table and is clearly the focal point in the shot. Audiences see Pippin enjoying the attention (and caring little if he looks foolish as he boisterously sings, stomps his foot to keep the beat, and drinks ale). At this point in the story, Pippin is as lighthearted as his song; he is most interested in the frivolity of the moment.

In a similar scene in *The Return of the King*, at a celebration by the people of Rohan following their victory at Helm's Deep, Merry and Pippin equally participate in a tabletop demonstration of dancing and Shire drinking songs.[32] Again, Pippin seems at ease in this situation—full of joy, as well as ale, and exuberant as the focal point of attention. These two scenes show Pippin's youthful enthusiasm for life as well as his comfort in front of others while he performs. Film audiences like this Pippin—he is lively and "Hobbity," quite a contrast to many more serious characters.

However, a different Pippin sings at the command of Denethor in Minas Tirith.[33] There Pippin states that the songs of the Shire are not appropriate for the halls of stewards (or kings, he implies, although he has no trouble entertaining the revelers of Théoden's court). Pippin must be commanded to perform. His heart is not in the song for enjoyment, and instead, he sings a lament meant to revere Faramir as he charges toward death. Pippin performs because it is his duty, and his becomes the lone, sad voice of reason overlaying the intercut scenes showing Faramir's suicidal charge against overwhelming numbers of Orcs while Denethor sits in comfort, savagely eating his meal. At this point, Pippin recognizes the evil in Denethor, and he mourns the noble Faramir. As a newly mature Hobbit, Pippin completes his duty—alone and sorrowfully—but he recognizes what is really happening in the city. As he finishes the song, a tear slides down his cheek, marking a notable change from the carefree young Hobbit to a mature soldier realizing the gravity of life in Minas Tirith.

Pippin sings no more in the trilogy, although he is shown back at the Green Dragon once the Quest is completed.[34] Here he is thoughtful over his ale and seems appreciative of home and the closeness of his comrades, but he is not moved to sing and dance as he once might have been. The mature Pippin is quieter and more thoughtful. Although still social, he no longer needs to be the center of attention and seems content to stay with his comrades.

The vocals added to the soundtrack also allow Jackson to find another way to incorporate more of Tolkien's poems and songs into the films. These songs not only provide another link to Tolkien's work, but also provide insights into characters that show their feelings and vulnerabilities. The performances deepen the characters' development and provide a multifaceted view of heroic characters when they are not in action, especially battle.

The Structure of the Story

Adaptation of the books into film scripts not only has to involve cinematic possibilities for telling the story, but also such expository items as dialogue and plot arcs that will work on screen. Not everything in a book can, or should, be filmed, and the massive number of characters, plot layers, and scope of settings in an adaptation of *The Lord of the Rings* once led many people to think that a successful live-action film—or film series—would be impossible to do well. Director/scriptwriter Peter Jackson comments that "adapting was . . . a blessing because they were great books." Trying to create a story of this magnitude would have been far more daunting: "we could never have come up with something as good as the raw material" with rich characters and a complete world with its history.[35]

Even with a script in place, the final on-screen story is the result of directorial and editorial decisions. As Philippa Boyens who, along with Fran Walsh and Peter Jackson, adapted the books into a screenplay, explains, "It's not about what you write; it is about what is shot . . . then it's about how the director cuts the story together."[36] With dozens of important characters across the three films, the essence and purpose of each character must be clear in both the scriptwriters' and finally the audience's minds. Coauthor Fran Walsh summarizes the writers' dilemmas in adapting such a large, complex work with the simple truth that "cinema is an entirely different medium than prose." The writers "honor the books" and do their best to "make the moments work as they were written . . . if they didn't translate into exciting and entertaining cinema, then we would make a change."[37]

Some changes include the deletion of scenes that illustrate a hero's growth or add depth to readers' understanding of a character's personality. Sometimes dialogue added to a scene creates a different perception of a character than readers may have from the books' description of that character. Specific changes in the depiction of the unsung heroes are discussed in later chapters, but all characters differ in some ways by being adapted to a cinematic story.

Jackson's resulting trilogy modernizes the heroes and sometimes changes the focus of their development. Tolkien's trilogy develops different plot arcs for many of the unsung heroes. However, in both trilogies, the less-often-discussed characters have their important heroic moments.

Modern Heroes in a Classic Tale

Through these films, Jackson produces another version of the myth, a fictitious history that seems as real as any documented history that has evolved into mythic proportions. Jackson creates a mythology for modern times, one full of heroes who do not always have the greatest number of lines or the most scenes. Through the medium of film, Jackson's adaptation becomes especially appropriate for those who are new to *The Lord of the Rings*. Young audiences, in particular, are interested in action and adventure; they prefer the faster pace of videogames and television in their films. They also are an audience more used to images than prose, having been brought up as visual consumers. Turning an epic like *The Lord of the Rings* into images that film audiences enjoy and remember helps promote Tolkien's characters as modern heroes.

Jackson's depiction of historic heroes and heroism fits more closely with current Western conceptions of a modern hero. Although the events are set millennia ago, the personalities often seem modern. The heroes are not only strong and resilient, they are also sensitive. Aragorn, for example, frequently doubts his ability to be a king, and even on his coronation, sighs mightily before turning to face his subjects. Despite this occasional self-doubt and ongoing regret about the emotional impact of war on innocents, including Hobbits and children, Aragorn always acts heroically. Audiences immediately know that Aragorn will save the day in *The Return of the King* when he leaps from a Corsair ship and charges the waiting Orcs.[38] The music swells, and a heroic fanfare punctuates the shot of Aragorn charging, sword raised. Even Frodo's final acts at Mount Doom seem anticlimactic compared to Aragorn's wistful whisper, "For Frodo," before he leads the charge against Sauron's hordes at the Black Gate.[39] Jackson clearly highlights one popular definition of a male hero: strong, but not silent; sensitive but courageous.

However, heroes defined in popular terms do not have to display stereotypical male or female traits. Not all male heroes have to act like, for example, John Wayne or Arnold Schwarzenegger. In *The Lord of the Rings*, Tolkien "reject[s] traditional heroism," but his "love for the idea of heroes, men of prowess and courage fighting a desperate battle for the right against seemingly overpowering odds" is one part of the story. Another important part of the heroic struggle "is internal and spiritual."[40] Tolkien, using the conventions of a book (e.g., internal dialogue, long descriptions), more easily shows the internal struggle of heroes, whereas the nature of film is better suited for action and outward displays of heroism.

Nevertheless, the male characters in *The Lord of the Rings* often show some "feminine" attributes. The Hobbits are openly emotional; they frequently embrace or gaze lovingly at each other. This tendency to share every emotion gives rise to fan-written homoerotic stories on the Internet pairing two or more Hobbits, and frequently other species as well. The characters in Tolkien's trilogy display strong emotions, and some critics find that although the Frodo–Sam relationship is actually stronger in the books, "the films still offer a powerful visual depiction of affectionate male-male partnership." Audiences looking for erotic interpretations "can restore the sexual union of Frodo and Sam (as well as the other pairings, such as Merry and Pippin, Gimli and Legolas, Aragorn and Boromir)."[41] It seems difficult for modern Western readers or filmgoers to accept intense male friendships and love without an overt sexual interpretation. However, some filmgoers find that the closeness of the characters and their openness to showing emotion, especially love and loyalty, make them more heroic. The characters are not afraid to show what they feel or to express their concern for others. In modern Western culture, that ability alone may make the characters seem heroic. In a society where greeting strangers with a cheery hello may be a suspicious act, or impulsively hugging a colleague may be grounds for sexual harassment, frequent friendly touches and broad emotions seem out of the normal range of expression. Tolkien's and Jackson's heroes do not have to be stoic to be real heroes.

Sam is often singled out in fan fiction, because he is especially devoted to Frodo. Filmgoers familiar with allusions to other movies might even view him as a Stepford Hobbit or "good wife"—he cooks and gardens, mends wounds and hearts, and is deferential to his "master." However, Sam also is physically strong, blindly stubborn in his loyalty, and clearly focused on the goal of destroying the Ring. He cries more than any character in the films, but he also is the only one capable of ensuring the Ring makes it to Mount Doom. Sam is honest with his emotions and expressions of concern and affection.

Legolas is a handsome Elf with fair features, but he is a deadly warrior. His grace in onscreen battle is featured in special effects sequences that audiences cheer in *The Two Towers* and *The Return of the King*. Only Legolas can gracefully "skateboard" down a stair during the Battle of Helm's Deep, shooting arrows at the same time.[42] His acrobatics in climbing a charging mûmakil not only allow him to surprise the Haradrim, but to entertain the audience.[43] Legolas's grace and beauty do not make him look like a typical male hero, yet he is decidedly "one of the guys."

Throughout Jackson's trilogy, even manly, heterosexual Aragorn shares meaningful glances with Legolas as well as Arwen; he discusses his doubts about his ability to overcome his family history with the Ring; he relies on the emotional and spiritual support of Arwen to help him become the man he wants to be. In the books and occasionally in the films, Aragorn is a

healer who personally nurses his friends—most significantly, Frodo, Faramir, Éowyn, and Merry. He is gentle and understanding with Éowyn, and,
in the film version of *The Two Towers*, takes time to comfort and offer hope
to a child soldier before the battle at Helm's Deep.[44] Whereas the Hobbits
may be "forgiven" their emotional outbursts because they look childlike and
are physically smaller than other characters, and Legolas may be beautiful
because he is an Elf, Aragorn is very much a human male. As a hero, he
importantly balances his fierce war persona with a gentle, caring, thoughtful
side. Tolkien's books celebrate male bonding and close friendships, and
Jackson's films give modern audiences a look at the power of same-gender
friendships. These close bonds often inspire heroic acts.

A variety of expressions of "womanhood" are also evident in the trilogies. Éowyn is beautiful, nurturing, and undoubtedly womanly, yet she is
a trained warrior and clearly has a mind of her own. She can rule a people
as well as follow her king's commands. Especially in the cinematic version
of *The Return of the King*, she is alternately lovely in love, happy to consider
a future as a wife, and determined to defend her people by going to war.
Éowyn illustrates both male and female characteristics. In books and films,
Tolkien's characters succeed as heroes because they embody a complete
personality with both male and female traits. Both trilogies show that
heroes are not limited to gender expectations or stereotypes that can be
found in Western cultures.

Critics or scholarly authors typically emphasize the most likely examples of heroes. Aragorn is an obvious role model of a "modern" hero,
whether as a grubby ranger, a battle commander, or a beloved king. Gandalf,
as guide and mystical director of much of the action, also serves as a type of
hero. He is a kindly father figure to Frodo, wise counselor to Aragorn, and
even a gruff but loving mentor to Pippin. Usually, Frodo is viewed as a
sacrificial hero, although ultimately he fails to destroy the Ring. More recently, Sam has been viewed as a modern hero in Jackson's trilogy (and
through actor Sean Astin's portrayal); many readers and filmgoers believe
that Tolkien's tale is really Sam's story and that his devotion to Frodo,
strength in overcoming adversity, and sheer stubbornness are the true mark
of a hero.[45]

Jackson also gives female characters more to do and enhances their
action-hero potential. Literary analyses most often concern male heroes,
and Tolkien has been roundly criticized for failing to develop his female
characters. In contrast, in the cinematic trilogy, the female characters' expanded roles allow them to seem more heroic. The inclusion of the behind-
the-scenes machinations of Galadriel and Arwen, for example, fits well in a
modern world in which heroes are often those who work quietly in the
background and may not immediately be recognized for their contributions.

Popular heroes are often public servants, such as police officers, fire-fighters, or co-workers in an office, who perform extraordinary acts of heroism while doing their regular jobs. When placed in life-threatening conditions or situations well beyond their previous experience, they rise to the task of helping others. They have no supernatural gifts, but their very nature allows them to respond heroically. Unlike the superhuman hero (e.g., Wonder Woman, Hulk, Spider-Man, Batman) whose identity must be kept secret and who regularly uses a super power to save innocents, everyday heroes have no secret lives or superhuman powers. The "every-person" hero can be found throughout Tolkien's and Jackson's trilogies.

Creating a Modern Definition of *Hero*

If definitions used by respected literary critics do not completely fit the range of popularly defined heroes in *The Lord of the Rings*, perhaps a new definition should be used in a discussion of these characters. Modern, everyday heroes, as well as heroes from literature or film, might be described in these words: knowledgeable, capable, loyal, courageous, and charismatic. They also meet these criteria:

1. They have the ability to act on their convictions.
2. They can plan a strategy and successfully carry it out, even if this strategy is planned on the run. They are thinking heroes who may have to plan spontaneously as a crisis occurs or think on their feet during a crisis.
3. They sacrifice themselves if necessary, but they do not seek to become martyrs.
4. They grow as characters; their heroic qualities have always been a part of their makeup, just dormant until the time when these qualities are needed to protect and nurture others, further a noble cause, or right a wrong.
5. They value love of family and home, which provides the impetus to act—to protect the people and places they love. "Places" does not indicate a willingness to conquer new lands nor to take land for personal gain. Instead, it refers to homelands that are being assaulted or destroyed by outsiders. These heroes defend their homeland and serve on behalf of their people.

In popular terms, all of the "good guys"—male and female characters—in *The Lord of the Rings* can be classified as heroes in these terms.

Are heroes only defined as such if they are heroic all the time? In the popular mindset, the answer has to be no. Other than Aragorn, who is always a hero, all good guys become heroes sporadically, sometimes when they are leaders, but more often when they are ordinary followers or doing everyday tasks. What makes most characters heroes in a popular sense is not their breeding or consistency in performing daily heroic deeds, but their ability to rise above their limitations—experientially, physically, mentally, spiritually, or emotionally—to perform a valiant act. Heroes may be defined by particular moments of action, not merely their history of past deeds, lineage, or noble characteristics.

The criteria outlined by literary critics such as Frye, Campbell, and Raglan apply most readily to classic heroes found in books, and these definitions have a limited value in defining heroes in Tolkien's or Jackson's trilogies. The criteria listed in this section are used in the following chapters to define Tolkien's heroes; they illustrate the qualities of heroes that reflect current Western cultural values and the qualities that readers and audiences value in *The Lord of the Rings* characters.

Unsung Heroes in *The Lord of the Rings*

I agree with Anne C. Petty that Tolkien's *Lord of the Rings* is the story of many heroes of different types.[46] However, even Petty left out a few important characters in her discussion of Tolkien's varied heroic types. Female characters, most notably Galadriel and Éowyn, often are overlooked as their roles are not perceived as large or important enough in light of the many examples of male heroism. Arwen, who is more of a creation for film, is seldom considered a hero, except by fans. Merry and Pippin are featured in side stories and, sometimes, quite frankly, do not seem capable of surpassing their fun-loving antics. Their growth throughout books and films is not often discussed by critics, and their early actions and attitudes do not indicate their future roles in the War of the Ring and later, in Tolkien's trilogy, in the post-Quest Shire.

Even the characters themselves decry their heroic potential at times. Sometimes, in Tolkien's story, Pippin or Merry laments his role in the Quest, believing that he is merely luggage to be carted here and there, in the way and with no real purpose.[47] In the film *The Two Towers*, Éowyn scornfully tells Aragorn of her fears for her future as a protected woman in a "cage," with no more chances for valor.[48] Nevertheless, these characters act in important ways to further the story and set in motion events without which the Quest would fail. They work both up front and behind the scenes, and they display heroic qualities.

Jackson's adaptation has reignited recent worldwide interest in *The Lord of the Rings*, which is not surprising considering the popularity of Tolkien's books for a half century, plus the cinematic wizardry in this latest version of the tale. Whether people come to love the characters as they are developed in print or on screen, the many heroes of *The Lord of the Rings* are worthy of study as well as affection. They, more than ever, illustrate heroic qualities needed in a chaotic modern society.

So we look at these unsung heroes—two Hobbits often used for comic relief in the films and sometimes maligned in the books; two female Elves, one who owes most of her existence to Jackson's cinematic visions; one woman who often has to shoulder the responsibility of representing all of womanhood because she is the most developed female character in book or film; a warrior Elf; and a gruff but kindly Dwarf. The following chapters delineate the heroism in Tolkien's books and Jackson's films of Merry, Pippin, Éowyn, Galadriel, Arwen, Legolas, and Gimli, and describe their place as popular heroes.

2

Merry as a Knowledgeable Hero

J. R. R. Tolkien envisions the Hobbits as gentle beings, different from Men or others in Middle-earth, who enjoy family life with all its simple pleasures: hearty food (and plenty of it), fine ale, the famous pipeweed Old Toby, and longstanding friendships. Hobbits live close to the land, sometimes quite literally within smials burrowed into the hills, but more importantly, share a love of the land. Tolkien writes that Hobbits "love peace and quiet and good tilled earth"[1] and are "apt to laughter, and to eating and drinking."[2] Thus, they live in relative harmony, aside from the usual scrapes and arguments created by different personalities, and have little desire to leave the considerable comforts of home.

In this type of society, Tolkien introduces Bilbo Baggins as an anomaly—a Hobbit who enjoys (or at least survives), adventures with Dwarves, Elves, and a Wizard no less. However, Tolkien also explains that other members of Bilbo's family fail to fit the description of typical Hobbits. There are his cousins, the Brandybucks, who themselves are perceived as eccentric, and the Tooks, who, although socially the most important family in the Shire, have their share of quirks. Bilbo's closer relative, Frodo Baggins, takes after his adopted parent through his love of reading and dreams of travels away from the Shire. It is no wonder that Tolkien's chosen Hobbits for the journey told in *The Lord of the Rings* each make their own interesting impact on the Quest story and provide readers with characters who both seem like everyday people and illustrate qualities that some readers or filmgoers might wish to emulate.

The Hobbits are the focus of Tolkien's trilogy, and Middle-earth is perceived through their life experiences. Peter Jackson's Hobbits, however, sometimes seem left in the background of the action epic that is his trilogy. Frodo and Sam Gamgee, as they travel ever closer to Mordor, are developed more completely, and the emotional impact of the Hobbits is most often left to these two characters' interactions with each other and Gollum. In Jackson's trilogy, the "Big Folk," especially Aragorn and Gandalf, are more obviously heroic and direct much of the story, especially in *The Two Towers* and *The Return of the King.*

Although film critic Roger Ebert's review of *The Fellowship of the Ring* is generally favorable, he comments that "the movie is about powerful men and wizards who embark on a dangerous crusade, and take along the Hobbits."[3] A review of *The Two Towers* continues, "the hobbits spend much of the movie away from the action."[4] Much of the dialogue and action involves Men, with Elves, a Wizard, and a Dwarf backing up the armies of Rohan and Gondor. Mainstream film audiences may be more comfortable with Big Folk as main characters; even full-size adult actors play the Hobbits.

Nevertheless, the two "lesser" Hobbits play important roles, and they are heroic many times over, despite their limited on-screen time. Merry Brandybuck's and Pippin Took's story is a third arc in *The Two Towers*, and their individual stories are told for much of *The Return of the King.* Through Merry and Pippin filmgoers are reminded not only of what it means to be a Hobbit, but what happens to such gentle beings who face previously unimaginable events, both good and bad. They provide an important link to Tolkien's concept of Hobbits and a different view of the War of the Ring. Whereas Frodo is changed because he carries the One Ring, and Sam therefore changes in response to Frodo's needs and trials, Merry and Pippin remain more typical Hobbits—at least until they face war directly. Through the youngest Hobbits' stories, individually and together, filmgoers learn not only how drastic world changes, including battle, affect the characters and their relationship, but also understand the value of holding onto friends and family in times of crisis.

In writing about Tolkien and everyday heroes, whom she dubs "Everyclods," Deborah C. Rogers's explains that one reason for Tolkien's popularity is that "he does not focus on the cloddish, though he does focus on hobbits," that aspect of naive, rustic society. "Bilbo, Frodo, Sam, Merry, and Pippin are all to greater or lesser extent billed as Everyclod at the beginnings of their stories, but . . . each of them becomes a hero."[5] Rogers correctly notes *each of their stories.* Not only do the Hobbits participate in the overall story of the Ring and act in various ways to further the Quest, but each character also has an important individual role. Each Hobbit is a hero in his own way and faces changes differently from the others as a result of the journey.

One of the most interesting evolutions as a character is the story of Meriadoc Brandybuck, a promising young Hobbit of the Shire at the beginning of the tale. Merry eventually becomes the character most affected by battle, yet, especially in Jackson's trilogy, he is able to learn and grow positively from even the most horrific warfront experiences.

Merry as a Literary Hero

Tolkien provides readers with a basic framework of the social structure of the Shire, in which the Brandybucks and the Tooks play a major role. Tolkien describes such titular roles as the Master of Buckland and, most important, at least ceremonially, the Thain. Readers can gather that, although there is not a monarchy in the Shire, a clear upper- and lower-class system is in play. The leadership roles of Master of Buckland and Thain of the Shire do not have to be hereditary, as Tolkien's family trees in the appendixes show, but most of the time the title is passed from father to son. Only the role of Mayor is an elected position, and shirrifs, or peacekeepers, seem to be appointed to their task.[6]

Readers come to understand that Merry one day becomes the Master of Buckland, and his first cousin Pippin becomes Thain. Within this social system, then, Merry is a member of the upper class. Merry's parents, Esmerelda (formerly a Took) and Saradoc trace their lineage back a few generations to Mirabella Took and Gorbadoc Brandybuck (according to the appendixes to *The Return of the King*), and so Merry can trace his lineage to the most prominent families in the Shire.[7] Merry's social status and family are well established in the Shire. Jackson's adaptation forgoes all these details, but at least Merry's clothing and his demeanor indicate that he is from a higher social class than Sam, who is clearly identified as a gardener and seems deferential to the other characters he perceives as "above" him. Merry does not defer to anyone, at least early in Jackson's adaptation. Tolkien's Merry is provided an extensive background that suggests he is expected to act as a leader or role model in Hobbit society, and generally he lives up to this expectation. Only Jackson's Merry seems to have far too much leisure time for his own good and is more scamp than future Master of Buckland.

Although the definitions of a typical literary hero do not always apply to Tolkien's characters, as discussed in the previous chapter, Merry does follow Joseph Campbell's sequence of departure, initiation, and return, although again, the framework should be modified to fit a more modern, popular view of heroes.[8] Like the other Hobbits' development, Merry's journey follows Campbell's departure, initiation, and return phases of a Quest, although in Merry's case the departures, initiations, and eventual return refer to more than a physical journey. Merry's greatest journeys are emotional and mental, and the events throughout *The Lord of the Rings* challenge his self-awareness and self-concept, as well as the most meaningful relationship in his young life, that with cousin Pippin. Both Merry and Pippin grow more than other characters in the story (both in maturity and physical height—Tolkien uses the Ent draft as a device to illustrate just how much Merry and Pippin literally grow up during their adventures). Their development goes beyond the typical growth from childhood to adult responsibilities. They not only grow up, but they grow into heroic figures who are forever changed by the events culminating in the War of the Ring.

Their rapid maturity and their enduring friendship with each other make Merry and Pippin fan favorites. They may remind readers or film audiences of their own children, younger siblings, or even themselves at a youthful age. Through these Hobbits, readers and film audiences see the great contrasts between the ideal of home and the harsh reality of a turbulent outside world. Tolkien, in particular, illustrates Merry's maturity from using knowledge to gaining wisdom, which he applies to his post-Quest life and leaves as written documents and libraries for those who follow him.[9]

Merry is a very loyal Hobbit, which helps make him endearing, especially in Tolkien's trilogy. Although Merry is not appointed to take the Ring to Mount Doom or to accompany Frodo on the Quest, he nevertheless goes along as a companion. The Quest is not his, but he participates in the journey, and indeed, his quest becomes more personal—to discover how he fits into a much larger world than he envisions back in the Shire. Throughout *The Lord of the Rings*, Merry struggles with changes in his awareness of the world, the many races and cultures within it, and more personally, with his place in the whole scheme of the Quest, the Fellowship, and even his relationship with Pippin. Merry's true quest becomes one of self-discovery, complete with its resulting losses and achievements. By the end of *The Return of the King*, Merry is well on his way of knowing who he is and what his role will become in Hobbit society and in Middle-earth. His journey is the one that every person must face in young adulthood—coming to terms with self-identity.

Joseph Campbell's phases of a hero's Quest (departure, initiation, return) are particularly applicable to Merry's physical and emotional/mental journeys. His growth as a character is largely due to a series of initiations to new dangers and cultures. As well, he departs from and returns to the Shire physically—with life-changing experiences in between that give new depth and maturity to his personality; these experiences also pave his way to an important future role in Hobbit society. His departure-initiation-return sequence includes an important journey of self-awareness as he is made to depart from his familiar role as half a duo and to stand alone (one type of initiation) for much of *The Return of the King*, only later returning to his role as half of the Merry-Pippin entity. Even then, the relationship has been redefined significantly by the time of the return. Tolkien brings Merry's cycle of departure-initiation-return to a satisfying conclusion that seems a natural outcome for a worldly Hobbit. With the description of the scouring of the Shire and the appended history, Tolkien emphasizes Merry's change from unchallenged, naive youth to enlightened, battle-tested leader; Merry truly is a returning hero in Tolkien's *The Return of the King*.

For Merry, not only is the return home a physical reentry into Shire life, but his reunion first with Pippin and later with the other members of the Fellowship helps him return to the familiar. "Home" becomes more than Buckland or the Shire in general; it is the security and love of those who understand how he has changed and love him as he is. His relationship with Pippin, which withstands many separations and tests, provides Merry with a solid foundation for the rest of his life. This is one relationship that Tolkien emphasizes not only in his tale of the Quest but also in his notes about the Fellowship's later years. Pippin remains a constant in Merry's life post-Quest until his death, and indeed, the two continue to balance each other's strengths and weaknesses to form an effective lifelong personal and professional partnership.

In Tolkien's trilogy, Merry is a responsible young Hobbit who, more than any other member of the Hobbit contingent among the Fellowship, plans as much as possible a safe way for Frodo and the Ring to leave the Shire. Marion Zimmer Bradley notes that Merry "seems less vital at first. . . . Yet on second evaluation it becomes obvious that Merry . . . performed his quiet background activities in a perfectly consistent way . . . [and] has, in fact, played a very quiet part in all [the Fellowship's] adventures."[10] Throughout the books, Merry continues to show his quick thinking, and by the end of the tale, he has been the battle strategist for the Hobbits' successful reclaiming of the Shire. However, Merry is much more than just a good planner who is finally able to put his knowledge to use in crises. He is a fun-loving, faithful companion who makes the journey easier on his fellow Hobbits. He is a caretaker, as well as a partner in the most celebrated familial friendship in the books. However, his ability to surpass his everyday nature and to act heroically in ways he never could imagine make Merry a hero in the books.

The following descriptions from Tolkien's trilogy illustrate Merry's responses to many stressful situations along the journey and indicate his ability to act as a hero. Tolkien highlights these aspects of Merry's character: (1) He is articulate, intelligent, and able to converse about many subjects. His ability to plan ahead and to express himself clearly serves him well throughout the trilogy. (2) Merry embraces what readers today might label "family values," and his actions often are the result of holding these values dear. (3) Merry, like all Hobbits, has a peaceful nature but will fight when necessary. He does not want to go to war for glory in battle but because his friends have gone to war; he wants to fight with and for them. He does not choose war, but will fight bravely to protect his friends and his homeland. War as a glorious activity is not part of his mindset. (4) Merry unhesitatingly will sacrifice himself to save another.

As a linguist and scholar, as well as teacher, Tolkien must have valued knowledge and the ability to gather, interpret, and share information. With Merry, Tolkien develops a character who, among his other abilities, is knowledgeable and values books and maps. Merry fits Tolkien's definition that "being heroic ties into being scholarly,"[11] and one of Merry's strengths as a character is that he respects knowledge and throughout the journey offers insights and helpful tidbits that further the Quest.

Merry is intelligent and perhaps the best planner of the Hobbits. Although heroes cannot plan for the crises they will face, their wisdom and previous life experiences help them when they face new, life-threatening situations. In particular, Merry uses his knowledge to help others on the Quest, sometimes saving their lives in the process. His knowledge of social courtesies and the necessity of protocol helps him to cultivate allies and to further his arguments with races that he has never before met. Finally, his growing knowledge of warfare and development of the skills needed in battle help him lead the Hobbits in a final battle to clear the Shire of the polluting influence of Saruman/Sharkey. Knowledge in these areas helps Merry serve as a leader, and his ability to act heroically is enhanced by his ability to think quickly and use the information gathered throughout his life to save those dear to him.

Of all the Hobbits, Meriadoc Brandybuck has the quickest wit and, especially post-Quest, takes the greatest pleasure in attaining and producing knowledge. Much like his cousin Frodo, Merry values books and later in life becomes a writer.[12] He also knows a lot of trivia about old stories from the Shire. Merry may benefit from Bilbo's storytelling of his travels or Frodo's retellings of Bilbo's adventures. He absorbs information, and when the need arises, he can quickly bring forth the most pertinent information and use it to his advantage.Merry initially shows his resourcefulness and courage early in *The Fellowship of the Ring*. As Frodo, Pippin, and Sam move Frodo's belongings to Crickhollow, they are frightened by a Black Rider. Pippin suggests escape through Farmer Maggot's land, stating that Maggot knows Merry well and will recognize Pippin if they are stopped because of his close association with Merry. This in itself shows that Merry is different from many Hobbits, who usually shy away from Big Folk. (That Merry cultivates a friendship with Maggot is testimony to his ability to communicate with many races, but this also shows that Merry is indeed "stranger" than the average Hobbit.) The Hobbits are detained by Maggot, who shepherds them close to Buckland and confesses that he also has seen mysterious visitors nearby. When Merry comes looking for the travelers, he talks easily with Maggot and does not seem frightened by the news of the Black Riders. A calm Merry ferries the Hobbits closer to Crickhollow, which he has made homelike for Frodo.[13] Tolkien's Merry is very much in command of the situation and has no trouble leading his kin safely home. His prior good relationship with Farmer Maggot and his familiarity with the area, as well as his success in setting up Frodo's household at Crick-hollow, indicate that he is a Hobbit used to responsibility. He is willing to take charge and seems to be successful in business and community affairs.

While the Hobbits await Frodo's recovery in Rivendell, Merry probably spends time in the libraries. Tolkien notes that the Hobbits stay in Rivendell for a few months, and Merry and Pippin are out in the community while Frodo meets with Bilbo. The Hobbits also listen to the Elves' stories during the evenings, as well as feast with Dwarves, Elves, and Men when Frodo is able to attend a banquet with the representatives who have gathered for Elrond's council.[14]

Merry undoubtedly learns much culturally during his stay. Much later, after he and Pippin escape the Orcs and are wandering in Fangorn Forest, Merry acknowledges that Pippin has been resourceful in aiding their escape, but now it is time for Merry to shine. "Indeed Cousin Brandybuck is going in front now...I do not suppose you have much notion where we are, but I spent my time at Rivendell rather better."[15] Merry then explains where they are, based on his knowledge of the maps he must have recently viewed.

Tolkien develops examples such as these of Merry's strengths as a planner and a student of books. Based on such descriptions, the concept of Merry as a lifelong student who one day collects information from other peoples, analyzes languages, and studies the Elves' tomes about botany, among other subjects, is not surprising. Neither is Merry's following in Frodo's and Bilbo's footsteps by writing books for the Shire.[16] Tolkien's trilogy emphasizes Merry's intelligence and makes his decision making throughout the Quest seem reasonable and well reasoned. The Meriadoc from the books has information that helps the Quest succeed.

Meriadoc Brandybuck's lineage helps readers to understand Merry as a knowledgeable hero. Katharyn W. Crabbe comments that "the backgrounds of Pippin and Merry are traced in the Prologue in such a way as to establish their status as descendants of some of the first families in the

Shire."[17] Although Tolkien does not provide readers with stories about Merry's early life, much can be discerned from the context of Shire life and the nature of Buckland. With his family's status and the expectation that one day he will be running the family "business" as Master of Buckland, only child Merry undoubtedly receives a fine education. He likely is expected to read, write, and figure accounts, but more importantly, know how and why everything at Brandy Hall operates. As the focus of attention within his family and in Buckland, Merry has to develop poise as the future Master. He must be well versed in the traditions and ceremonies in which he someday will play an important part.

In addition to knowledge gained as a result of his position within Buckland, Merry is blessed with Frodo and Bilbo as cousins. Bilbo maintains a library at Bag End and writes books. He has traveled with Gandalf on adventures and is personally acquainted with Dwarves and Elves, not to mention a certain dragon. With visits to see older cousin Frodo at Bag End, Merry most likely becomes well acquainted with Bilbo's books and maps. His extended family gives him the opportunity to learn, and his social status probably gives him the leisure time to explore the finest resources in the Shire. Merry's early family life helps prepare him to become a knowledgeable hero.

As part of his training for his eventual responsibilities as the head of the family business, Merry has learned how to deal with many different types of personalities, even among the Hobbits, and to represent himself and his family to their best advantage. Because Buckland is located in one corner of the Shire, close to the river and the old forest, the Bucklanders, in particular the Brandybuck family, are perceived as rather strange by the inhabitants of the more "reasonable" areas of the Shire. Hobbits by nature are not fond of water, yet those in Buckland go boating or even swimming.[18] The forest is a forbidding place, yet those who live near it seem unconcerned, if not downright familiar with the mysterious elements lurking among the trees. The idea that his family and those around him are perceived as strange by other Hobbits probably makes Merry aware at a young age that he may need to rely on logic and be able to convince others through his words and deeds that he is, in fact, a quite reasonable Hobbit and one who should be respected as a leader.

Merry further shows an understanding of beings outside his experience with Hobbits. For example, Merry correctly understands the anger of the trees in the Old Forest. He knows that the hostility shown by Old Man Willow is based in part on the general anger of the trees. Because he remembers that the trees are said to communicate with each other, he is able to predict to Pippin that the Ents are possibly highly dangerous and should not be disregarded as combatants:[19] "True to his prediction, the stored power of nature to strike back in its own defense is indeed cataclysmic."[20] Merry is able to remember and apply information about beings different from himself. This ability to recognize possible actions, in enemies or friends, is helpful in a potential hero.

Merry's later connection to the Rohirrim is well established through his personal affection for and service to Théoden, King of Rohan. Although Gandalf warns Théoden that Hobbits, in particular Merry, love to spend hours talking,[21] Théoden finds Merry an interesting, articulate companion. Théoden accepts Merry as esquire after Merry follows the protocol of offering Théoden his sword in service. Merry is invited to share with Théoden his knowledge of the Shire, and at their parting, Théoden expresses his regret that he and Merry will not be able to talk together at Meduseld.[22] Merry's ability to find common ground with kings of other lands (including Théoden, Éomer, and Aragorn/Elessar) is indeed helpful to his future role as a Shire leader. His devotion to Théoden in particular, however, sets in motion a series of events that brings Merry to the Pelennor and, thus, to his most heroic act. Merry cannot know how his service to and affection for Théoden will end, or to what future his actions take him, but it is fortunate for the people of Rohan that Merry develops this relationship and ultimately is with Théoden as he dies, as well as with Éowyn when she faces the Witch King.

In Tolkien's appendixes, Merry becomes known as Meriadoc the Magnificent, well-respected Master of Buckland, a representative of the Shire at the court of King Elessar (Aragorn), and author of scholarly works about history, linguistics, and herblore. After the Quest he travels to Rivendell, Rohan, and Gondor and thus maintains at least his contacts with Men and Elves.[23] His ability to understand the customs and actions of different societies helps him guide Pippin, Frodo, and Sam through at least part of their individual and collective journeys. More than any other character in Tolkien's *The Lord of the Rings*, Merry grows into the role of knowledgeable hero quite respectably. He becomes one on whom others can count for advice and protection.

Merry's devotion to his fellow Hobbits is well documented throughout Tolkien's trilogy. Here are but a few illustrations. As Frodo is planning to slip away quietly to take the One Ring from the Shire, Merry, Pippin, and Sam confess that they know about the Ring and plan to accompany Frodo. When Frodo protests, thinking to protect the others from impending peril, Merry tells him, "You can trust us to stick to you through thick and thin. . . . But you cannot trust us to let you face trouble alone, and go off without a word. . . . We are horribly afraid—but we are coming with you."[24] By the time of *The Return of the King*, Merry is the only Hobbit riding to battle as a member of the Rohirrim. During this time he especially misses

Pippin and longs for someone with whom to talk. In his imagination, he pictures Pippin also as lonely and afraid, the only Hobbit in Minas Tirith. Merry wishes that he could be "a tall rider like Éomer . . . and go galloping to [Pippin's] rescue."[25]

After the battle and his reunion with Pippin, Merry seems much like his pre-war self; he and Pippin chat about what has happened to them and how they are not well suited for such a life. They still prefer the Shire, although they now value what else is in the world. Pippin takes care of Merry, but he also banters with him. The scene in which Merry awakens in the Houses of Healing is a good example of the bond between the cousins and their typical interactions. Merry awakes hungry, and he and Pippin try to make light of the situation in front of Aragorn. The two plan to share a meal and a pipe. Although Merry has been seriously wounded and is now mending, neither he nor Pippin seems overly anxious; they enjoy being reunited and sharing simple pleasures.[26] This quiet family scene provides a contrast to Tolkien's later description of a despondent Merry who watches Pippin march to war, because he himself is not well enough to accompany the armies. Even after Pippin and the others are long out of sight, Merry remains on the spot: "everyone that he cared for had gone away . . . [and] little hope at all was left in his heart that he would ever see any of them again."[27] Merry's life revolves around his family and friends, and his emotions reflect whether he is with them or alone, if they are endangered or safe. These "family values" initially motivate Merry to become part of the Fellowship and later to serve the peoples of Middle-earth as best he can.

In Jackson's films, there is no scouring of the Shire, a chapter Tolkien uses to highlight Merry's and Pippin's new roles as leaders within the Shire. In the book, *The Return of the King*, Merry successfully plans the offensive and leads the Hobbit troops to attack Saruman's flunkies. Because of the Ent drafts, he is a good head taller than other Hobbits, and he wears the armor of the Rohirrim. His experiences during the Quest prepare him as a leader of Hobbits and as a returning warrior/protector. Consistently throughout Tolkien's chapter, Merry is the one to step forward and confront the ruffians, question them, threaten them, or explain what is going to happen. Of course, Pippin is usually right behind him, but Merry takes the initiative in what can be possibly explosive situations. He continues to act heroically by being the one to question what is happening in the Shire and to say clearly that the ruffians are not allowed to continue their work. Then he backs up his words with action.[28]

Whereas Frodo hopes against hope that the ruffians invading the Shire can be stopped without bloodshed, Merry understands all too clearly that this view most likely is naive. He tells Frodo that it will take more than "being shocked and sad" to rescue the Shire from danger.[29] Merry's plan is to raise the Shire to action against the invaders. He issues orders, sets up roadblocks, and confronts the ruffians. After riding throughout the night to gather more Hobbits to the cause, Merry plans their strategy and helps lead the charge. Warrior Merry also kills the ruffians' leader and thus brings the Battle of Bywater to a close. Merry can put his new battle skills to work, but he also displays his ability to develop strategy and gain the confidence of the Shirefolk as a leader.

Merry, and Pippin as well, display characteristics of the leaders who have influenced them throughout their journey: "Merry's firmness and Pippin's courage show echoes of Théoden, of Aragorn, even of Denethor and Gandalf."[30] Other authors note that Merry and Pippin "have learned the tricks of battle, have earned great courage, and are ready to lead."[31] They have "come to prominence" and are able to motivate the normally passive Hobbits to "show unexpected courage and ferocity" under their leadership.[32]

Merry seems able to do what must be done, but he acts as protector and defender instead of bloodthirsty warrior. It is a role he takes because he has more knowledge and battle skill than other Hobbits and can use his wartime experiences to save the Shire. Tolkien writes matter-of-factly about Merry in battle: "Merry himself slew the leader, a great squint-eyed brute."[33] After Saruman has been destroyed, Merry comments that he hopes this is the last of the war; however, during the "cleanup" of the Shire, Merry and Pippin seemingly are appointed to root out any remaining troublemakers. Tolkien writes only one sentence of their job: "The task of hunting out the last remnant of the ruffians was left to Merry and Pippin, and it was soon done."[34] Merry's actions as a warrior are required to save the Hobbits.

Tolkien's Merry is able to return to his pre-Quest nature, even if he likes to ride about the Shire wearing his shiny armor and singing songs learned during his travels. He and Pippin grow in stature, physically and within Shire society, but otherwise are no different, unless they are "more fairspoken and . . . full of merriment than ever before."[35] Merry is a warrior by necessity, and he is able to remain true to his Hobbit nature once the threat to his friends, family, and homeland has been silenced.

Merry as a Cinematic Hero

One review of Jackson's *The Return of the King* compares perceptions of Tolkien's vision with Jackson's. The critic notes that, "Tolkien hated war. He had personal experience of it and saw many of his best friends killed during World War I. He uses war as a crucible for heroism in his books; just as Narsil is reforged into Anduril, so are the hobbits into heroes."[36]

Another reviewer comments that "it's clear that up on the big screen [the Hobbits] are revered icons of courage and hope. Merry and Pippin . . . don armor and fight in battles where they are by far the smallest creatures on the field."[37] Although Merry's role as hero goes beyond a few moments of battle action in the third film, the character's portrayal and Jackson's highlighting of his emotions and actions in the Battle of the Pelennor Fields emphasize the culmination of the hero's growth. When Merry returns home, he takes with him the firsthand knowledge of warfare as well as his experiences with other races and cultures.

Actor Dominic Monaghan, who portrays Merry in Jackson's trilogy, explains his interpretation of Merry's role as hero: "I don't think he sees himself as a hero . . . he probably thinks that he's a survivor."[38] Indeed, Jackson sets up the character as one overwhelmed by the true face of war but who nevertheless performs nobly throughout the battle and especially in a moment of great crisis. This depiction makes Merry a sympathetic character as well as one who provides film audiences with a unique perspective on all aspects of what it means to be a battle veteran.

The cinematic Merry is portrayed as less heroic than his book counterpart, but he nevertheless is a hero in one particular climactic action sequence, as well as in smaller ways throughout the trilogy. Jackson's adaptations clearly show Merry throughout Campbell's sequence of initiation, departure, and return, and the cinematic versions do a good job of playing up Merry's emotional journey and responses to a variety of traumatic situations. Cinematic Merry is more vulnerable in many ways, perhaps because he is perceived as much younger-acting than the character found in the books. Monaghan thinks of the character as "an innocent and lovable 11- or 12-year-old boy who wanted to be funny and always looked on the bright side of things."[39] A youthful, vulnerable, but still knowledgeable hero resonates more with young filmgoers, who can identify with Merry's struggles as well as his role as an older sibling/role model for younger cousin Pippin. (It also does not hurt that Monaghan is charismatic in personal appearances and has become an ongoing favorite of young film fans who continue to follow his career post–*Lord of the Rings*. In 2004, more than thirty fan Web sites are listed just for this actor; this number does not count his inclusion in more general *Lord of the Rings* official and fan Web sites. His popularity builds Merry's popularity, but he became more visible to worldwide audiences because of this role.)

The Hero's Journey

The sequence of departure, initiation, and return, as described by Campbell, is an important journey for a character who becomes a hero. As in

Tolkien's trilogy, Jackson's trilogy shows Merry's personal quest, during which he matures and is able to act heroically through this structure. Jackson's trilogy portrays Merry's journey in a series of physical, emotional, and psychological departures, initiations, and returns, but develops a different dramatic arc than Tolkien's structure for Merry's journey. (See chapter 3 for a comparison of Merry's and Pippin's story arcs; Jackson develops the character of Pippin in more scenes than those used to highlight Merry's growth as a hero.) Because Merry is a "lesser" character in Jackson's adaptation, many scenes from Tolkien's trilogy that involve Merry have been deleted or reworked so that, on screen, this Hobbit has fewer pivotal moments of character development, but these moments are dramatic and emphasized by Jackson's filmmaking style.

Physical Departures in Jackson's Trilogy

Merry's physical departure from the Shire is abrupt—running from a series of dangers. In an early scene in the first movie in Jackson's trilogy, Merry almost literally falls headfirst into adventure. While escaping from Farmer Maggot after raiding the farmer's garden, Merry prompts partner-in-crime Pippin, as well as Frodo and Sam (who just happen to be cutting through the farmer's fields) to flee from Maggot's wrath.[40] Running even farther from home is simply the result of a prank, not the action of a future hero. After that escape and a brief respite in which Pippin, Sam, and Merry find a treasure of mushrooms, Frodo alerts the unsuspecting members of the little group to get off the road and hide from the Black Rider. Just when it appears that the evil Rider will discover the group, Merry diverts attention from the Hobbits' hiding place by throwing the sack of mushrooms in the opposite direction. The Black Rider thus is drawn away from Frodo and the Ring. The Hobbits escape again, running as fast and far as they can. When they stop to catch a breath, Merry confronts Frodo about the Rider and learns that Frodo and Sam are traveling to Bree.[41] Merry understands that Frodo is in danger, and he wants to be told of the danger. Although Frodo only mentions that he and Sam must leave the Shire, Merry is smart enough to understand that it must be a grave danger to drive Frodo from his home. Without hesitation, Merry plans a way for the Hobbits to avoid the Black Rider and head for Bree. Merry directs the Hobbits to a ferry, by which they safely journey closer to Bree. Once again, the Hobbits barely manage to escape several Black Riders as Merry steers the raft away from danger.

Merry's departure from the Shire is unplanned and the result of a series of escapes. Even this early in the film, however, Merry shows the quick thinking and ability to command others that saves the Hobbits—and the

Ring—from initial capture. He is knowledgeable and puts his knowledge to good use. Although Merry does not act forcefully—such as attacking the Riders—he does act heroically by using his mind to help his friends escape danger. Running away from danger may not seem to be the mark of a hero, but Merry's actions as a leader keep the Hobbits from harm. He also runs with them, not away home to safety. He is willing to assist, and by thinking quickly and knowing the area, he is able to serve Frodo well.

In Bree, Merry could leave Frodo in Strider's keeping, especially after the Black Riders depart. However, Merry goes along on the next part of the journey. He first shows a protective streak toward Frodo as the Hobbits travel with Strider toward Rivendell; he asks Frodo how he knows that Strider is truly a friend and voices his suspicions about the ranger.[42] Merry seems reluctant to let Frodo go off on his own, although how Merry can protect Frodo if Strider truly wants to harm him probably never enters his mind. Merry is shown trying to piece together the bigger story, to under-stand how Frodo fits in with this ranger and the greater danger.

The departure from Bree and entry into a darker part of the journey is Merry's first deliberate departure. It may not be a difficult decision to stay with his cousin, but it is the first of many choices that become progressively more dangerous and require him to recognize probable danger to himself, and to tagalong Pippin, who seems content to follow Merry's lead. Unlike Frodo, at many points in the story Merry could choose to leave the Fel-lowship or abandon the Quest, but he always elects to further the journey and continues to put himself forward in more dangerous situations. Having knowledge of potential danger, even in the abstract, and still choosing to go forward is one mark of a hero.

At Rivendell, Merry makes another decision about continuing, now with a much larger group of Men, a Wizard, an Elf, and a Dwarf. Other than Gandalf, Merry is only well acquainted with the Hobbits; even Aragorn/ Strider is a fairly new acquaintance. The customs and even statures of the other races must seem daunting to him. Although the chance for adventure may be an important part of his desire to undertake the Quest (Jackson's story is unclear about Merry's motivations), Merry also has become a bit more aware of the importance of Frodo's mission. His desire for knowledge, even if gained through eavesdropping on Elrond's council, helps him make his decision. Merry announces his commitment to accompany Frodo, al-though he must have some idea of the possible dangers—at best they are abstract concepts to him. At that point in the story, Merry has not yet seen much death or been forced to endure many hardships. As the Fellowship is established, Merry again runs headlong into a departure, stating that he (with faithful follower Pippin, of course) would have to be "tied up in a sack" and sent home before he would be left behind.[43]

A final physical departure takes place at the end of *The Fellowship of the Ring*, when the Orcs capture Merry and Pippin. Once more, Merry quickly decides what to do and accepts—at least theoretically—the possible consequences of the departure and his self-sacrifice. Merry and Pippin hide from the Orcs, and when they see Frodo hiding behind a nearby tree, urge him to share their more secluded hiding place.[44] Frodo shakes his head, and Merry realizes immediately that Frodo plans to leave the Fellowship and strike out on his own. Merry reluctantly accepts this decision and probably would have stayed hidden until the battle ends.

However, impulsive Pippin cannot accept Frodo's plan and leaps from cover to protest Frodo's leaving on his own. Once in the open, Pippin belatedly notices the approaching Orcs, who could spot him at any moment. It seems likely that the Orcs would see Pippin before he could return to his hiding place, and his loud exclamation as he leaps from hiding probably does not go unheard by the Orcs. Merry then has to make a potentially fatal decision regarding his departure from other members of the Fellowship. He can stay hidden, perhaps survive the battle (provided the Orcs do not find Merry's nearby hiding place), let Frodo escape on his own (which Frodo seems capable of doing), and leave Pippin to his fate. Or he can try to protect Pippin, or at least not let him die alone, and possibly create a diversion that allows Frodo an even better possibility of escape. Merry must realize that his action most likely is suicidal, but he hesitates only a few moments before standing alongside Pippin and urging Frodo to leave while he and Pippin draw away the Orcs. Left on his own, Merry most likely would not have chosen to battle the Orcs heroically; his preferred method of survival seems to be running and hiding. However, when Pippin is endangered, Merry acts bravely to at least try to keep him alive as long as possible, even at the risk of his own life. Merry's capture by the Orcs is his final departure in *The Fellowship of the Ring*.

The series of physical departures is part of Merry's development as a hero and allows him to show some budding heroic traits: quick thinking, the willingness to act in a crisis, and self-sacrifice. Every event propels Merry further into the Quest and farther not only from his home but also from safety, security, and innocence.

Merry's quick thinking and decision making in unexpected points of crisis also mark him as a hero for modern times. This Merry does not go looking for danger or brag about how many Orcs he might kill. He tries as much as possible to keep himself, his cousins, and his friends out of harm's way and, in the larger scope of Middle-earth, to make sure the One Ring gets to Mordor and its destruction. He is much like the everyday hero who only tries to do what is right at the moment and must rely on prior knowledge and the ability to think on his feet in a crisis.

Jackson's Merry is not afraid to act without hesitation, but his actions are not calculated to show his bravery. Merry does not put himself in dangerous situations for the possible glory of victory or because he thinks of himself as brave and strong. He simply reacts bravely to situations as they arise and does the best he can to protect others.

The first film in the trilogy best represents Campbell's departure phase of heroic development, and the series of physical departures from the Shire, Bree, and Rivendell truly set Merry on his journey as a hero. At this point, he really cannot turn back physically from the Quest, and the challenges he faces as a result of these physical departures shape him emotionally and psychologically so that he can act more heroically in the future.

Emotional and Psychological Departures throughout Jackson's Trilogy

Although in Tolkien's books Merry is thirty-six, three years past his coming of age in Hobbit society, Jackson's Merry acts more like a human adolescent, especially in *The Fellowship of the Ring*. He is a prank-pulling, self-indulgent young Hobbit. Dominic Monaghan describes his portrayal of early-trilogy Merry as "charming and cheeky," the type mothers both love and dread seeing appear on their doorstep.[45] He "represents a simple, beautiful way to think about life, which is to just be nice to people, eat good food, and celebrate being alive."[46] Although his charisma and the potential to charm his way through situations hint at the leader he someday will become, Merry in *The Fellowship of the Ring* is inexperienced and unaware of anything but his own interests.

The initial physical departure from the Shire—unplanned, spontaneous, with no regard to probable consequences—mirrors Merry's mindset early in the trilogy. Monaghan explains that this early Merry "often takes on a big brother sort of role and likes to suggest things to Pippin to see if he'll try them. Pippin is a little more naïve and willing to do things to impress Merry."[47] In the first scene in which filmgoers see Merry, he prompts Pippin to steal the largest firework in Gandalf's cart and, moments later, to light the firework inside a tent. Merry does not seem to think of the consequences for himself or his younger cousin. Merry appears soon afterward, powder covered and knocked to the ground, but with an appreciative grin on his face. "Let's get another one," he suggests to a willing Pippin just before Gandalf saves them from themselves by dragging them off to a suitable punishment.[48] This type of mischief seems to be a typical activity for Merry, and he drags Pippin along with him. He leads Pippin into and out of Farmer Maggot's fields and over a cliff; moments later he unceremoniously pushes Pippin aside to be the first to reach the mushrooms that Pippin happily discovers a few feet away. Merry leads Pippin into the

Fellowship, not for any noble idea of saving Middle-earth or even the Shire—he simply does not want to be left behind. Merry assumes, as an older "sibling" often does, that Pippin always will follow and that no real harm can come to either of them.[49]

Once Merry leaves the Shire, he begins to see the dangers of the outside world (such as the Black Riders and their ongoing attempts to murder Frodo), but with Pippin next to him, he seems unconcerned about their future well-being. He appears incapable of thinking of a situation that the two of them together cannot face. Merry's role in the Merry–Pippin relationship early in *The Fellowship of the Ring* is that of best friend, older sibling, and role model—he can push Pippin around and get him to do anything. However, not long into the journey, Merry's relationship with Pippin begins to change, as does Merry's awareness of the importance of the Quest and his place within the larger world.

Throughout *The Fellowship of the Ring*, Merry looks after Pippin as an older brother or parent does. When Pippin worriedly questions Merry about Strider's appalling lack of understanding about second breakfast, Merry deftly catches the first apple that Strider tosses to the Hobbits as they continue their march, immediately giving the fruit and a pat on the shoulder to Pippin.[50] When Pippin and Merry practice swordplay with Boromir, Merry is quick to praise Pippin's progress and playfully tackles Boromir to get him back for accidentally nicking Pippin's hand.[51] In the mines of Moria, when the Fellowship rests while Gandalf gets his bearings, Pippin whispers, "Merry, I'm hungry," and later questions whether they are lost.[52] Merry has to provide for Pippin's immediate needs, whether for food or comfort. After Gandalf falls in Moria, a distraught Merry holds Pippin as he cries.[53] Merry serves the role of parental caretaker—the one to whom Pippin turns for everything from the next meal to answers to his questions.

Jackson's direction, as well as script (cowritten with Philippa Boyens and Fran Walsh), emphasizes Merry's role as surrogate parent and information provider throughout the first film, a role Merry willingly accepts. Much more so than in Tolkien's trilogy, Merry looks after Pippin, who is less of an equal partner than a willing accomplice for much of the trilogy.

In *The Two Towers*, Merry still acts as a font of knowledge for Pippin. When the trees in Fangorn Forest protest the Orcs' murdering of their friends, Pippin wonders aloud, "What is that noise?"[54] Merry immediately recalls an old story about trees that can talk and move. He correctly answers Pippin's question by comparing current experience with the groans and creaks of the trees to a Hobbit tale probably used by parents to scare their inquisitive little ones away from the forest. Merry's ability to recall this information instantly is especially amazing considering that he has recently suffered a gash to the forehead and spent much of the day unconscious.

The ability to retrieve information not only helps Merry to protect his kin, but to reassure him, as only a knowledgeable parent/older sibling can. Understanding a danger and making it manageable can have a calming affect, particularly on children. Merry's ability to recall bits of information has the added benefit of soothing Pippin.

The pattern of parental concern is prevalent throughout much of *The Two Towers*, especially when the Orcs hold Merry and Pippin captive. Merry suggests that Pippin not worry about him, even when he is badly wounded.[55] Because Merry understands Pippin's impulsive nature, he most likely worries that Pippin will say or do something to put himself in danger, and Merry does not want to be the reason for any impulsive act. As Merry and Pippin stand before the bickering Orcs, including those who want to munch on Hobbit for dinner, Pippin whispers to Merry that the Orcs think that the Hobbits carry the One Ring.[56] Merry quickly shushes Pippin with the warning that they will be killed if the Orcs realize that they do not have the Ring. Moments later, when the chance for escape comes their way, Merry prods Pippin into crawling away from the infighting Orcs.

Throughout this part of their ordeal, Merry continues his parental role of looking after Pippin. He correctly understands the possible consequences of their acts and the growing danger to their situation. Merry adapts his newfound understanding of the big bad world to steer Pippin and himself as much as possible away from unnecessary danger. These changes in Merry's responses to danger and to Pippin indicate his increasing maturity, a tremendous emotional and psychological departure since the beginning of *The Fellowship of the Ring*. At this point in the trilogy, Merry accepts responsibility for Pippin and himself, and although he has not abandoned his natural inclination for fun, he is taking the world much more seriously.

When the Hobbits encounter Treebeard, Merry is forced to depart from his purely parental/big brother role to enter a relationship as co-partner. As the Hobbits run away from a lone Orc intent on capturing or killing them, Merry tells Pippin to climb a tree to escape or to at least hide. However, by remaining a moment too long before starting to climb the tree himself, the menacing Orc captures Merry.[57] Once again, he nearly sacrifices himself while making sure Pippin is safe. After the Hobbits are reunited with Gandalf the White and left in Treebeard's care, the Hobbits' relationship shifts, and Merry faces his first real departure from the role of all-knowing caretaker.

The extended version of *The Two Towers* further illustrates Merry's unease with changes in his role in Pippin's life. When Pippin drinks the Ent draft first and is disinclined to share the secret of his physical growth, Merry for the first time is "smaller" than his younger cousin. Merry does not initially know what makes Pippin taller, although he quickly figures it out. For once, Pippin can look down on Merry, which forces Merry to reconsider his role in the relationship. He has relied on being taller, older, and smarter than Pippin. In fact, Merry tells Pippin that "everyone knows that I'm the tall one; you're the short one."[58] This taller Pippin seems more self-confident and less likely to need Merry as a parental figure. Only when Merry drinks the draft and regains his height advantage over Pippin does he feel that "the world is back to normal."[59]

In a cute bit of business in the extended version of *The Two Towers*, once Isengard has been secured and Merry and Pippin are slogging through the flooded castle, Merry measures his height against Pippin's as his cousin stands, back turned, before him. Merry smiles in relief when he has proof that he remains the taller. Confronting this "challenge" to his authority, or more likely, Pippin's need for him as an authority figure, is an important emotional departure for Merry. It forces him to think of Pippin and, consequently, his own role in this relationship in a different way.

Merry may be seen as a "hero" to the young-acting Pippin, and this type of heroic role is one that Merry seems to covet. A modern hero is often a role model for younger people, whether they be siblings, a teacher's students, or a sports figure's fans. Whereas in Tolkien's trilogy the author shows how Merry and Frodo look out for Pippin, the Fellowship's youngest Hobbit also looks out for his own interests. In fact, Pippin often seems self-centered in his pursuit of comfort. He does not rely only on Merry; he can think on his own. Therefore, although Tolkien's Merry is a close friend as well as cousin to Pippin, he is not the same type of caretaker shown in Jackson's trilogy.

The emotional/psychological seesaw between which Hobbit is currently "bigger" or "dominant" in the relationship is not found in Tolkien's books. Tolkien takes great pains to show the parallel heroic development of Merry and Pippin, and their strengths and weaknesses always balance each other so that they have an equal partnership. Jackson's trilogy emphasizes the modern preoccupation with being "first" or "better," in which either Merry or Pippin is usually dominant in a scene between the two, even in small ways. Their relationship is balanced in the sense that the two characters together make a well-rounded, complete, efficient "whole"—a working partnership that accomplishes what neither could do alone. However, the blending of the actions is what is equal; within a given scene, one Hobbit or the other is shown as smarter, larger, more successful, more powerful, or physically stronger. The emotional/psychological aspects of this departure from what Merry has come to believe is the way the world (and his relationship with Pippin) ought to be is a crucial departure.

Merry's vulnerability as he begins to relinquish his role as authority figure also echoes a modern view that a hero also can be vulnerable and does not always have to know all the answers. He does not have to be a hero all the time, even though his insights and actions, especially in a crisis, are valued.

Although he is older, more knowledgeable, and more experienced than his cousin, Merry comes to realize that these facts alone may not make him successful. He also has to rely on Pippin in order for his objective to be achieved. Merry's speech before the Ents in *The Two Towers* is his longest and most impassioned dialogue in the trilogy, and it marks a clear turning point in the Merry–Pippin relationship as Jackson portrays it.[60] For all his impassioned words, Merry cannot sway the Ents to go to war. Pippin, however, manages to make Treebeard see Saruman's destruction, which persuades the Ents to fight. However, Merry's failure to move the Ents does not lessen his heroic potential; if anything, it shows the modern hero's need to work with others instead of having to do everything himself.

In a complex world, people cannot act alone to achieve their objectives; real heroes are not like the superheroes from comic books or films who best work well alone, with their true identities hidden. In Jackson's trilogy, all heroes, whether great or small, need to work together. Even in a relationship as close as Merry and Pippin's, in which Merry is accustomed to being the older sibling/surrogate parent, there is a realization that sometimes he cannot solve a problem on his own. No matter how intelligent or experienced, Merry, as all heroes, needs help sometimes.

The greatest emotional/psychological departure for Merry comes during the third film, after Pippin's fateful gazing into the palantír. Although Pippin at first fails to realize that he alone is to accompany Gandalf to Minas Tirith, Merry is all too aware that Pippin's impulses may not only alert Sauron to Pippin and possibly endanger the Quest, but they also separate him from Pippin. Dominic Monaghan explains the significance of this separation: "Merry and Pippin are like brothers; they love each other and draw on each other for strength. For them to be separated . . . is very traumatic. It's like losing the other half of [his] personality."[61] Nevertheless, parental Merry stands by Pippin's side while Gandalf passes judgment and sets the battle plan for Aragorn in motion. Merry, not Pippin, immediately realizes the gravity of the situation and its possible consequences for the Quest. As Pippin tags along after Gandalf to the stables, an angry Merry asks Pippin why he always has to follow his impulses without thinking of the consequences.[62] In part, Merry probably is afraid that Pippin's impulsive behavior will doom him once he is away from his watchful care, but Merry, as a surrogate parent, also may be berating himself for not protecting Pippin from himself.

Nevertheless, Merry gives Pippin his tobacco pouch and the last of the prized Longbottom Leaf to take along on the journey. Not only is this gift everything of value that Merry has to give Pippin, but it is a reminder of their beloved Shire. If Merry cannot be Pippin's remaining link to home, then at least his gift can help Pippin feel a bit less alone on the journey to Minas Tirith. Pippin's last question, "But we'll see each other soon. Won't we?" finally breaks Merry's composure, and Merry's uncertain reply, "I don't know what's going to happen," highlights a further departure from Merry's comfort zone as Pippin's protector and source of knowledge. Merry, who usually has all the answers to Pippin's many questions, is shown as uncertain and afraid.

Jackson films this pivotal scene so that filmgoers are looking down on Merry, making him seem smaller and more vulnerable. As Gandalf urges Shadowfax to bolt from the stable and away from Merry, audiences see and hear the scene from Merry's perspective—Pippin's terrified cry of "Merry!" as Shadowfax swiftly carries him away and soon out of view.[63] For Merry, the physical departure is matched by the emotional/psychological departure from the role he has played since Pippin's birth.

When Pippin and Merry are reunited on the Pelennor, Jackson emphasizes Pippin's reaction to discovering the wounded Merry. This time Pippin becomes the caretaker and comforter, assuring Merry that "I'm going to look after you."[64] For Merry, this is yet another significant departure from his previous role in the relationship. Instead of looking after Pippin, now and in the future, Pippin is capable and willing to look after Merry. Again, one in the pair is dominant; this time Pippin is physically stronger and better able to care for Merry. However, as noted earlier in this section, the two characters balance each other to form a complete unit. The two become equals in their responsibility to each other, as well as to others. Merry realizes that he can rely on Pippin as much as be relied on.

This shift does not lessen Merry's impact as a knowledgeable hero. Modern heroes can and will act heroically given the need; they have the ability to act. In Merry's case, he is still knowledgeable, but he also can draw strength from being a partner, not a full-time caretaker, which gives him a strong foundation for future actions.

In the final scene showing Merry and Pippin, after Frodo embarks on the ship from the Grey Havens, the cousins together turn to head home.[65] They walk side by side toward their future. Although Tolkien provides more closure by emphasizing Merry's and Pippin's heroic roles in the scouring of the Shire and by describing their later lives, Jackson closes his version of *The Lord of the Rings* with this final glimpse of Merry and Pippin as partners.

Initiations throughout the Trilogy

In Jackson's cinematic trilogy, Merry is shown through a number of initiations, some pleasant, some disturbing. Culturally, he learns about the ways of Elves, Dwarves, Wizards good and bad, Orcs, Ents, and Men from different kingdoms, speaking different languages. Geographically, he learns from his travels, and culturally he enjoys or survives many habitats. He travels to Rivendell and Lothlórien, and throughout Rohan and Gondor. He lives in splendor for a time in Edoras and Minas Tirith, as well as survives harsh conditions in the bush, from the midge-ridden marshes to the snows of Caradhras to the battlefields of Gondor. More importantly, he is initiated into the ways of evil and a much larger, potentially deadly world away from his comfortable, supportive home.

One ongoing series of initiations illustrates all these new experiences: Merry is initiated in the ways of a warrior. In Jackson's *The Fellowship of the Ring*, Merry learns to handle weapons. At Weathertop, when Strider first hands him a dagger/short sword, he does not know what to do with it and basically is pushed away by the Black Riders eager to get to Frodo and the Ring.[66] Merry is not only ineffective as a warrior, but his concern for a late supper helps the Black Riders find the Hobbits by their campfire. Later in the film, Merry learns to handle a sword in practice sessions with Boromir.[67] However, Merry's first real initiation into what it means to be a warrior comes in Moria when Frodo appears to have died at the hands of a cave troll. Merry leaps onto the troll and stabs him repeatedly.[68] Although Merry is tossed away, almost like an insect buzzing around the troll's head, he first learns what it means to be in battle and possibly to suffer the great loss of a kinsman. Shortly thereafter, he is initiated into the cost of battle, when the loss of Gandalf seems too much to bear.[69]

By *The Return of the King*, Merry becomes a warrior with the Rohirrim, although Jackson's theatrical version does not show Merry offering his service to Théoden. (This scene is included in the extended version, and a brief clip is shown as part of the special features included in *The Two Towers* theatrical DVD.)[70] Instead, once more Merry almost accidentally goes to battle. Merry echoes his book counterpart's claim that because all his friends have gone to war, he will be "ashamed to stay behind."[71] Nevertheless, he has no opportunity to go to battle until Éowyn plucks a despondent Merry as she rides off to war; he has little choice at this point but to hold on and ride with Éowyn.

By the time Merry is literally lifted into battle as a companion to the disguised Éowyn, he probably thinks that he understands war and its dangers. Already he has faced minor battles, capture, and deprivation, but none of these prepare him for the overwhelming magnitude of the armies on the Pelennor Field. Before the battle begins, Jackson moves for a close-up of a trembling Merry, bolstered only by an unsure Éowyn's mantra of "Courage for our friends."[72] Merry's first up close glimpse of warfare is frightening, a realistic view of what being a warrior truly involves.

Jackson downplays Merry's role in slaying the Witch King, a brief but honorable act to protect/save Éowyn. Nevertheless, unlike other times in battle when Merry is defending himself while surrounded by Orcs or taking the reins so that Éowyn can slash at the mûmakil, Merry takes the initiative to wound the Witch King. He chooses not to hide from the Nazgûl, but to stab him, a move that leaves Merry wounded and weaponless when his sword burns away. With this act of bravery, Merry accomplishes what no man can do—help kill the most fearsome Nazgûl. His previous choices and understanding of the probable outcomes of his actions lead him to become a hero in battle. He does not seem to enjoy the battle, but he fights for those he believes he is helping to save: Pippin, who is living in the besieged city; indirectly, Frodo and Sam; and much more abstractly, the Hobbits back home, as well as his new friends in Middle-earth. Specifically, he stumbles on the opportunity to save a member of the Rohirrim. In Tolkien's trilogy, that soldier is known as Dernhelm; in Jackson's trilogy, it is Merry's friend Éowyn.

In Tolkien's *The Return of the King*, Merry does not recognize Dernhelm, the young soldier who befriends him and allows him to ride along to battle. Merry only recognizes Dernhelm/Éowyn after she removes her helmet and after Merry has stabbed the Witch King.[73] In the book, Merry is not saving the woman Éowyn, with whom he has a closer relationship; he is not being chivalrous in his heroism. Instead, Merry selflessly acts to take down a terrible enemy who threatens King Théoden and another soldier.

Jackson emphasizes the personal aspect of Merry's heroism by including two scenes that highlight the growing friendship between Éowyn and Merry. In one scene at Dunharrow,[74] Éowyn outfits Merry as one of the Rohirrim warriors and encourages him to sharpen his sword and prepare for battle. In the aforementioned scene, when Éowyn literally sweeps Merry off his feet, he instantly recognizes her.[75]

Barrie M. Osborne, a producer of the film, explains that the creative team "tried hard to make [the huge battle] personal. We really needed to have it affect our characters, so the audience can have empathy with what's going on."[76] Building the relationship between Merry and Éowyn not only simplifies the story and frees it from details not needed to further the plot, but it also strengthens the emotional impact of the scene. Unfortunately for Merry, it turns his spontaneous, selfless heroism described in the book into more of a protective reflex. The act is still heroic, but it has a different motivation.

In the cinematic version of *The Return of the King*, Merry participates in one last battle. He joins Pippin at the Black Gate and, in fact, helps lead the suicidal charge to buy Frodo some time. Although displaying a lesser form of battle heroics, Merry and Pippin also are shown as bolting first toward the enemy as the battle begins. Their battle cries are heard first, with the rest of Aragorn's forces adding their own cries as they charge. The Hobbits are not hungry for war, but they show the other warriors by example that they will do all that they can, as Aragorn promises, "for Frodo."[77]

The Return Home

After this series of initiations, Merry returns home to find the world a very different place. The Hobbits receive a raised eye at their finery when they ride back into the Shire,[78] but there is no cheering or even a feeling that they have been missed. For the Hobbits left at home during the great changes in Middle-earth, life has simply gone on much as it always has. Only the returning heroes (although they are not recognized as such at home) know how much the larger world has changed and what their roles have been in implementing those changes. Jackson illustrates the sadder but wiser Hobbits in a postreturn scene at the Green Dragon. Whereas in *The Fellowship of the Ring* Merry and Pippin entertain patrons with their rowdy drinking songs and dance on a table as the center of attention, in *The Return of the King*, the cousins sit quietly with Frodo and Sam and share knowing looks over their ale.

Dominic Monaghan explains that the "characters are dealing with many emotional difficulties at the third film's end. They're all confused and lost. . . . To go back [home] now feels odd to them."[79] The travelers accept their sacrifice of innocence for a good cause while acknowledging that no other Hobbits can ever understand what they have gone through. They know that their experiences have changed them, and they can never go back to being the Hobbits they once were.

This scene mirrors what often happens to returning heroes in communities today. No matter if the returning hero is a medaled veteran or a local police officer, today's newsmakers are often displaced by the next breaking story. In a world looking for heroes, media coverage is often for the most recent hero, not the brave everyperson who made yesterday's news and now must return to everyday life, forever changed by the crisis that prompted the act of heroism. Jackson's scene at the Green Dragon reminds filmgoers that the everyperson heroes are seldom remembered for very long by the communities they serve, but that they must live with their memories and lingering wounds even as life goes on.

In the case of the four post-Quest Hobbits, Sam gets on with life sooner than the rest; Jackson shows Sam leaving his comrades to talk with Rosie Cotton at the tavern.[80] The next vignette takes place at Sam and Rosie's wedding, and by the end of the film, Sam and Rosie have two young children. Frodo, at the other extreme, is too badly wounded to return to normal life in the Shire. He can only find healing in Valinor. Merry and Pippin seem to find solace and healing with each other and at the end of the film are shown heading home side by side.[81] Jackson's film has a sadder ending than Tolkien's book. Although "life goes on" is a theme in both Tolkien's ending to the book and Jackson's ending to the film, the ramifications of war and the ongoing effects to its smallest heroes are implied more heavily in the film.

Differences between Book and Film Merry

On the surface, Jackson's Merry appears much like his book counterpart. Until he dons battle gear, Merry wears a yellow vest and green coat; Tolkien writes that Hobbits are fond of bright colors, especially yellow and green.[82] Actor Sean Astin, who plays Samwise Gamgee, comments that Dominic Monaghan's portrayal of Merry is a "sweeter, more faithful interpretation" of true Hobbit nature.[83] Whereas Sam and Frodo do not behave as typical Hobbits because of their ordeal on the way to Mordor, Merry responds to adversity more stereotypically. He also seems more intelligent than Pippin—or at least less of a mindless follower—and so can better represent the thoughts and actions of the Hobbits as Tolkien describes them. However, critics and fans complain that the cinematic trilogy changes both Merry and Pippin beneath the typical Hobbit attire and superficial demeanor. One author grouses that "Jackson felt compelled to flatten these good-natured and generally upbeat hobbits into the buffoons who provide the major comedy in an otherwise fairly serious story," whereas Tolkien's trilogy, in contrast, develops Merry and Pippin into the "most complex and personally inspirational characters."[84]

As in the books, Merry performs at least one valiant act that labels him as a hero. However, Jackson's trilogy presents a different Merry, one who is at first more foolish but who eventually grows into a responsible Hobbit. Like Tolkien, Jackson creates a Merry who has knowledge that the other Hobbits, especially Pippin, lack, and the cinematic Merry also values family and friends to the point of self-sacrifice. In the film trilogy, Merry differs in four important ways: (1) Merry serves as comic relief; (2) Merry acts younger and less responsible than Tolkien's character; the ages of the Hobbits have been compressed so that they are younger and closer in age; (3) Merry becomes more broken by warfare and seems subdued when he returns to the Shire; and (4) the importance of the Hobbits, including Merry, is greatly diminished in ridding the world, or even the Shire, of evil.

Comic Relief

In Jackson's trilogy, Merry seems the second least likely Hobbit (Pippin is the least likely) to become a hero. Even old Bilbo has a sword and mithril "armor" to give to Frodo.[85] Merry at first not only seems ill prepared ever to be able to fight, but he is self-indulgent to the point of recklessness. Merry and Pippin usually provide comic relief through physical humor, such as in the fireworks incident in *The Fellowship of the Ring* and their antics with song, dance, and drink in both the first and third films. In the extended version of *The Two Towers*, Merry mimics Treebeard and the cousins laugh wildly at their own jests as they feast at Saruman's overthrown Isengard.[86] Early in *The Return of the King*, a drunken Merry welcomes Gandalf, Aragorn, Gimli, Legolas, Théoden, and others to Isengard.[87] He and Pippin return briefly to their comfortable roles as fools, seemingly unconcerned with the Quest once the siege of Isengard is over. Their current interests are food, drink, a full pipe, and each other's company. Although Merry displays typical "Hobbity" virtues of love of pipeweed, ale, and food, Jackson's scenes develop these interests to an extreme.

When he is not the focus of the low comedy, Merry acts as foil or straight Hobbit (man) to Pippin. For example, as the boats are loaded with supplies from Lothlórien (in the extended version of *The Fellowship of the Ring*), Legolas shows Elvish lembas to the cousins, telling them that only a small bite can fill a man's stomach.[88] A moment later, Merry casually asks Pippin how many he has eaten. "Four," Pippin belches, to Merry's knowing nod. This behavior is typical of Jackson's Merry.

Even in scenes very similar to those in the book, in which Merry plays a more clever role, Frodo is sometimes given Merry's lines from the book, establishing Frodo, not Merry, as a problem solver or thinker. In a scene before the Fellowship's entry into the Dwarvish mines at Moria, Gandalf fails to open the hidden entryway, and the Fellowship sits stalled next to a large body of water.[89] Acting like bored children, Merry and Pippin toss stones into the water, accidentally rousing the Watcher, an octopus-like monster who soon attacks Frodo. In the film, Frodo figures out the riddle to open the door, but in the book, Merry solves the riddle. Throughout the films, Merry is much more prone to comic relief and lesser regard by other characters, at least until a crisis propels him to hero status.

A review after *The Return of the King*'s release in December 2003 compares Merry to his book self. Merry is deemed approximately seventy-four percent accurate in the translation from Tolkien's trilogy to Jackson's. The final determination is that in the book, Merry is "fatter, more sensible," whereas film Merry is a "sensible and svelte Hobbit who keeps Pippin out of mischief" and "suffers a lot from being a second-rank character."[90]

Jackson adds lighter scenes, such as the Ent draft and flotsam and jetsam scenes in the extended version of *The Two Towers*, which flesh out characters and add scenes adapted from the books. However, the largest character shifts occur with one-liners created specifically for the film adaptations, such as Pippin's response to lembas or the Dwarf-tossing jokes in *The Fellowship of the Ring* or *The Two Towers*. The jokes break the film's tension for filmgoers and play to the sensibilities of younger audiences who enjoy not only rooting for the good guys in gory battle scenes but also laughing at the low humor and modern references. The humor helps audiences, especially younger ones, to identify with these heroes and share "in" jokes with them. They do not laugh at the characters but share the joke with them. If humor "is almost exclusively associated with goodness in *The Lord of the Rings*," then Pippin and Merry, as the youngest, purest, and liveliest of Hobbits in the Fellowship are fine examples of this goodness, which makes their introduction to war first hand, and their reactions to it, all the more poignant. Readers and filmgoers may wonder about the cost of these characters' heroism as they sacrifice the purity and innocence of youth in the power struggle for Middle-earth.[91]

Age Differences

According to Tolkien, Merry is eight years older than Pippin, two years younger than Sam, and fourteen years younger than Frodo at the start of the Quest. At the beginning of the journey, Merry is thirty-six, three years past his coming of age in Hobbit society.[92] Following this structure, at the time of Bilbo's grand birthday party, which also marks Frodo's coming of age at thirty-three, Merry is seventeen and Pippin, nine. Compare these ages in Tolkien's *The Fellowship of the Ring* with Jackson's adaptation, and the age differences show up dramatically. Although young, Pippin looks much older than nine, even if Hobbits age at a different rate than humans, and Merry acts much younger than Sam, who already has an eye for Rosie Cotton. Merry's voice is much higher in the party scene than at any other time in the films, and his antics with the fireworks make him seem closer to Pippin's age than to Sam's. In the films, Merry seems only a bit older than Pippin, when in fact, Tolkien gives him an eight-year headstart on his closest friend.

Jackson uses this age compression to good advantage. A fifty-year-old Frodo may seem too old for younger filmgoers to identify with; a teenaged Elijah Wood playing an indeterminate age Frodo appeals to teenaged audiences. As well, the four Hobbits' friendship seems more plausible today if their ages are closer together. In a culture in which cousins or even siblings may be split up and reared in different parts of the country, the strength of the familial bond may not seem like enough of a motivation for the cousins to follow Frodo on his journey. The closeness among extended families often is lacking in modern society. In the same way, relationships in which the friends' ages span a decade or more may not seem as likely in today's contexts for close relationships, which are often built among people of similar ages through educational, sports, and introductory work experiences. In Western societies, twenty-eight (Pippin's age, according to Tolkien) and fifty (Frodo's age) are very far apart. The younger, closer ages of the Hobbits on film makes them seem a more likely group of comrades to younger, Western audiences and much more likely for audiences to relate to them.

Personality Changes as a Result of War

In Tolkien's *The Return of the King*, Merry and Pippin grow up, and by the time they are ready to lead in the scouring of the Shire, Gandalf notes that his work as mentor and protector is completed.[93] Tolkien does not dwell on Merry's battle injuries or any recurring emotional or physical problems as a result of being a warrior. Merry seems to be on the mend after Aragorn heals him in Minas Tirith.[94] Indeed, Tolkien takes great pains to explain that Merry successfully returns to Hobbit life, getting married and participating fully not only in the Shire but also within Middle-earth. His life and contributions to the larger world continue long past the Quest. Although the end of the Third Age marks a turning point in his life, as well as in the history of Middle-earth, Merry retains his true Hobbit nature. He does not appear to be scarred permanently by the events during the War of the Ring.

Jackson's depiction of battle, by the very nature of film, is more graphic. Merry, as the only Hobbit in the Battle of the Pelennor (Pippin is a defender within Minas Tirith as it is invaded), is the focal point for the way hand-to-hand combat on the huge battlefield affects the littlest soldier.[95] Before the battle, Merry's eyes grow large at his first sight of all the Men and Orcs, as well as the destruction already wrought on Minas Tirith. As he calms enough to yell "Death" as a battle cry, he is rushed into battle, having no time for thought as the onslaught begins. A series of fast cuts shows different characters in action, and Merry is quite briefly (less than a second of screen time) shown slashing at Orcs surrounding Éowyn's horse.[96]

In a later battle scene, Merry clutches his arm and falls to the ground after stabbing the Nazgûl.[97] Although injured, Merry still appears whole. This is quite a contrast to audiences' next view of Merry, as Pippin finds him on the battlefield. With bloodshot eyes, milky face, bloody mouth, and lifeless limbs, Merry truly seems to be destroyed.[98] He is only a shell of his former self. Jackson lessens Merry's strength as a hero by having him found, at first apparently dead or near death, by Pippin on the battlefield. Whereas Tolkien allows battle-fatigued Merry to wander the streets of Minas Tirith until Pippin finds him, film Merry falls on the battlefield, completely felled by his heroic deed.[99] He is unable to go to the city under his own power.

Although Merry appears in remaining scenes in the third film—indeed, he is shown to be jarringly playful and jubilant at the recovering Frodo's bedside—he only has one line, "Frodo!" cheered in recognition of Frodo's apparent success in destroying the Ring.[100] Scenes in the Shire show him subdued at the Green Dragon,[101] happy at Sam's wedding, and tearful at Frodo's departure to Valinor.[102] Outside of the raucous reunion with Frodo, Merry seems much changed by his experiences, possibly because of his direct exposure to battle. Jackson's Merry is a battle survivor, and a more somber post-Quest Merry is the final view filmgoers have of this character.

In several interviews prior to the release of *The Return of the King*, Dominic Monaghan explains that Merry's exposure to battle and death dramatically changes the character. In one interview Monaghan describes Merry as slightly "broken" by his experiences and "lost along the way in the world he's forced to face." Further, "he gets weighed down with the magnitude of everything—more so than any other hobbit."[103] During a television special about the making of the films, Monaghan elaborates that the final film, for his character, is about "loss of innocence. He just goes so far down into the depths of war and death and darkness that . . . [audiences] don't even know if that guy is going to come back again."[104] Merry's heroics come at a personal cost.

This interpretation is understandable to world audiences who can see battlefronts on CNN or BBC at almost any hour of any day. In a world in which veterans may often be diagnosed with posttraumatic stress disorder, a reticent, somewhat traumatized Merry seems logical to filmgoers. As Monaghan elaborates, "At the start of the [trilogy] . . . , Merry is very sure of himself. . . . But as soon as he leaves his home, he realizes the world is nothing like he thought it would be." Merry's experiences mirror what Monaghan thinks "symbolises what people go through in a time of war. So many young men think it's going to be the making of them but a lot of the time it ends up destroying them."[105] Merry's life does go on, but his heroism is downplayed and simply surviving the horrors of the journey is increased in significance. This is another large departure from Tolkien's works.

Lesser Importance of the Hobbits

Even at the end of Jackson's *The Return of the King*, the Hobbits are not recognized by their peers as returning heroes. Tolkien brings all of the Fellowship Hobbits full circle with his description of their individual departures, initiations, and returns, to use Campbell's terminology. Especially with Merry and Pippin, Tolkien emphasizes their growth as characters and their ability to use the experiences gained throughout the Quest first to protect the Shire and later to serve it as respected leaders.

In addition to Merry's successful return home, Tolkien provides several examples when Merry's heroism is recognized and rewarded. Gandalf explains to Pippin that Merry has achieved more than what Gandalf expected, and Gandalf himself carries Merry to the Houses of Healing.[106] As Pippin prepares to go to battle with Aragorn, Merry laments that he must be left behind. Aragorn tells him to let Pippin have a chance for such renown as Merry has achieved.[107] As the Fellowship, post-War, leaves Éowyn and

Éomer, Éowyn rewards Merry with the family heirloom of a silver horn. Éomer, now a king, regrets that Merry will not take such treasure befitting his deeds and notes that "indeed I have no gift that is worthy."[108]

In contrast, film Merry is never called a hero specifically, or his heroic deed mentioned at all. His action stands for itself on screen, but it is never mentioned directly by other characters. This detail is not important to the overall outcome of the cinematic epic, but it nevertheless undermines Merry as a strong character. In a memorable climax to the coronation scene, Aragorn bows, and thus so do all his people, before the Hobbits, but this action seems more to honor Frodo and Sam, with Pippin and Merry receiving only peripheral attention.[109] Dominic Monaghan's expression during this scene is one of rather uncomfortable awe, which is fitting for book Merry's humble demeanor in not accepting gifts from Éomer. In spirit, if not in specifics, Merry receives some recognition in the film, although his role is reduced drastically not only from the book but also in relation to the roles of the other Hobbits in the Fellowship.

In Jackson's version, no one back home seems to have missed the travelers or even been aware that the foursome has been gone. Life in the Shire has not changed while the Hobbits of the Fellowship are away; there is, and seems never to have been, no apparent "wrong" to right. The rest of the Shirefolk seem to have no idea that their homeland and very lives have been to the brink of extinction.

Perhaps this is a reasonable depiction of at least some segments of Western society. Although news media can bring pictures of all of the world's crises into homes, unless the battle moves into the local neighborhood, people often choose to turn off the television or browse another Web site. Disconnection from world crises is one possible choice. In Jackson's scenes of the Shire post-Quest, this disconnection is prominent. Although the Hobbits of the Fellowship understand each other and their experiences, those who have not lived through the War of the Ring or any aspect of the Quest can never understand the sacrifices made or the recognition granted by foreigners.

Merry and a Modern Definition of *Hero*

In both trilogies, Meriadoc Brandybuck is a special type of hero, the knowledgeable hero. His acquisition of information gives him the ability to remember important tidbits when called on to supply answers or quickly solve problems. His growth through new experiences supplements his previous knowledge.

In Tolkien's trilogy, Merry eventually shares his wisdom with others through his writings and counsel. He uses his knowledge and experience to fight enemies and finally to liberate the Shire during wartime, but he also serves as a new type of hero in the dawning Fourth Age, a time of peace when warriors can "put away their weapons and begin to study simply for the sake of study."[110]

In both Tolkien's and Jackson's trilogies, Merry fulfills the role model aspects of a hero for modern times through his willingness to sacrifice himself to save others and the personal characteristics that inspire loyalty and friendship from kings and commoners throughout the Quest. Under the definition of a modern, popular hero listed in chapter 1, Merry indeed is a hero. Not only does he prove himself to be capable, loyal, courageous, and charismatic, but he also frequently meets the five "action" criteria for a hero:

1. He acts on his convictions.

Many times, Merry follows his words with action—by joining the Fellowship, pledging his allegiance to King Théoden, and planning ways to free the Shire from ruffians. Although many such actions are absent from Jackson's films (or are included as added scenes to the extended versions), Tolkien amply illustrates Merry's ability to follow through with his commitments and his growing dedication to the Quest.

2. He can plan a strategy and successfully carry it out, even if this strategy is planned on the run. He is a thinking hero who may have to plan spontaneously as a crisis occurs or think on his feet during a crisis.

Again, most notably this item is illustrated in the Tolkien's trilogy as Merry plans not only Frodo's departure from the Shire but also plans how he might go along on the journey. The scouring of the Shire also shows Merry's ability to plan a battle strategy and carry it out. His later activities, such as building the library at Brandy Hall and documenting much of what he learned throughout his many travels, also show long-range planning skills.[111] In Jackson's trilogy, Merry often has to think on his feet, especially when he must attempt to steer Pippin away from danger. As shown in his explanation to Pippin of what will become of the Shire if Saruman and Sauron are not stopped, Merry understands the importance of the Ents' participation and passionately urges the Ents to go to war.[112]

3. He offers to sacrifice himself, if necessary, for the cause.

Several literary critics note Merry's stabbing of the Witch King as a possibly self-sacrificial act. After all, Merry does not know that he will survive when he attacks the Nazgûl. Jane Chance Nitzsche writes that Merry's "love for another" allows him to accomplish this "most charitable and heroic act."[113] Author Randel Helms describes Merry's action as the "bravest deed of the

day, . . . thereby saving the life of [Éowyn] . . . and turning the tide of battle."[114] Although the nature of the act changes in Jackson's adaptation,
Merry still is shown as possibly sacrificing himself with this act. As mentioned earlier in this chapter, throughout Jackson's trilogy, Merry often is
willing to sacrifice himself if it means he may save his friends or family.

> 4. He grows as a character, showing under extreme circumstances the heroic
> qualities that always have been part of his makeup, but have not been
> recognized until these qualities are needed.

The size issue is discussed by yet another critic, who notes that Captains Merry
and Pippin, during the scouring of the Shire, courageously defeat "men twice
their size."[115] Merry grows physically, emotionally, and psychologically to
become a hero by the end of the tale. He has redefined his relationship with
the world and with Pippin, his closest ally. Both trilogies illustrate Merry's
growth, although Tolkien develops the character in much greater detail.

> 5. He embodies the values of love of family and home, which provide the
> impetus for him to act to protect the people and places he loves.

Merry does not fight for love of war, riches, or conquest. He never starts a fight
or eagerly participates in battle. Instead, he fights only to protect those closest
to him. This approach to conflict is apparent in Tolkien's and Jackson's
trilogies. Although Tolkien portrays Merry ultimately as a strategist and
captain in the final Battle of Bywater, Merry only does what has to be done. He
tries to save as many Hobbit lives as possible, and he refuses to allow the
ruffians to destroy the peaceful, agrarian lifestyle that defines the Hobbits.
After the conflict has been settled and the Shire headed for recovery, Merry
does not become a tyrant or a bully, but returns to his "Hobbity" nature,
settling down into his responsibilities within the Shire and in the larger world.
Merry consistently works to save his family and friends, and if violence is the
only means, he is quite capable of protecting his loved ones and home. One
mark of a modern hero is not the love of violence or vengeance, but the ability
to protect endangered loved ones or strangers. Merry easily displays this ability.

In Jackson's trilogy, Merry is shown protecting his fellow Hobbits and
other comrades. The depth of his love for others is most easily shown in
scenes with Pippin, but his loyalty to other members of the Fellowship and
the friends he makes throughout the journey also is portrayed in the films,
especially in *The Return of the King*.

As a hero for today's readers and filmgoing audiences, Merry serves another purpose: youthful role model. Jackson first portrays Merry as a playful

rule-bender who eventually matures. Tolkien emphasizes Merry's background, which shows he is more of an outsider who eventually becomes an insider. Because the Brandybucks are considered eccentric by Hobbits in other parts of the Shire, young Merry must have felt himself outside the "normal" parts of Hobbit society. Although his family is aristocratic, that fact also makes him different from working Hobbits his age. His future role as Master of Buckland also separates him from other wealthy, high-class Hobbits. Even within the Shire, Merry is perceived as different, a fact that only increases when he returns home post-Quest much taller than any Hobbit has ever been, but also changed by his wartime experiences. For Merry to become one of Tolkien's responsible leaders, a Hobbit not only revered later in life within the Shire but within the kingdoms of Rohan and Gondor, is an important step in his development. This change shows that even those who adults think are incorrigible or eccentric can grow up into fine citizens who might even become famous. Young readers in particular can identify with Merry's "outsider" qualities and admire him as he becomes an effective "insider" later in life, without having to conform to the expectations of others. Merry is successful, but he is also true to himself.

During the Quest, as shown in both book and film trilogies, Merry often is overlooked because of his size. Aragorn compares him to a human child,[116] Théoden deems him too small to go to war,[117] and Treebeard even mistakes him for a little Orc.[118] Merry is belittled by almost every non-Hobbit character at some point. However, part of Merry's significance as a hero is that he overcomes his physical limitations and status as an outsider to achieve great deeds. Young people who identify with the "otherness" of Merry—someone too short, too insignificant, too young—also can see that Merry believes in himself and accomplishes a great deal, no matter what other people initially think of him.

Merry is an everyperson hero who takes care of his family. He guides Pippin through the muddy waters of adolescence as well as the flotsam and jetsam of Isengard. Merry becomes the ideal community leader, a local hero who continues to work to improve the lives of others. In addition, he is an effective reminder that the best (re)actions are based on reason and that reason needs to be steeped in knowledge—not just the gathering of information, but the analysis of pertinent information combined with personal experience to form a wise plan of action. Because Merry incorporates new knowledge into his understanding of the way the world works, he can act wisely and quickly in emergencies and in peacetime. Meriadoc Brandybuck should be recognized as a knowledgeable hero who acts nobly and efficiently and one who can serve as a role model today.

3

Pippin as Impulsive, Youthful Hero

Poor Peregrin Took. Many critics over the years, and especially since the release of Peter Jackson's trilogy, have denounced the young Hobbit as nothing more than a fool. Shanti Fader notes that fools are necessary in Tolkien's story and that, in fact, Pippin and his cousin Merry are the type of fools who prompt the action and ultimately save the day. Fader explains that the wise (such as Gandalf) can be annoyed by the antics of foolish characters and "want to push the fool aside, but to do so is to deny the fool's power—and that denial can be fatal."[1] In several instances in both Tolkien's and Jackson's trilogies, Gandalf pushes Pippin aside. For example, in the book *The Return of the King*, Gandalf pushes Pippin back after his emotional outburst before the mouth of Sauron, when Frodo's clothing is displayed to taunt Aragorn's army.[2] In the film version, Gandalf uses his staff to push Pippin back after he impulsively offers his service to Denethor.[3] Pippin, however often he may seem a fool, plays an important part in the story and is a necessary character for the ultimate success of the Quest. However, Fader's praise of the necessity of fools seems faint at best.

There is no getting around the fact that Pippin is indeed foolish. Like many children and youth, he acts without thinking and only later, if at all, realizes the consequences of his actions. He responds with his emotions, not his mind, and in Pippin's case, his heart is truly great enough that he responds frequently, impulsively, completely. Although in some cases scattered throughout *The Lord of the Rings* this impulsive nature sets in motion actions that further the story, or even result in the salvation of another character, most often Pippin is perceived by the great thinkers, such as Gandalf, as irritating and bothersome. Nevertheless, even Gandalf, often

Pippin's harshest critic, finds enough good in Pippin for him to be worth the trouble. Why else would Gandalf look after Pippin on the way to Minas Tirith, not merely drag him along as the baggage he fears that he has become? Why else would Gandalf care enough to berate Pippin when he does something foolish? He both criticizes and praises Pippin at different points in the tale. Gandalf spends a great deal of time with the youngest member of the Fellowship and acts as a father figure during much of the trilogy.

Although Pippin needs quite a bit of looking after, especially in *The Fellowship of the Ring* and *The Two Towers*, he also does quite a bit of good, and for all his misplaced intentions and rash behavior, he often wins the affections of those around him. The Fellowship do not merely indulge Pippin's childish behavior or youthful foibles. They love him and, as he grows up during the journey, recognize his increasing maturity. By the time Pippin returns to the Shire, he is a mature Hobbit, even if he has not yet come of age as recognized by Hobbit society. Pippin, as much as Merry, changes during the Quest and returns home more thoughtful, and more effective as a budding leader.

Readers and audiences also seem to love Pippin. In the many times I have read *The Lord of the Rings*, at different points in my life during the past thirty years, I identified with different characters. During an early reading, I found that I understood Pippin's dilemma quite clearly. I, too, wanted "Big Folk"—parents, teachers, older relatives—to take me seriously. Sometimes my grand plans did not work out as I wanted, or what seemed grand to me seemed irritating and childish to others. I understood what Pippin was going through. I must not be alone in my identification with the young Hobbit. Shortly after the release of the first film, I discussed it with one of my former students. She mentioned that she was eager to get to the part of the trilogy with Éowyn, but her younger sister really liked Pippin. He acted like she did, and often got into trouble without meaning to. That response seems common among my university-aged students who have grown a little past the "Pippin" stage but fondly recall the character and how his misdeeds often seemed similar in spirit to their own. Pippin, possibly because of his cheerful nature, does not seem to be a bad sort, just careless, much like children who keep saying "I'm sorry. I won't do it again" the third, or fourth, or fifth time they knock over a lamp roughhousing indoors or accidentally paint the dog green.

Seeing Pippin grow into a heroic young Hobbit, winning the respect of those who previously thought him only a fool, is a wonderful story all its own. As actor Billy Boyd, who brings Pippin to life in Jackson's trilogy, says in an interview just prior to the release of *The Return of the King*, "In the first movie [Pippin] said he felt like luggage, but by *The Return of the King*...there are things he does that really influence the end of the movie."[4] Young readers or filmgoers may feel the same way: Just wait until we grow up, and you will see how great we will be!

However, in the book and film trilogies, it takes a long time for Pippin to believe in himself in dangerous situations. As the journey progresses, Pippin eventually understands how perilous the Quest will become. Even more than Merry, Pippin questions whether he can be an effective participant in the Fellowship. As the journey continues, Pippin seems to fail with alarming regularity, yet he keeps trying and does not once ask to return home. He makes mistakes, which can have tragic consequences. He fails in his closest relationship, with Merry, when he looks into the palantír and then is taken from his cousin to accompany Gandalf to Minas Tirith. Especially in the beginning, Pippin seems hardly heroic and more likely to foil any heroic activities; in fact, he more often seems to need saving than to be likely to save others.

Nevertheless, later in Tolkien's trilogy, Pippin alerts Gandalf to Denethor's madness, allowing Gandalf to intercede in Faramir's imminent immolation.[5] Pippin protects a Gondorian soldier on the battlefield at Cormallen, slaying a troll and nearly dying in the aftermath.[6]

In the scouring of the Shire, Pippin works closely with Merry to create a workable defense against the ruffians; he travels alone to Tuckborough to raise a small army for the battle and later fights alongside Merry to rid the Shire of Saruman's/Sharkey's evil.[7] Pippin's heroism in the books is revealed not through a sudden shift in his nature or the revelation that he must learn to think before he acts. Indeed, Pippin continues to jump willingly into situations, good or bad; however, he does learn how to temper his impulsive nature with the ability to take care of himself and others.

Pippin's greatest gifts are stealth, empathy, and love. Pippin can sneak vegetables from a field[8] or the palantír from under Gandalf's nose.[9] He understands what others need to see or what they want; he can perceive the needs of others, ranging from Grishnakh the Orc[10] to Treebeard the Ent.[11] Pippin is fully alive and feels emotions deeply. His actions are based on emotional responses to a situation, whether they be love, curiosity, fear, sorrow, joy, or pride. Pippin is a sensualist who lives each moment fully and emotionally. One of his best qualities is what Merry describes as the "unquenchable cheerfulness of Pippin."[12] In many ways Pippin retains his optimistic outlook on life, but eventually understands how to use his impulses positively to inspire and help others. Tolkien's trilogy emphasizes these qualities in Pippin's development as a hero in *The Return of the King*, in which the author allows Pippin to achieve greatness by growing up while not changing his fundamental good-hearted, fun-loving nature.

Jackson's trilogy also shows these characteristics but goes to extremes in portraying Pippin as comic relief during much of the first two films. A member of the Tolkien Society, and a devout reader of the books, derides this portrayal as "Billy Boyd's standup comedian Peregrin McTook,"[13] and complains that if the film had been "dumbed down" any further, Peter Jackson "would have been catering for fans of LotR McDonald's happy meals."[14]

In the first two films, Pippin is a fool who seems to offer little but a naive, silly counterpoint to the serious nature of the Quest. However, Jackson also does an effective job of showing Pippin's development as a hero in *The Return of the King*. Pippin's story is featured much more prominently than Merry's in the third film, although the characters receive about the same amount of screen time in the first two films. Once he rides to Minas Tirith with Gandalf, Pippin is often a key element in the scenes involving Denethor, Faramir, and Gandalf. Although Jackson's Battle of Cormallen does not follow Tolkien's structure, and so troll-slaying Pippin is not a part of the film, he is shown in new or adapted scenes that allow him to perform heroically. Even though Jackson's film does not include the scouring of the Shire, an important section of the book for heroic Pippin, the young Hobbit is recognized as a hero in the Minas Tirith scenes of the third film.

As part of the Merry–Pippin dynamic in books and films, Pippin brings emotion and quick action to the partnership. He enlivens Merry's more serious nature and provides an empathetic understanding of others to balance Merry's more logical approach to problem solving. As he and Merry grow to their full stature as adult Hobbits during the Quest, Pippin is an inspirational character who proves that even a fool can become a hero.

Pippin as a Literary Hero

Pippin's value as a hero cannot truly be measured using the typical definitions of a literary hero. The importance of this character lies not in his ability to serve as a classic literary hero preordained for greatness, but in his ability to overcome his fear and self-doubt to grow up and into a heroic young adult. Pippin is truly the everyperson hero who, at least early in his life, might be voted least likely to do anything worthwhile for others, but who matures into a leader capable of heroic action in crises.

Like his cousin Merry Brandybuck, Pippin Took is from a leading family in the Shire. His father, Paladin, is a descendant of the Tooks who have ruled the Shire for generations.[15]

Although Pippin tells Bergil, son of Beregond and a guard of Gondor, that his father "farms the lands around Whitwell," at the time of the Quest, Paladin Took also is Thain of the Shire.[16] The role of Thain has been described as the leader who "represents the high king's interest in the Shire and sees to it that his laws are obeyed,"[17] a "Chief Executive" whose "authority began where that of the Mayor ended."[18] It is the highest title in the Shire, and Pippin should inherit this role later in life. In a way, Pippin's family can be considered the "royalty" of the Shire. The title *Ernil I Pherianneth*, or Prince of Halflings, as the people of Minas Tirith call him, is not entirely incorrect.[19] Although Pippin does not like that title, he is rather familiar with Gandalf, Denethor, Faramir, Aragorn, and others of high rank, and he treats them as equals, as befitting the demeanor of a prince. By birth, Pippin might be anticipated to act heroically, like classic literary heroes, but by nature, he does not strive to be a hero. Pippin has the aristocratic background similar to that of a classic literary hero, but his true stature as a modern hero comes from his personality and actions in times of crisis.

Tolkien's More Heroic Pippin

Tolkien's Pippin displays a true Hobbit nature. He is especially emotional and experiences life sensually. He revels in experiencing the pleasures of life; he loves a hot bath, a good pipe, fine food several times a day, a soft bed, and the pleasurable company of his kin. He is a somewhat spoiled young Hobbit, but he also has never had more responsibility than helping out his family and apparently spending a great deal of time with Merry. Tolkien writes that the Tooks are a "numerous and exceedingly wealthy" clan who receive some notoriety in at least every generation by giving the Shire "strong characters of peculiar habits and even adventurous temperament."[20] Pippin, in his generation, certainly fits this description and is a fine match for cousin Merry, who is one of the eccentric Brandybucks. Pippin is described in his youth as often hiking through the Shire with Frodo and seems to enjoy an uneventful early life with his family and friends.[21] There are no astounding feats of bravery indicating that he is, or may become, a local hero. His later Quest-related heroics may be surprising to those who watch him grow up in the Shire. As Pippin matures throughout *The Lord of the Rings*, he begins to temper his emotional responses to situations and to use his cleverness to help get him out of dangerous situations. His growth as a heroic character is not always an easy journey, but by the end of the tale, Pippin emerges as one on whom others can rely and as a strong leader.

Pre-Fellowship Pippin

Pre-Fellowship Pippin's personality is revealed as Pippin and Sam help Frodo move his belongings to Crickhollow, where Merry awaits after initially setting up the household there. Interestingly, neither Frodo nor Merry lets Pippin get away with too much, although he boisterously tries to get special treatment. Pippin comes across as indeed the youngest Hobbit among his closest cousins, the one who winsomely tries to be babied or sneak an extra treat, but who also is not so spoiled that he is sullen when he does not get his way.

As Frodo, Sam, and Pippin make their way from Bag End to Crick-hollow, they camp out at night.[22] After the first night on the road, Frodo cheerily wakes up the other two Hobbits. Pippin asks to sleep in, but Frodo pulls off Pippin's blanket and rolls him over, effectively getting him started on the day. Pippin then asks if Sam has a hot bath ready. Sam, ever eager to please his master—or his master's cousin—is startled awake and into action, but Frodo tells Pippin to accompany him to collect water. Pippin does, and he helps out around the campsite in other ways as the Hobbits prepare to hike another day. When the travelers finally arrive at Crickhollow, Merry has anticipated their needs and prepared hot baths for everyone. Pippin already has requested being the first in the tub, so Merry's solution is indeed efficient and allows everyone time to wash up before dinner.

Tolkien captures Pippin's personality beautifully when he writes about Pippin's bath time. The youngest Hobbit loves to sing and, with Merry's encouragement, cheerfully runs through many verses while he splashes. Merry notes that so much water is on the floor at the end of Pippin's bath that his young cousin must hurry to mop it all up before dinner. Pippin loves a good meal and quickly complies before joining the others for the meal that Merry and Fatty Bolger have prepared. At dinner, Pippin tries to snag more than his share of mushrooms, but Frodo guards his favorites well and will not let Pippin take all that he wants. This homey scene early in *The Fellowship of the Ring* shows how normal or common Pippin's early life has been. He is high spirited and clearly asks for what he wants, but he is very much a typical young Hobbit.

Along the journey from Bree, Pippin does what he must and tries to act tough enough for Strider. In Bree, before the Hobbits agree to let Strider accompany them, Pippin tells Strider that he does not look like the man described in Gandalf's letter to Frodo, but concedes that anyone who lives on the trail as much as Strider probably would not look any better. Strider replies that it would take more than living in the wild for Pippin to look as tough as he is; in fact, Strider adds, Pippin would probably die in the wilderness "unless you are made of sterner stuff than you look to be."[23] Pippin is not confident or toughened enough yet to be able to survive on his own, but he keeps trying. Unlike Merry, who becomes Strider's companion as a scout, Pippin usually stays with Sam or Frodo to prepare the campsite during the journey to Rivendell. When a crisis occurs, Pippin is terrified, but not any more so than Merry or the other Hobbits. For example, when the Black Riders attack Frodo at Weathertop, both Merry and Pippin collapse in fear and are ineffective in helping Frodo. However, once the crisis is past, the two diligently tend Frodo by heating water and bathing his injured shoulder and arm. Although Pippin is not ready for facing such crises, and he clearly cannot fight as a warrior, he completes little tasks well and is as devoted as the others to accompanying Frodo.[24]

Even Tolkien's humor, such as it is, is gentle when describing the foolish Pippin. On the way to Rivendell, Merry and Pippin walk ahead of the little group to scout the trail. A moment later, however, they run back in fear, telling Strider about the trolls on the path before them. Strider pokes fun at the Hobbits by reminding them of what they know about trolls, including the fact that trolls do not walk about in the daylight. He then shows the Hobbits the stone trolls, including one with a bird's nest on its head. Pointing out Merry and Pippin's folly is a gentle joke, and Pippin is not any more foolish in this instance than is Merry. The group shares a laugh, but it is not at Pippin's expense.[25]

Although Pippin lightly complains about the hardships of the journey, he nevertheless fights to become included in the Fellowship. After the Council of Elrond, as Frodo's companions are carefully chosen, Elrond wishes to send Merry and Pippin back with a warning to the Shire.[26] Pippin does not agree to be left behind simply because he does not understand all the potential dangers ahead of the Fellowship, and he tells Elrond that no one can anticipate what will befall them. Surprisingly, Gandalf supports Pippin in this argument, and Elrond reluctantly agrees to let both Pippin and Merry accompany Frodo. This scenario is far different from Jackson's scene, in which Pippin is equally determined to go along, but is sillier in his expression of his desires. Tolkien's Pippin is more articulate and, although he cannot know all that will happen in the future, nevertheless has some idea of the danger and knows exactly where Frodo is headed. There is no humorous tag line to close Tolkien's scene; after telling Elrond "you will have to lock me in prison...for otherwise I shall follow the Company," Pippin is allowed to become the final member of the Fellowship.[27]

Growing Pains during the Quest

A final example from Tolkien's *The Fellowship of the Ring* indicates Pippin's youthful foolishness but also has a different tone than the "fool" comments included throughout Jackson's trilogy. In the mines of Moria, Pippin is "curiously attracted" to the well in the room where the Fellowship rests while Gandalf determines their next move. As many young people do when confronted with something strange, new, and potentially harmful, they take a closer look, and Pippin is no different. He first peers over the edge and feels cool air arising from the well. "Moved by a sudden impulse," Pippin drops a small stone down the well. Tolkien writes that, many moments later, the stone makes a "*plunk*, very distant, but magnified and repeated in the hollow shaft."[28] Gandalf wonders what happened, but Pippin quickly confesses that he dropped a stone into the well. Gandalf is first relieved, then angry, calling Pippin a fool, as the sound of a hammer next alerts the Fellowship that they are not alone. Some type of communication is taking place, and others in the mines know that the Fellowship is there.

As punishment for creating the noise, Pippin keeps first watch. Although afraid that something bad will crawl out of the well and get him, Pippin nonetheless stands guard. After only an hour, however, Gandalf tells Pippin to go to sleep and keeps the watch himself. By this time, Gandalf's anger has waned, and his tone with Pippin is quite gentle. Although Pippin is often labeled a fool in Tolkien's work, his foolishness indicates the curiosity of the young and inexperienced, not a general lack of intelligence. In fact, in *The Two Towers*, Pippin is often resourceful and clever.

Several prime examples occur in scenes of Pippin and Merry's captivity among the Orcs. Pippin thinks quickly when the Orcs fight among themselves about what to do with the Hobbits. When one of the Orcs is killed and falls near him, Pippin's arm is nicked by the dead Orc's knife. Tolkien explains that Pippin feels the blood trickling down his arm, but more importantly feels the knife itself. When no one is watching him, he finds the blade and cuts the rope binding his wrists, then pretends that the bonds have not been cut. Tolkien adds that Pippin's wits are "wide-awake."[29]

During the forced run toward Isengard, Pippin takes a brief opportunity for either escape or a "message" for Aragorn. Tolkien writes that a "sudden thought leaped into Pippin's mind, and he acted on it at once."[30] Acting on this impulse, Pippin manages to flee his keepers long enough to drop the Elven brooch from his cloak in an untrammeled place where Aragorn is more likely to find it. Pippin cannot know for certain that his effort will be rewarded, and he is whipped and threatened for his brief escape. Readers soon learn that his action does help Aragorn, Legolas, and Gimli find what has become of the Hobbits. Pippin's impulsive action does pay off, although not immediately, and is a worthwhile impulse to have followed. In this situation, Pippin's quick wit and impulsive action make a difference in the way the plot unfolds; if Pippin had played it safe, the youngest Hobbits might have had a very different future, and even the War of the Ring might have turned out differently.

Finally, Pippin speaks impulsively, which might anger Grishnakh, one of his captors, but ultimately provides Pippin and Merry with a means of escape. Grishnakh wants to take the Hobbits for himself instead of allowing them to go to Isengard. Pippin understands at once what Grishnakh wants when he begins to search the Hobbits. Tolkien acknowledges Pippin's anxiety while furthering readers' understanding that Pippin is quite an astute young Hobbit: "Cold fear was in Pippin's heart, yet at the same time he was wondering what use he could make of Grishnakh's desire."[31] Pippin then begins talking to Grishnakh, mimicking Gollum and hinting that he knows the location of the Ring. A moment later Merry understands Pippin's strategy and plays along. The exchange is enough to convince Grishnakh to abscond with the Hobbits as his prize. However, as he drags them away from the rest of the Orc encampment, Éomer and the Rohirrim arrive, and Grishnakh is killed in the ensuing fight.

The result of Pippin's quick thinking is that the Hobbits are much closer to Fangorn Forest and can escape the battle unharmed. Tolkien shows that, although Pippin continues to be impulsive, he is not stupid or even merely foolish. He has moments of cleverness and quick thinking that save him, and Merry, from what otherwise might be a foolish act. As Pippin grows up through his experiences on the Quest, his impulses become less self-serving and more outwardly directed. He uses his impulsive nature to solve problems or to jump into a situation from which other characters may shy.

Pippin's impulses often lead him into foolish trouble, and indeed, the outcome of the previously mentioned scenes in *The Two Towers* could have ended much differently. Pippin might have easily been killed for his escape attempt or simply gutted by an angry Grishnakh; his impulsive actions at best might have been vain attempts at escape or rescue. However, Tolkien creates scenes in which Pippin's impulsive speech or actions sometimes work out well not only to assist Pippin and Merry on their part of the journey, but to further the overall story of the Quest as well. These scenes also endear Pippin to readers, who might empathize with the youngest Hobbit because he seems to want to do what is right, but often also seems to be at the mercy of his impetuous nature. Everyone knows a Pippin, someone whose intentions are good but who may be a bit too naive or unaware for his own good.

Wartime Heroism

Throughout Pippin's time in Minas Tirith (*The Return of the King*), he acquits himself well.[32] Pippin sees that Denethor plans to kill both Faramir and himself and knows that he alone cannot stay this madness. Pippin runs through the city to alert Gandalf, who does have the power to save Faramir. Pippin is the messenger and backs up Gandalf, but he alone does not save Faramir (in contrast to events in Jackson's adaptation).

Although Pippin displays bravery in a few chapters in *The Return of the King*, he is most noted in two different battles: the Battle of Cormallen in Gondor and the Battle of Bywater in the Shire. In Pippin's first full-fledged battle, he saves a comrade from being killed; Pippin steps forward and mortally wounds a troll.[33] The Hobbit is later recognized for his heroism and self-sacrifice by being dubbed a Knight of Gondor.[34] At the Battle of Bywater, Pippin brings troops from Tuckborough to create an army large enough to rally against the ruffians in the Shire.[35] Pippin acts as one of two captains (Merry is the other) who not only fight admirably and lead the Hobbits in scouring the Shire of the immediate danger, but also in rooting out the last of the evildoers after the battle.[36] Pippin effectively helps make the Shire safe for a return to normal life. Readers may approve of "grown-up" Pippin, who at last is successful and heroic. The cheerful Hobbit has tempered his mischievous nature but is still vibrant and lovable. He has redeemed himself for the indiscretions of his past, a fact that readers may applaud.

Post-Quest Heroics

As Gandalf tells the Hobbits before they reenter the Shire without him, they have been trained to take care of the problems in the Shire and will be successful. He adds that the Hobbits "are grown up now . . . among the great you are, and I have no longer any fear at all for any of you."[37] This high praise from Gandalf is directed to all four Hobbits, but it is especially applicable to Pippin, who is now taller than most Hobbits and most recently spent a great deal of time with the Wizard. Gandalf no longer needs to look after him; Pippin acts like an adult with the ability to use his experiences more wisely and to know when to act on his impulses. In the remainder of the tale, Tolkien's Pippin indeed lives up to Gandalf's words by assisting first in the scouring of the Shire and later in its peacetime rebuilding.

Although Tolkien creates in Pippin a youthfully foolish Hobbit who acts on impulses that older Hobbits or characters representing other races might easily repress, Pippin is not solely a fool. He matures and on many occasions shows that his impulsive speech and actions are based in an understanding of a potentially dangerous situation. His nature always will be to respond emotionally to a situation, but he has learned how to channel these emotions into more appropriate actions. Pippin's motivations are never malevolent, even when they lead to problems for the Fellowship. However, by the end of Tolkien's trilogy, Pippin learns to temper his impulses so that his actions are more focused. His attention is more outer directed in times of crisis, although once the crisis is past, Pippin returns to his fun-loving ways.

In his last descriptions of Pippin in the trilogy proper, Tolkien again shows Pippin's range of emotions. The young Hobbit laughs to have "outsmarted" Frodo from giving Merry and him the slip as he leaves for Valinor, but Pippin also cries to see Frodo leave. Pippin, Merry, and Sam stand quietly as the ship departs, but once on the road home, Pippin begins to sing again.[38] As the emotional barometer for the Fellowship, Pippin is full of life. He successfully grows from an inner-directed young Hobbit to an outer-directed adult who nonetheless retains his enjoyment of what he values in life. Throughout Tolkien's trilogy, Pippin is impulsive in speech and deed, but he also grows in the ability to use his wits to think so that his impulsive actions are more likely to succeed.

Pippin as a Cinematic Hero

In Jackson's trilogy, Pippin remains impulsive, but the results of his impetuous behavior are split into two sections: Possibly Dangerous to Downright Disastrous, and Dangerous but Potentially Heroic. The first section comprises all of *The Fellowship of the Ring* and the beginning of *The Two Towers*. Pippin's impulses begin to pay off, even in unexpected ways, during the Hobbits' dealings with Treebeard and lead Pippin to heroic behavior in *The Return of the King*. Jackson's Pippin, therefore, has a much more dramatic personality change by the third film; he becomes more mature, and although he retains his Hobbity good nature, he becomes noticeably more somber after his arrival at Minas Tirith, the point when he truly becomes an adult. Many of Pippin's actions are Dangerous but Potentially Heroic in the third film, as his impulsive nature helps him intervene on behalf of others.

At first, Jackson's Pippin is much sillier than his book counterpart. Throughout *The Fellowship of the Ring* Pippin seems to have few ideas of his own, and those that do pop into his head often prompt impulsive actions that get him into trouble. However, Jackson develops new scenes, or twists book-related scenes, that allow Pippin honorably to redeem himself and become a true hero by the end of the trilogy. Jackson's Pippin differs from Tolkien's depiction of the character in these ways: (1) he is sillier and frequently serves as comic relief, (2) his impulsive acts are exaggerated for good or ill; however, his later impetuous actions in the trilogy become more heroic as he is able to save important characters, and (3) Pippin becomes a strong character, physically and emotionally, in different ways than Tolkien's Pippin shows strength of character.

Fool of a Took

As Gandalf repeats several times in the first and third films, Pippin truly is a "fool of a Took." He blindly follows Merry into adventure, or he is so curious or impulsive that he acts on his own without thinking. Especially in the first film in the trilogy, Pippin is childlike and has the self-centered interests of the very immature. He seems aware of little else but his own needs and the reactions of others to him. However, Jackson does allow this depiction of Pippin to change dramatically by providing glimpses into Pippin's increasing maturity and, by *The Return of the King*, to become a young adult who leaves behind the single-minded self-interest of the un-aware and not fully formed. Jackson provides Pippin with a dramatic arc for growth, which serves the character well without changing his basic nature. The buffoon of the first film eventually gives rise to a hero in the third, but first, Pippin is the comic relief.

The first scene Jackson shows of Pippin is the fireworks scene, when Pippin boisterously is boosted into the back of Gandalf's wagon to steal a rocket.[39] Safely hidden in a nearby tent, Pippin first lights the firework and then asks Merry what they should do, not the wisest sequence of actions. Through luck, neither he nor his cousin is more than singed by the rocket, and neither apparently has the sense to realize what a close call they have had. Pippin is all too eager to steal another explosive immediately after the first one takes off unexpectedly.

Another early scene, in which Pippin and Merry flee after they filch vegetables from Farmer Maggot's fields, ends only slightly better. Pippin is pushed off a steep embankment, tumbling down to land near a fresh pile of manure. "Ooh, that was close," says an undaunted Pippin, not worried about the consequences of the fall so much as the luck of not landing in something deep and fragrant.[40] That brief occurrence could be rather symbolic of Pippin's early film life as a tagalong to Merry. Wherever Merry leads, Pippin eagerly follows, sharing in all pranks and adventures, some of which could lead him into deep trouble. Of course, a moment later in this scene, Pippin spies mushrooms and is cheerfully squashed by Merry and Sam in their eagerness to get to the mushrooms. Pippin acts as if this is a normal occurrence, and as he is the youngest in the group, it probably is. Pippin follows along as fearlessly as any young lad eager for acceptance in the group and foolishly willing to prove his worth in whatever scrape they get into.

At the inn in Bree, an eager Pippin again tries to keep up with older cousin Merry, who proudly returns to the Hobbits' table with a full pint of ale.[41] Pippin, just beginning a half pint of his own, immediately jumps up to retrieve an even larger tankard. Even if half a pint would be plenty, he must keep up with Merry. Unfortunately, as he gets his drink, Pippin is overheard rather loudly explaining his relationship to Frodo, who desper-ately, if poorly, tries to conceal his identity. Oblivious Pippin spouts all the family information, causing Frodo to rush forward to shush him. However, when Frodo trips, the Ring accidentally flies upward and onto his finger, making Frodo disappear. Pippin's careless actions and inability to understand the seriousness of Frodo's meeting in Bree nearly doom the Quest before it truly begins.

As the journey to Rivendell begins in earnest, Pippin is appalled that their leader, Strider, does not allow the Hobbits their customary number of meals.[42] As Strider throws apples back toward the Hobbits, expecting them to munch as they hike, an apple smacks Pippin squarely in the head. Pippin is oblivious as to where the apples originated, looking up in a daze at the sky, as if it might be raining apples. This action is repeated during the flotsam and jetsam scene in the extended version of *The Two Towers* when Pippin spies apples floating in the debris.[43] He glances up at the sky, as if to make sure one more time that apples are not falling.

Because Pippin is only concerned with his stomach, not the possible danger at Weathertop, he only is indignant that Frodo gets ash on the tomatoes that Sam, Merry, and Pippin have been preparing over the fire.[44] Although Frodo sees the fire as a beacon to their enemies, the other Hobbits, especially Pippin, who complains to Frodo, only see that their hot meal is ending early. Pippin's foolish self-interest blinds him to real dangers.

At Rivendell, Pippin once again dashes after Merry into Elrond's council, agreeing to go on the Quest without understanding anything about the undertaking.[45] As Pippin self-importantly explains that the Fellowship will need some person of wisdom on the journey, Merry needles him by commenting wryly, "Well, that rules you out, Pip." Pippin immediately agrees—it seems like he automatically agrees with anything Merry says—before realizing that he is insulting himself. The final tag to the scene takes place after Elrond's solemn pronouncement about the creation of the Fellowship and their dangerous mission, when Pippin pipes up with a cheerful "Where are we going?" His exclamation not only lightens the somber nature of the scene, which is becoming ponderous, but it also shows just how little Pippin understands.

In the extended version of *The Two Towers*, Jackson uses the interplay between Merry and Pippin for the film's lighter moments. Interestingly, these scenes are added to the extended version, where there is time for audiences to see them, unlike in the theatrical release, which focused on the darker themes and ended with the Battle of Helm's Deep. In the extended version, the structure of the film is changed, and the overall pace slowed, by the inclusion of the extra Pippin–Merry scenes.

The Ent draft scene highlights the playful sibling rivalry of the pair and provides more character development.[46] Both characters are delightfully silly in their one-upmanship. Pippin blissfully ignores Merry's inquiries about what he is drinking and, quite childishly, does not want to share his secret, or the draft. Pippin acts innocent about what he is doing and, once it becomes apparent that the draft is making him grow taller, is delighted by the outcome. Filmgoers can understand why this scene has been cut from the original theatrical version, as it slows the pace of the film and does nothing to further the plot. However, it does provide quiet moments of lively character interaction that let audiences learn more about the lighter side of the Hobbits and the depth of the Pippin–Merry bond.

This type of light humor is again evident in the flotsam and jetsam scene at the conclusion of the extended version.[47] Pippin is not humorous in the same way he is as a fool in *The Fellowship of the Ring*. Instead, his true nature provides the lighter moments, as he scavenges for food for his insatiable appetite, glories in pipeweed, and laughs uproariously with his cousin.

This tone is maintained in Pippin's and Merry's first scene in *The Return of the King*, which is basically a continuation of where audiences left the duo in the previous film, or more explicitly, in the extended version.[48] The cheerfully sensual Pippin, living fully in the moment and gleeful in his complete enjoyment of food, drink, and good company, does not apologize for his lack of propriety in addressing royalty when Aragorn, Théoden, and others arrive at Isengard. Instead, Pippin simply rejoices in the captured bounty and reunion with his friends. His previous captivity seems a far-off memory, and Pippin is a lighthearted example of someone with the childlike capacity to enjoy life to its fullest at a given moment. The "fool" quality is lacking in the latter part of the trilogy, but any lighter moments are most likely to be Pippin's.

Pippin's "foolish" optimism in the face of almost certain defeat is inspirational in a later *Return of the King* scene.[49] Pippin fully believes that good will triumph in the end, and even that the soldiers of Minas Tirith, as well as the good folk of Middle-earth itself, will prevail, if only because Gandalf is on their side. At Minas Tirith, Pippin discusses the upcoming siege with the Wizard one evening. "Is there any hope, Gandalf, for Frodo and Sam?" Pippin softly asks, most likely wanting a comforting reply. "There never was much hope. Just a fool's hope," says Gandalf. Pippin may be the fool in the story, but his ability to bounce back after each hardship and challenge, and to keep believing in the hope that Frodo will succeed, not only keeps Pippin from despair but also makes a fool's hope seem desirable. Filmgoers may very well feel that they should be as foolish as Pippin to keep believing in miracles, especially when times are difficult. He may be a fool for believing that he and his cousins will survive the war, or that Middle-earth can be saved from Sauron, but he is markedly less foolish in his behavior.

Even at the end of *The Return of the King*, in a brief scene without dialogue, Pippin once again acts the fool but in a more subdued way than how he is portrayed earlier in the trilogy. As Merry, Frodo, and Pippin witness Sam's wedding, Jackson uses the modern (and not specifically Hobbity) convention of having the bride's bouquet thrown into the crowd of guests.[50] In many Western cultures, the female who catches the bride's bouquet is supposed to be the next to be married, and this interpretation is what Jackson requires for the humor to work. Pippin catches the bouquet, looks momentarily embarrassed, but then also catches the eye of the lovely Hobbit lass standing next to him. Pippin then smiles in a more interested way and rocks back and forth on his heels. It is a sweeter version of the Pippin-as-fool scenario and may presage Pippin's marriage to Diamond of Long Cleeve. The character is not identified as such in the film's credits, but readers of the book may like to draw that conclusion.

Jackson's humor is broader than Tolkien's, and in fact, Tolkien is not effective with humor in the books. Derek Robinson writes that Tolkien's style "is almost totally resistant" to humor. Dialogue is the natural place to insert humor, which is where Jackson most often makes Pippin look the fool, and Robinson adds that Tolkien is not a strong author of dialogue. Tolkien "is quite definitely bad at handling lively exchanges where views are challenged or where temperaments clash."[51] Jackson breaks up Tolkien's long speeches and modernizes the dialogue. However, Jackson's tone is occasionally so broad as to be embarrassing for a character who is normally dignified (see chapter 4, about Éowyn, for example, in which her culinary skills become the focus of humor). In Pippin's case, his book self is often foolish, too, but not the buffoon that Jackson sometimes has him be for the sake of comic relief. The sweeter, lighter moments in the films, often found only in the extended versions, are truer to Tolkien's depiction of Pippin as a young character whose exuberance often gets him into trouble. Yet even this fool behaves heroically by the end of the story. Pippin's "foolish" nature allows him optimism in facing a dangerous future, and sometimes his seemingly foolish acts or words lead to the right course of action.

In fact, Pippin's quiet optimism and childlike exuberance are an effective foil for other characters who face the grim realities of Middle-earth. Although Pippin is much less heroic in the first half of Jackson's trilogy, his foolishness is not only useful for showing a contrast with other characters, but it also dramatically contrasts his more somber demeanor in later scenes in *The Return of the King*.

Although Pippin's foolish behavior, especially in *The Fellowship of the Ring*, may be a bit disconcerting to film audiences, his self-absorbed, unenlightened enthusiasm for adventure does help endear him to audiences. He seems to need to be protected, and because he is completely unaware of the true dangers lurking outside the Shire, audiences may worry about his safety and root for him as he encounters characters and situations far beyond his limited experience. Pippin's impulsive acts also indicate his youthfulness and remind audiences that even the youngest within a group may play an important role in a crisis, or may surprise their elders with their ability to adapt and spontaneously help others when need arises.

Pippin's Impulsive Nature

Throughout Jackson's trilogy, Pippin is especially impulsive in both action and speech. In *The Fellowship of the Ring*, his impulsive actions are self-serving, owing to his insatiable curiosity and his simple lack of awareness of the darker meanings of situations. In *The Two Towers*, his impulsive actions sometimes help—or are motivated by his desire to help—others. In *The Return of the King*, Pippin's impulsive words and deeds eventually serve the good of many and lead to specific heroics. Jackson does well by Pippin in the third film by allowing his heroic deeds to shine; Pippin, more than Merry, is allowed to showcase his heroism with more onscreen time, and as a result, Pippin grows into a more fully developed adult Hobbit by the conclusion of the trilogy.

Through the Rivendell scene in *The Fellowship of the Ring*, when the Fellowship prepares to leave on the long journey toward Mordor, Pippin's impulsive actions are humorous. Nothing more serious than a bop on the head or a bruise to his pride happens to him, and although he is frightened by Frodo's attack at Weathertop, by the time the Fellowship departs Rivendell, Frodo seems to be relatively back to normal. However, midway through *The Fellowship of the Ring*, Pippin learns a difficult lesson, and his impulsive act puts into motion a series of events that have an impact on the rest of the story. Although Pippin's curiosity leads to a terrible loss, it also sets up events that ultimately work to the benefit of the "good guys" in Middle-earth.

In Moria, Pippin is given the task of holding Gandalf's staff while the Wizard reads the final entry in Balin's journal and learns the fate of the Dwarves who worked the mines.[52] On seeing a skewered skeleton nearby, curious Pippin reaches out to touch it. He is youthful in the need not only to see, but also to experience. He extends his fingers to grasp a bony hand, but the touch is enough to topple the skeleton, along with a chain and a bucket, into a deep well. Jackson provides a close-up of grimacing Pippin, chagrined beyond belief as the sound echoes for a long time.

Billy Boyd elaborates on the scene and the way that Pippin's inquisitive nature is expanded for the film: Director Jackson and Boyd discussed that "it would be great if I didn't actually push [the skeleton] but just touched something near it," starting the progression of head to body to chain to bucket falling into the well. "In the book, it was a stone; . . . [Jackson's version] tells the story in exactly the same way, but in a film, a stone wouldn't have the same effect that the skeleton had."[53]

Jackson plays up the sound effects in this scene.[54] All is quiet, save the ongoing clank as the objects knock against the side of the well. Finally there is a resounding crash. Silence is held for only a moment before a menacing, increasingly louder thump draws ever nearer to the Fellowship. Screeches begin to accompany the thumping. The next sound is Gandalf's slamming of the journal, admonishing Pippin: "Fool of a Took! Throw yourself in next time and rid us of your stupidity." A final shot of Pippin looking mortified and guilty closes the "quiet" part of the scene. The film's pace immediately picks up as first goblins and then the Balrog battle the Fellowship. Gandalf spectacularly fights this latter foe and appears to be lost in the great chasm before the Fellowship manages to flee the mine.

For the first time, Pippin keenly feels a loss and probably experiences remorse in alerting the hostile forces to the Fellowship's presence. Not only does Frodo come close to being killed by a troll,[55] but Gandalf is lost.[56] The sudden violence and tragic consequences must seem doubly shocking to such a kindly, gentle Hobbit as Pippin, who has first drawn his sword and effectively fought in defense of his friends and kin. Gandalf's fall, and Frodo's near death, are not Pippin's fault, but his curiosity does play a part in making the Fellowship's journey through Moria more hazardous. Jackson's tableau of the devastated group after leaving Moria emphasizes this first loss within the Fellowship. Music overlays the scene, which has no dialogue at first, as each character shows his grief or shock. Pippin has collapsed, weeping, and a shocked Merry holds him, rhythmically squeezing Pippin's arm. Despite this comfort, Pippin seems to be inconsolable.

However, this difficult life lesson does not curb Pippin's impulsive nature. During the battle scenes at the end of *The Fellowship of the Ring*, Pippin and Merry hide from Orcs—at least until Pippin bursts from their hiding place to protest Frodo's leaving on his own.[57] Even when Merry prompts Pippin to run so as to draw the Orcs away from Frodo, Pippin seems unaware of exactly how precarious their situation is. He seems to run not so much to keep away from the Orcs, but because Merry tells him to run faster. "It's working!" Pippin crows as he and Merry dash away, yelling for the Orcs to follow them. "I know it's working! Run!" Merry urgently replies, aware that they have too successfully encouraged the Orcs to chase them.

If nothing else, by the end of *The Fellowship of the Ring*, a captured Pippin now knows how deadly the results of his hasty actions can be. His impulsive speech and action do not kill Boromir, but Pippin's response to Frodo's departure sets in motion the need for Merry and him to be saved. The Gondorian fights bravely to try to save the Hobbits he has befriended. If Pippin, and therefore Merry, had stayed hidden, Boromir may not have died at that point. It is impossible to know how or if he would have died. Nevertheless, when the Hobbits are threatened and seem in imminent danger of death, Boromir charges forward, although he is greatly out-numbered, and gives his life in defense of the Hobbits.[58] This fact is not lost on Pippin.

Boromir's death prompts another of Pippin's impulsive actions later in the trilogy—to offer his service to Boromir's father, Denethor, in "payment" of his and Merry's debt.[59] Although Pippin is impulsive in his allegiance to the steward, Pippin at least realizes by the time he meets Denethor that actions have consequences, and one often gains responsibilities as a result of the consequences of one's actions.

Pippin's impulses are based less on curiosity or self-indulgence through-out *The Two Towers*. Instead, Pippin's few impulses shown on film come from his selfless desire to help others, or specifically to save another. This change continues throughout the end of the trilogy.

In the first scene in which film audiences see Merry and Pippin in *The Two Towers*, the Hobbits are tied to the backs of Orcs and are bouncing along rather uncomfortably toward Isengard.[60] In the extended version, when the Orcs pause in their run, the brute closest to Pippin drinks from his waterskin. Pippin is worried about the injured Merry. Pippin impulsively exclaims that Merry is ill and begs the Orc to give him a drink. However, the Orcs' cruelty turns Pippin's request into a form of torture for Merry, as a foul brew instead is forced down his throat. Pippin then urgently commands the Orcs to leave Merry alone. This draws the attention of an Orc captain, who warns Pippin to keep quiet. Only slightly subdued, Pippin barely waits for the captain to turn away before he gets Merry's attention and checks to see if he is badly injured. Pippin's outburst does not get the result the young Hobbit desires, but it is done for the good of another, not to help himself. His impulsive speech comes from his concern for his cousin. It may not be wise to confront his captors, but Pippin does not seem concerned about the possible harm to himself if his actions would help his cousin.

Once the Hobbits are brought before the Orc leaders taking the pair to Saruman, Pippin's impulsive speech almost gives away information about the Ring.[61] The Orcs argue about what should be done with the Hobbits—including the possibility of eating them—to which the stronger of the captains announces that the Hobbits are to be spared because they have a weapon that Saruman wants. Pippin stage whispers to Merry, "They think we have the Ring," certainly not the most intelligent admission to make when surrounded by hungry Orcs. Merry immediately shushes Pippin and reminds him that they will be killed if the Orcs find out they do not carry the coveted weapon.

However, Pippin's impulsive speech does not always put someone—usually himself or Merry—in danger. Pippin is more effective when he and Merry meet Treebeard.[62] After the Ent moot, Treebeard carries the Hobbits to the edge of Fangorn Forest so they may return home. Pippin suddenly commands Treebeard to stop and turn around so that the Hobbits will be left at the forest's closest border to Isengard. Treebeard and Merry think that Pippin is being foolish to come so close to Saruman, but Pippin has worked out that Treebeard needs to see the destruction wrought by the Orcs in order to be motivated to go to war. Billy Boyd explains that Pippin has "the lovely ability to look at people and almost know what they need at that moment in order to continue." This ability comes in handy when Merry has been unsuccessful in persuading the Ents to go to war. "Although Pippin hated showing Treebeard the dead trees, he realized he had to make it immediate for the Ents to get them involved."[63] By asking Treebeard to drop off the Hobbits near Isengard, Pippin succeeds in getting the Ents to go to war. The resulting battle destroys much of Isengard and pins Saruman and Wormtongue under the Ents' control. This understanding of Pippin's strengths behind Boyd's approach to the scene may not be apparent to viewers, who only see that Pippin has come up with a strange idea that will seem to put the Hobbits in Saruman's path.

Jackson downplays Pippin's intelligence and empathy in this scene by making Pippin's confidence that he and Merry will not be caught if Treebeard takes the Hobbits closer to Isengard seem inexplicable. Pippin cannot tell Merry about his reasoning or Treebeard also will hear. When Treebeard exclaims that Pippin's change in direction will take the Hobbits closer to danger, Pippin replies nonsensically that "the closer we are to danger, the farther we are from harm."[64] Treebeard echoes what at least some audience members must be thinking: "That makes no sense to me." Jackson's version of the Ents' motivation to go to war gives Pippin a larger role in the battle for Middle-earth; however, even when Pippin is behaving rationally and thinking before he speaks, his foresight seems more like luck than intelligence.

The changes marking Pippin's passage into maturity and the beginning of using his impulses in heroic ways all take place during the third film of the trilogy. In *The Two Towers*, Pippin vacillates between being insightful with the Ents to unthinking in what he blurts aloud; however, his demeanor grows progressively more serious in this film. Nevertheless, once danger is at bay for the moment, Pippin reverts to his carefree, playful self. In the Ent draft scene in *The Two Towers* extended version, Pippin is annoyingly vague about the draft and shows how he and Merry probably interacted like siblings back in the Shire—slightly competitive and teasing. Also in the extended version, Pippin's thoughts turn to food as soon as Isengard has been secured; he delights in the discovery of Saruman's larder. Although Pippin is maturing in *The Two Towers*, there is no true sense of the adult Hobbit he will become.

The question about Pippin's adult persona is answered by the conclusion of the trilogy. Pippin's development is clearly shown through several
revealing scenes, and in *The Return of the King*, Pippin is given much more
to do than in the previous two films.

At the beginning of *The Return of the King*, Pippin drinks, eats, and
cheekily welcomes royalty to Isengard.[65] His behavior is laughably understandable by his friends in the Fellowship, who are relieved to find the
Hobbits in such good spirits after their captivity. Nevertheless, Pippin's
speech and actions are not appropriate for greeting Théoden and Éomer at
least, but Pippin is more concerned with the virtues of salted pork rather
than with royal protocol. He appears as impulsive and self-involved as ever.

Slightly later in scenes at Isengard, Pippin spies the palantír as he rides
behind Aragorn. Pippin slides from the horse to wander in wonder toward
the shiny orb beneath the flood. Pippin seems transfixed by the palantír as
he holds it, and he looks both downcast and resentful as Gandalf demands
that he hand over the treasure. Once Pippin sees the palantír, he is attracted
to it, and his curiosity gets the better of him. It nags him so that he cannot
sleep, and the only way he will be satisfied is to give into the urge to look
into the orb. Pippin's later "borrowing" of the palantír is done to satisfy his
curiosity; it is not an act of treachery.[66] Pippin tells Merry that he only
wants to see the palantír, with plans to return it to Gandalf as stealthily as
he took it. Pippin even brings his prize to Merry's makeshift bed to remain
under his cousin's watchful eye. As film audiences know, the consequences
of that impulsive act are immediately painful, physically and mentally. Only
Gandalf can bring Pippin back to himself after he has encountered Sauron
through the palantír. Although Sauron could have learned of Frodo and the
Ring, instead, Gandalf learns of Sauron's plans. Gandalf also knows that
Pippin does not lie to him about the encounter; terrified he may be, but
Pippin is, as Gandalf tells the others, only "an honest fool."

Pippin pays for his impulsive action, and this great lesson perhaps
tempers his behavior for the rest of the film. Pippin learns that he must take
responsibility for his actions, and if they are hasty and ill thought out, then
he still must pay the price. The two scenes that show how Pippin moves
from the remnants of childhood to adulthood occur sequentially in the film,
with a thematic bridge between them.

Pippin is still nearly childlike as he trots after Gandalf to leave for
Minas Tirith.[67] He asks Merry what is happening and seems unhappy at
his cousin's ire, but filmgoers, or readers of the book who see the film,
probably have the idea that Merry has scolded Pippin for misdeeds in the
past, but has gotten over his anger before long. This time, however, Pippin
cannot get Merry to slow down or stop being angry. When Merry asks why
Pippin looked into the palantír, Pippin's reply is the typical wayward child's

"I don't know. I couldn't help it." Pippin then makes the rash promise of all children who want to be back in good graces, even if they are not sure what they did wrong: "I'm sorry. I won't do it again, all right?" This time, Merry cannot so easily forgive, and Pippin comes to realize that one on-going consequence of his impulsive act is to be separated from Merry. For him, that is indeed a high price to pay for being inquisitive.

This is the last scene of childlike Pippin. The journey on Shadowfax to Minas Tirith provides a bridge between Pippin's rather sheltered early life and an adulthood in which he must stand on his own. Jackson shows Pippin and Gandalf riding through woods and across plains to arrive in Minas Tirith.[68] The physical journey also represents Pippin's journey from childhood into greater maturity. In Minas Tirith Pippin still is impulsive; he almost immediately offers his service to Denethor, who readily accepts.[69] However, this action is motivated by more than self-interest.

Although Pippin disobeys Gandalf when he tells Denethor what be-came of Boromir, he does not do so in open defiance of his mentor/father figure, but because he feels he must repay a great debt. Boromir was his friend and protector, and Pippin pledges his allegiance to Denethor not out of wounded pride, as in Tolkien's book, but out of the need to meet his and Merry's obligation to Boromir's family. Pippin wants to make right, even in a small way, the great loss of Boromir. As Pippin later touches his new uniform and gingerly handles a sword, he comments that he does not want to fight and hopes that he will not be expected to serve as a warrior.[70] Gandalf mocks him as a "guard of the citadel"; nevertheless, Pippin plans to fulfill his commitment to the best of his ability. He honors the obligations that he impulsively makes.

Billy Boyd also adds another important motivation for Pippin's actions throughout the Minas Tirith scenes in Jackson's trilogy. Pippin has to make the best of a bad situation, and if Minas Tirith is not the place where he would like to be, he understands why he is there and strives to act hon-orably and responsibly. According to Boyd, Pippin learns about war and "tries to deal with it without Merry. He doesn't do it to become a hero. He does it to see his friend again and shows himself to be . . . a noble charac-ter."[71] Pippin is very much the modern hero who is placed in a situation and must act; he does not seek situations in which he may act heroically; his motivation is much simpler—to be reunited with family and to have his actions make them proud along the way.

Pippin is losing his innocence throughout the Quest, but even in Minas Tirith he is not likely to understand how Denethor might use him as a pawn against Gandalf or how his service to Denethor may worry the Wizard. Pippin's impulse to offer his service is purely motivated; for once his im-pulsive act is not for himself, and it is a successful action. Pippin's service to

Denethor, and Gondor, is a positive deed, although Pippin does not know that his voluntary offer of service will eventually lead to heroic deeds.

For all his increasing maturity, Pippin's does not abandon his impulsive nature. Now it is directed in such a way as to make him more heroic. Through scenes adapted from the book or written only for the film, Jackson increases Pippin's stature as a hero. It seems fitting that Pippin's entry into full maturity takes place at Minas Tirith. In Sindarin Elvish, *Minas Tirith* means "tower of guard."[72] Pippin truly becomes a "tower" of a guard by saving Faramir and Gandalf from death, and by taking on the task of lighting the beacon to call for aid from the rest of Gondor and Rohan.

Even Pippin's change in costume indicates his older, more serious persona.[73] When Pippin becomes a guard of the citadel, he is given the uniform of a Gondorian soldier, including mail and a black tunic emblazoned with the white tree of Gondor. In a scene in which Pippin looks over the uniform he must wear the following morning, he is wearing a soft white shirt with blue embroidery. His "civilian" clothes are soft and white, reflecting Pippin's innocence and a gentle connection to his home. Pippin does not want to fight; the Hobbits are "essentially 'civilian' temperaments, unsuited to combat and danger yet forced into them by circumstance. . . . [Audiences] admire them for their aversion to fighting, not their love of it."[74] As he dons metal and dark cloth, Pippin takes on the serious responsibilities of an adult, especially one who realizes the hazards of troubled times and the demands of being part of the larger world. As with youths exposed to the adult problems of the world at an early age, Pippin is forced to grow up faster than usual and deal with issues he should not have to face until he comes of age, if at all. During his time in Minas Tirith, Pippin grows into a powerful, honorable, yet still deeply caring hero. He towers above his previous buffoonish behavior and acts responsibly and nobly. He has become an adult.

Four Heroic Deeds

In Jackson's trilogy, Pippin is a hero through four actions: lighting the beacon, alerting Gandalf to Denethor's madness, saving Faramir from the pyre, and saving Gandalf from an Orc's blade. Each heroic act is impulsive, but each turns out well. Jackson allows Pippin to act heroically, without thought to his own safety, to protect others; the director emphasizes Pippin's actions and expressions in key scenes in Minas Tirith. Although every hero's spontaneous action might be deemed "impulsive," Pippin's nature throughout the trilogy is consistently impulsive; his spontaneous exclamations or deeds are typical, not an atypical response to crisis. This is not true of other heroic characters in the trilogy. However, only in the latter part of the third film do Pippin's impulses become a consistently effective force, one that has positive consequences for the forces of good. Pippin's response to crisis is to act impulsively, but his instincts for what to do and when to act have improved greatly by the conclusion of battle scenes at Minas Tirith and Cormallen.

Gandalf gives Pippin his first opportunity for heroism by shamelessly playing on Pippin's need for Gandalf's approval.[75] Gandalf explains that there is a task only Pippin can accomplish, one that will give another opportunity for the "Shire-folk to show their great worth." Of course, Pippin, who has had self-doubts about his worth on this journey, readily agrees without asking what is to be done or how dangerous it might be. Indeed, possibly only a Hobbit could climb the great tower, which is more like a raw cliff face, to light the beacon without being set upon by the beacon's guards or seen by others in the city. The audience's attention is directed by the camera movement, which provides different views of the cliff/tower. The shot moves up and around the tower as Pippin climbs; then the camera looks down on the Hobbit to show just how far and steep an ascent he has made.[76] Pippin accomplishes the task, and Jackson's shot of Pippin (highlighting Billy Boyd's expression and body language) once the beacon catches fire perfectly shows Pippin's state of mind. Pippin's first reaction is to grin in quiet pride in accomplishing the task, only belatedly to realize that he is standing atop a burning stack of logs, with a long climb to safety before him. The rapid shift in expression from joy at his success to awareness of danger, and the change in body language from confident stance to awkward maneuvering away from the flames, is a purely "Pippin" moment.

Much of Pippin's heroism in Minas Tirith is the result of a literal baptism by fire. His position as one of Denethor's guards gives him the opportunity to sneak closer to the procession carrying Faramir's wounded body toward the family crypt. Pippin rushes forward when he overhears Denethor's plan to burn Faramir and himself before the city is overrun by Sauron's forces. A horrified Pippin vainly tries to scatter the kindling, but Denethor drags the Hobbit to the door and releases him from service.[77] Pippin, however, does not give up. His first impulse to save Faramir by himself has been thwarted, so Pippin thinks through his next move—to have Gandalf intervene.

Pippin braves the battle already taking place in the city's streets to find Gandalf and tell him of Denethor's plan. Pippin is shown dodging debris and conquering his fear in order to locate the Wizard.[78] When Gandalf and Pippin, riding Shadowfax, finally break into the chamber where Denethor is igniting the wood, Gandalf first knocks Denethor from the pyre. Seeing the flames so close to the unconscious Faramir, Pippin leaps from Shadowfax directly onto the pyre. He pushes Faramir away from the flames and frantically smothers the fire already consuming Faramir's clothes. He does not stop, even when Denethor attacks him.[79] Pippin's trial by fire to leap into danger and save another is a true heroic act, one that Jackson rewrites from the book and one that gives Pippin a larger role in saving Faramir.

A final heroic act shows formerly passive Pippin saving Gandalf's life. Pippin does not become a bloodthirsty warrior during the siege of Minas Tirith, even as he sees carnage around him. In fact, he only runs to the battlefront because Gandalf summons the soldiers, and Pippin takes his duty seriously. However, when faced with the overwhelming assault by Orcs and trolls entering the city, Pippin freezes. He narrowly escapes death because Gandalf kills the Orc ready to skewer Pippin; the Hobbit's only response to the attack is to cringe and clench shut his eyes. A few moments later, however, Gandalf is about to be run through by an Orc. There is no time to shout a warning, and Pippin steps forward and stabs the Orc. As he stares at the blade, black with the dead Orc's blood, Pippin expresses shock, not joy or satisfaction. He only looks slightly pleased when Gandalf praises him—"Guard of the citadel indeed!"[80] Pippin acts heroically, impulsively, to save Gandalf, but he is not truly an effective warrior. Pippin eagerly accepts the Wizard's advice to return to greater safety higher in the city. Pippin acts bravely when necessary and has found his courage. He fulfills his duty and, like Merry, can now defend his people, but his true role is not that of a full-time warrior.

In the final battle scene before the Black Gate, Jackson shows Pippin dashing toward the enemy.[81] In quick cuts of the fighting, Pippin is shown slashing at Orcs. However, the lengthiest shot of Pippin in this battle—and his only close-up—shows an anguished Pippin crying "Frodo" as he sobs on the field. Pippin realizes the cost of saving Middle-earth, as the destruction of Mount Doom and Sauron's tower likely also claims Frodo's life.

Throughout the trilogy, Pippin grows into an adult whose impulses are tempered by thought, but who is still willing to act on these impulses to save others. He understands actions and consequences and has learned the nature of duty and sacrifice. He becomes a hero during moments of crisis.

The Strength of Pippin

Jackson's trilogy also shows Pippin's growing emotional and physical strength. His transformation into an adult and a hero takes place gradually throughout the three films, with Pippin's strength peaking in the Minas Tirith scenes. As Pippin learns to trust his impulses and use them to better advantage, and as his confidence in himself increases, he moves from a character who is cared for to one who takes care of others.

As mentioned previously, throughout *The Fellowship of the Ring* Pippin is childlike and needy; he often relies on others, especially Merry, to meet his needs. Although Pippin is resourceful and seems more than willing to try to keep up with the older Hobbits, he also is used to having others look after him. Pippin looks to Merry to supply the basics, such as food; he turns to Merry, not Strider, when he is concerned about the lack of second breakfast early in the journey toward Rivendell;[82] he tells Merry that he is hungry in the mines of Moria.[83] He has a child's clumsiness when he tries to do what everyone else in the Fellowship does; he stumbles through the marshes and ends up getting drenched;[84] his footing slips as he climbs in Moria, earning him an exasperated "Pippin!" from Merry, who is the recipient of a faceful of dirt as Pippin climbs before him;[85] he is not as coordinated as Merry in learning to handle a sword under Boromir's tutelage.[86] Pippin is not a weakling, but he does not have the grace and stamina of those older or those used to long marches. Pippin is forced to become hardier as the journey continues.

Pippin's time in captivity does a lot to strengthen him. Merry is injured and unable to assist him or provide moral support for a while, but Pippin first shows his resourcefulness when he is on his own. Pippin is good at overhearing conversations, and he learns from the Orcs that Men are following the party of Orcs toward Isengard.[87] He rips the Elven brooch from his cloak and drops it so that Aragorn might find it. This is another example of Pippin's positive impulses, as he takes only a moment to decide what to do and drops the brooch apparently without worrying that his captors might see him. Pippin also seems physically stronger. When the Orcs are attacked by Éomer's troops, Pippin finds an axe on the ground, probably from a fallen Orc, and hastily saws apart his bindings.[88] Then he returns to Merry to untie him and help him to his feet. Pippin has begun to rely on himself in a tight situation and to assist Merry when he can. His emotional and physical strength increases.

However, Pippin's true physical strength is most evident in three scenes in *The Return of the King*. Pippin ably climbs the craggy face of a tower in Minas Tirith, lights the beacon, and returns to the city via another long climb.[89] As Jackson's camera shots emphasize during Pippin's ascent, Pippin scrambles capably up toward the beacon. This Pippin is much more confident and able to move more quietly and quickly than the young Hobbit shown slipping in Moria.

Even if Pippin's strength is adrenaline fueled in two other scenes in which he saves characters dear to him, he nonetheless is able to move bodies much larger than his to achieve his objective. First, Pippin pushes Faramir off the burning pyre, rolling the dead weight away from the fire and then smothering the flames on Faramir's clothes with his gloved hands.[90] Even with his fear for Faramir to allow him to do more than he would be able to under normal circumstances, Pippin prior to the Quest most likely would not be able physically to save Faramir. In the same way, when Pippin sees Merry buried under a larger body on the battlefield of the Pelennor, Pippin shoves the body away from his cousin and gently pulls Merry into his arms.[91] Pippin is physically able to do much more than he might have anticipated before he began his journey.

The physically strong Pippin in Jackson's final film is in contrast to Tolkien's view of Pippin on the battlefield.[92] Tolkien's Pippin is described as terribly smaller than other beings on the battlefield. Although Tolkien's heroic scene for Pippin pits him in a David and Goliath situation, Pippin's smaller size and lesser strength ultimately work against him. He is strong enough to attack a troll, but is unable to get out from under the troll when he falls. Instead, Pippin is crushed and only later is found by Gimli, who is able to free the Hobbit from such a gruesome place.[93]

Not only has Jackson's Pippin increased his physicality during the trilogy, but he has grown stronger through increasing self-confidence. As the Fellowship leaves Lothlórien and Galadriel provides gifts to each member according to his needs, Galadriel tells Pippin not to worry, that he will find his courage.[94] As with all youngsters who are unsure until they learn to rely on themselves and are tested in a variety of ways, Pippin does not know what he might be able to do, nor what he will have to do. Yet, when he is tested in battle, when he is the only Hobbit in a city of Men, when he has taken on responsibilities that only he is expected to meet— Pippin performs well. He is still a deeply feeling young Hobbit, as shown by his tearful understanding that Denethor is sending Faramir on a suicide mission,[95] his emotional responses to the wounding of Faramir[96] and Merry,[97] his curiosity about the afterlife Gandalf describes and his acceptance of his probable death in battle.[98] However, Pippin is much stronger emotionally, so that when he tells Merry, "I'm going to look after you," he can mean it.[99] Pippin is capable of looking after himself and others, and he now has the physical and emotional strength to be able to take on more responsibility.

Jackson's films build an upward arc for Pippin so that his strength, self-confidence, and skills increase throughout the trilogy, allowing Pippin to emerge as a young hero. Tolkien's trilogy provides more peaks and valleys to Pippin's growth. His physical strength is never emphasized, but his emotional strength is tested many times. For example, just before the Battle of Cormallen, Sauron's representative shows Aragorn's assembled army Sam's sword and Frodo's clothing, including the mithril shirt. When Pippin sees them, he rushes "forward with a cry of grief" and is pushed back by Gandalf; Pippin's outburst indicates to the messenger that the items hold great value for the army before him.[100] When Gandalf takes the tokens but does not bargain with Sauron's minion, Pippin is overwhelmed with grief but holds himself together for the upcoming battle. Nevertheless, he moves to the front rank next to Beregond, a Gondorian guard he has befriended, and thinks it "is best to die soon and leave the bitter story of his life."[101] He thinks of Merry and wishes that they could die together. This despair shows the formerly optimistic, cheerful Hobbit's emotional "weakness," although Pippin is determined to die well in battle.

His great act of heroism at the Battle of Cormallen is to save Beregond. As a troll is about to rip out Beregond's throat, Pippin kills the troll. He saves Beregond, but in the process is trapped under the dead troll's body, his last thought that his tale has ended as he thought it would. Tolkien writes that his thought "laughed a little within him ere it fled ... casting off at last all doubt and care and fear."[102]

Tolkien's Pippin does not achieve his greatest emotional strength in battle, as does Jackson's Pippin. Instead, Tolkien's little Hobbit is strongest emotionally when he is surrounded by those he loves. Of course, he does his duty and acquits himself well in battle, but his strongest emotions—and the ones that in turn strengthen others—are positive, happy, loving responses to life. War weakens Pippin's emotions in Tolkien's books, whereas Jackson uses warfare as a means of testing Pippin and allowing him to show his true worth. Tom Shippey writes that this type of story arc, as with all Tolkien's organizational/narrative structures, is "a part of his worldview" and explains that it "cannot be imitated on screen." Because mass-marketed film is essentially "triumphalist," the good guys have to win. Of course, Tolkien also has good triumph over evil, but Shippey notes that "Tolkien never thought this was inevitable."[103] Part of Pippin's growth as a hero is his realization that the story may not have a happy ending. Jackson shows Pippin awaiting what he perceives will be his death in the battle about to begin. In a quiet scene, Gandalf explains the afterlife to Pippin, whose response to impending doom is that this depiction of the afterlife "isn't so bad."[104] He is not overjoyed at the prospect of death in battle, nor looking to act as a hero in the coming fray, but he is not despondent about his fate.

Jackson's trilogy emphasizes Pippin's growth as a heroic character from weaker youth to stronger, more confident adult. Because Jackson's films only superficially show the bonds of Fellowship among the nine travelers and the familial bonds that motivate Pippin to come on the journey, Pippin's strength is directed more by outward forces than inward desires. Such is the nature of film—to show by action—and Jackson successfully shows Pippin's increased strength, which helps him act heroically in crisis. Tolkien's trilogy has Pippin gradually develop a responsible nature that allows him to act heroically in battle, but Tolkien makes it clear that

Pippin's ongoing strength comes from the bonds of love developed among his friends and kin.

The Structure of Pippin's Development in Book and Film

The tone of Pippin's character is mostly retained from Tolkien's trilogy, although Jackson emphasizes the silliness and comic aspects of the youngest Hobbit far more than Tolkien does. Jackson's Pippin is still irrepressible and lives life fully. He expresses his emotions freely and throughout the course of Jackson's trilogy displays a range of emotions. He never loses the capacity to feel deeply for his friends and to back his emotional responses one hundred percent with commitment—usually in impulsive actions. Billy Boyd explains that Hobbits express emotions differently than Men do, and Jackson and the cast infuse the films with Tolkien's ideas about what makes Hobbits unique: Hobbits "feel emotions more deeply and they will show their emotions easier than a human will. But Tolkien also said . . . that they're very quick at recovering from that."[105] Jackson's direction and Boyd's performance are true to that objective. Pippin retains his resilience and complete range of emotional responses to all joys and sorrows of the journey.

Although these elements of Pippin's nature (even if sometimes in exaggerated form) survive the transformation from book to film, the beauty of Tolkien's parallel structure in developing Merry's and Pippin's growth as heroes and future leaders is lost. Although many other differences between the book and film versions of Peregrin Took are outlined throughout this chapter, the parallel structure of events in Merry's and Pippin's lives after they are separated in *The Return of the King* is the greatest deviation in both characters' development. In Tolkien's second half of his *The Return of the King*, the events shown in table 3.1 take place. Although the events are parallel, the situations involving and motivations of Pippin and Merry differ, as do their personalities. Tolkien uses this structure to show the two Hobbits as equals who grow to full maturity during time of war. The structure illustrates the two Hobbits as an effective pair who grow up together, mature along similar lines, and then continue to serve their families and lands for the rest of their adult lives, all while retaining their unique personalities and strengths. Unlike critics, or even fans, who often cannot tell the difference between Pippin and Merry, Tolkien portrays the cousins as two sides to the same coin, similar in some ways, but unique in others. They are not interchangeable characters, and their actions and reactions during their parallel development indicate some important differences.

Table 3-1   **Pippin's and Merry's Parallel Development in Tolkien's Trilogy**

Event	Pippin	Merry
Offers service to the leader of a people	Offers to serve Denethor, Steward of Gondor (also in Jackson's trilogy)	Offers to serve Théoden, King of Rohan (only in the extended version of *The Return of the King*)
Once service is accepted, receives and performs duties to his liege lord	Acts as a page, waiting on Denethor, singing him a song, learning his way about the city (shown in a limited way in Jackson's trilogy)	Acts as a companion, telling stories and the history of the Shire
Continues to serve even after being released from service	Finds Gandalf to tell him of Denethor's plans to kill Faramir and commit suicide (also in Jackson's trilogy)	Sneaks off to war without the King's knowledge (also in Jackson's trilogy)
Saves the lord's child	Alerts Gandalf to Faramir's imminent death so that Gandalf saves Faramir (in Jackson's trilogy, alerts Gandalf but also saves Faramir from the pyre)	Stabs the Witch King, which diverts the wraith's attention for a moment, helps to mortally wound him, and allows Éowyn to finish off the Witch King (also in Jackson's trilogy)
Remains with the lord during his death	Is present as Denethor burns, being unable to save him (also in Jackson's trilogy)	Talks with Théoden as he dies, being unable to save him
Becomes recognized by the successor for heroic deeds	Serves the new King, Elessar, in battle; acts heroically in battle; becomes a Knight of Gondor (also in Jackson's trilogy, but only in a group battle scene and a group recognition scene)	Receives gifts from the new King, Éomer, as well as recognition for saving Eowyn; becomes Master Holdwine, a Knight of Rohan (only in a group recognition scene in Jackson's trilogy, but not recognized by Éomer)

Pippin impulsively offers his service to Denethor, who has basically insulted him as being too small and insignificant to matter.[106] Pippin's pride to do what he can and to show the Steward of Gondor his worth prompts him to act rashly. Nevertheless, it is an act that Gandalf later praises. Quite practically, his new role gives Pippin access to Denethor and all of Minas Tirith, which could prove helpful to Gandalf's plans and actions. Merry, however, feels great affection for Théoden and considers him a father figure; his offer of service is based on love and loyalty.[107] Although their motivations differ and reflect their different personalities, the events following their entry into the service of a lord are similar.

Neither Pippin nor Merry "serves" in active ways, at least during the formal part of their relationship with their respective lords. Pippin primarily prepares for his duties by learning about Minas Tirith, memorizing the passwords that allow him access throughout the citadel, gaining battle gear, and then waiting while Denethor talks with others.[108] Denethor requests a song from Pippin, who obliges reluctantly, but Pippin is not put into action. Denethor's motivation for accepting Pippin's offer is not out of affection for or curiosity about the Hobbit, but out of spite for Gandalf. Not finding a practical use for Pippin is only one result of this spiteful act. Merry fares better with Théoden, who agrees to allow Merry to serve him primarily so that Merry will be protected.[109] In this way Théoden acts as a father to Merry and indulges him in small ways. He allows Merry to dine with him and to be a part of the conversations in the king's tent; he shares stories with Merry about Rohan and learns about the Shire; he hopes that he and Merry will be able to discuss herblore and other topics at leisure (and later regrets not being able to do so).[110] Even though Théoden has no intention of taking Merry into battle, he allows Éowyn to fulfill Aragorn's request that Merry be outfitted as an esquire of Rohan.[111]

When battle is imminent, both lords release the Hobbits from their services. Denethor sees no further use for Pippin as the city is breached; the steward is too busy preparing for his and Faramir's deaths to waste time with Pippin. Denethor's parting words to Pippin tell him to prepare for death.[112] In contrast, Théoden sternly tells Merry that he is too small to go to war and he must stay behind to be safe.[113] Théoden consistently acts to protect Merry and values his friendship. Whereas Denethor's response to crisis concerns death, Théoden's response is to emphasize life.

However, both Hobbits stubbornly refuse this order, which ultimately is good for their respective lands, as they save the child of the ruler. Pippin brings Gandalf to Faramir's aid, and although it is too late to save the mad Denethor, Pippin is present as the steward's life is ended by his own hand.[114] Merry rides to war with Dernhelm, only later learning that the soldier is really Éowyn, Théoden's niece and adoptive daughter, in disguise.[115] Merry attacks the Witch King to save Dernhelm, who then reveals herself as Éowyn, and to avenge Théoden. When Éowyn is overcome with the pain and shock from fighting the Witch King, Merry is left alone with his king.[116] He talks with Théoden and hears his last words.[117]

The impact of these rulers on the Hobbits is measurable; they have seen the best and the worst of leaders and have based their responses to their lords' actions not on blind loyalty to a ruler but on their understanding of what is right and honorable. Both Pippin and Merry initially entered the service of their respective lords "out of the Hobbits' instinctive sense of what is right. Both demonstrate their determination to do what's right."[118]

Especially when the Hobbits defy their lords' wishes, they ultimately manage to do what is right for their lord, their people, and their own development. Pippin acts in spite of Denethor's wishes and commands, by valuing Faramir throughout their association, even if Denethor does not. Merry acts out of devotion to Théoden, protecting the king and his soldiers and trying to act as bravely and nobly as his lord.

Tolkien shows that the brave deeds of both Hobbits are individually recognized by the lords' successors, and the Hobbits are retained in service to Elessar and Éomer long after the War of the Ring. Pippin's and Merry's close association with their respective rulers gives them a deeper understanding of what it means to have responsibility for and power over others.[119] Again, the cousins serve as a balance to each other. Merry's experiences with Théoden are more positive than Pippin's with Denethor, but this range of pooled experiences will make them effective leaders in the Shire. Both rulers have a powerful, continuing influence on the Hobbits; they "learn what it feels like to have their hearts broken by the death of someone to whom they have sworn loyalty . . . Pippin's service to Denethor is . . . [more] an act of recognition of the ancient greatness inherent in the rulers of Gondor," but Denethor's death still deeply affects Pippin.[120]

Understandably, in a tale as complex and long as *The Lord of the Rings*, many characters from the book cannot be included in even the longest film. As well, Pippin and Merry are treated as secondary characters in Jackson's trilogy, and the intricacies of their development are simplified into key events or important personality traits. The most important action events, not the internal development of the characters, are best shown on screen and move the story forward. As a result, the parallel development highlighted across hundreds of pages in Tolkien's final book in the trilogy becomes limited to a few key scenes on film.

Pippin is much better developed than Merry in scenes from Jackson's trilogy. Pippin is shown offering to serve Denethor, and more of his time in the service of the steward makes it to the theatrical version. In particular, minor points in the book, such as Pippin singing for Denethor, become more poignant on screen.[121] Jackson uses the song as the soundtrack for Faramir's suicidal charge against the vast army of Orcs at Osgiliath, while Denethor savagely eats his dinner and Pippin tearfully sings. The juxtaposition of images overlaid with the sad song highlights not only the differences between Faramir and Denethor, but also between what Pippin knows a good father and ruler should do and what Denethor cruelly chooses to do instead. The scene takes on emotional power through this editing of images and inclusion of only the music to build emotion in the scene.

Pippin is given a fuller story arc in Jackson's trilogy, but the true strength of his growth and development as a hero is found only in Tolkien's trilogy.

Pippin and a Modern Definition of *Hero*

In chapter 1, an outline of the characteristics defining a modern hero, for film or book, lists these five items:

1. He acts on his convictions.

Especially in Tolkien's trilogy, Pippin acts on his devotion to Frodo and his desire to help Frodo in whatever way possible, even if the journey is difficult for him. As the Quest progresses, Pippin also becomes devoted to his friends in the Fellowship. His pledge of service to Denethor is honored, and Pippin later honors his liege lord Elessar with continued service. However, Pippin's heart truly lies with his family and friends, and although he does not prefer to be a soldier, he fights to regain his homeland. Pippin is a noble character who learns throughout the trilogy how to act responsibly and effectively on his convictions.

Jackson also shows that Pippin acts on his convictions, but they take the form of first being a devoted follower to Merry, no matter where that may lead him. As Pippin matures, he takes on new responsibilities that mirror new friendships and allegiances. Pippin provides possibly the greatest service to Boromir, who dies trying to protect Pippin and Merry. Pippin acts on his former friendship with Boromir and his new friendship with Faramir to save the latter from his father's madness. Throughout Jackson's trilogy, Pippin is shown as valuing his friends and acting in such a way that honors that value. Pippin fights for those he loves, not for an abstract ideal, and that bond motivates him to act heroically.

Modern, everyperson heroes find themselves becoming heroes when they protect those they love. They may intercede in a dispute or stop on the highway to aid accident victims. They may run into a burning building to save a neighbor or stand up for a younger sibling against a bully. Modern heroes act not because they feel obligated to act bravely because others expect them to do so. They react bravely to a situation because they want to protect others out of love for humanity in general, or more specifically, for friends or family.

2. He can plan a strategy and successfully carry it out, even if this strategy is planned on the run. He is a thinking hero who may have to plan spontaneously as a crisis occurs or think on his feet during a crisis.

Jackson shows a glimmer of Pippin's foresight and empathy, especially in his understanding of Treebeard and what it will take before the Ents march to war. However, this aspect of a modern hero is downplayed in Jackson's trilogy much more so than in Tolkien's. In the books, Pippin often shows wit and courage in following his impulses, but he never truly plans his actions. About halfway through Tolkien's trilogy, Pippin's impulsive words and deeds begin to come from an understanding of other characters or a crisis that necessitates quick action. Pippin is not a planner in the sense that Tolkien's Merry is a strategist, but Pippin does act on his thoughts and eventually becomes more successful with his impulsive actions. Of all five parts for the definition of a modern hero, however, Pippin is weakest in this area.

However, this fact also makes Pippin a character with whom young readers or filmgoers can more readily identify. Because Pippin's actions are impulsive and sometimes do not work out well, especially in the beginning of the trilogies, he is much like many older children or teenagers who mean well but are basically "lovable screwups." Seeing a character like Pippin, who is impulsive and does not have a plan mapped for every occasion, do well and save important characters, most notably Gandalf and Faramir in Jackson's trilogy, makes Pippin a lovable hero. Pippin can act heroically because of his devotion to others and his ability to jump in to help, almost as a reflex. His value as a modern hero for young people may be precisely because of his impulsive nature and his ability to surprise others by actually acting heroically without having the refined skills of a warrior or the wisdom of older characters. Pippin has not received much training to serve as a hero, although he develops new skills throughout his journey. His strength lies in his good heart and his willingness to intervene when he sees he can make a difference in a dangerous situation.

   3. He offers to sacrifice himself, if necessary, for the cause.

Pippin excels on this item in both Tolkien's and Jackson's trilogies. He does not seek out situations that might require his sacrifice, but he does not hesitate to protect those he loves. His impulsive nature often means that he might accidentally sacrifice himself in action, even though Pippin admits to Gandalf in Jackson's *The Return of the King*, "I don't want to fight."[122] If the sacrifice is necessary, Pippin will make it willingly; however, he is not reckless to the point of being suicidal.

In the same way, modern heroes sometimes die performing their heroic acts. The passengers who attempt to take over a hijacked aircraft, travelers who give life vests to others, or soldiers who take the time to drag comrades out of the line of fire do not always survive. Pippin does not know if he will survive when he runs toward danger, but that uncertainty does not stop him from acting.

   4. He grows as a character, showing under extreme circumstances the heroic
      qualities that always have been part of his makeup, but have not been
      recognized until these qualities are needed.

This is Pippin's strongest point as a modern hero, and one that makes him especially well suited as a role model for younger audiences, be they readers or filmgoers. As Tolkien aptly shows throughout the trilogy, Pippin grows up from Gandalf's "fool of a Took" into a Hobbit who Gandalf recognizes as an adult with all the skills and experiences necessary to take his place as a leader in the Shire. Jackson's Pippin truly finds the courage that Galadriel promises him will be there when he needs it. In both trilogies, Pippin faces more trials than he could possibly have imagined when he first leaves the Shire, or even Rivendell, and his experiences bring forth the best parts of his personality—his love of family and friends and his ability to live life to the fullest. When called on to act in a crisis, Pippin ably acts to save others. His growth indicates that he will not shy away from future dangers but will now act responsibly and possibly heroically in the future. Modern heroes do not go around looking for new dangers, but once they have faced danger, they often are willing to do so again if need be.

   5. He embodies the values of love of family and home, which provide the impetus for him to act to protect the people and places he loves.

Tolkien's early scenes of domestic life in the Shire best show Pippin's place within his family and the simple values that motivate him throughout the Quest. By the time Pippin returns to help scour the Shire of corruption, he can act more effectively to protect those he loves and to return his home to its former peace and prosperity. Although Jackson's scenes of the Shire post-Quest are mere vignettes that illustrate Frodo's isolation and eventual need to depart, they still show that returning battle veteran Pippin continues to participate in Shire life and support Merry, Frodo, and Sam in their re-entry into their former lives. Pippin is fiercely protective of his kin and new friends, and his words and actions in both trilogies emphasize Pippin's devotion to "family values." Modern heroes often display similar devotion to family and country and are willing to fight to uphold what they cherish.

   The arcs leading to Pippin's development as a heroic character differ greatly in Tolkien's and Jackson's trilogies, but they both arrive at the same point: Pippin has grown into a responsible Hobbit who still has impulsive behavior, but who directs his words and acts toward helping others. He is a worthwhile role model to those who feel out of place in the world of adults or other authority figures, but Pippin is not just a rebel without cause or justification. His early impulses often backfire on him, but his motivations are pure. When his impulses become directed outwardly, to help others, instead of inwardly, for self-gratification, Pippin becomes a true modern hero.

4

Éowyn as Action Hero

In the past year, I have heard two especially strong responses to Éowyn that represent the wide-ranging opinions about Tolkien's strongest female character in *The Lord of the Rings*. When photographs from Peter Jackson's *The Two Towers* became available to the media, some Internet fans began to link Éowyn with Xena, Warrior Princess, from the popular television show. One fan magazine even splashed a photo of Éowyn on its cover, asking "Is Éowyn the New Xena?"[1] Perhaps this connection occurred because the television series *Xena: Warrior Princess* also was filmed in New Zealand, or perhaps some fans who wanted to see another leather-clad woman warrior were thinking wishfully. The idea that all females who go to battle are automatically categorized as "Xenas" takes away much of Éowyn's strength as a character, for she is not Xena-like. Éowyn is strong, but not superhumanly so; she fights because it is her duty to protect her people and her destiny to be a leader. Eventually, Tolkien's Éowyn renounces war when the need for battle is over; ultimately, she rules as a peacekeeper and healer. The concept of "one size fits all" should not be applied to women in strong character roles, even if they are starring in what many filmgoers perceive as a sword epic.

The other response came from a devoted Éowyn fan, a young woman who sat next to me during Trilogy Tuesday—December 18, 2003—as the extended versions of *The Fellowship of the Ring* and *The Two Towers* preceded the U.S. general-release premiere of *The Return of the King*. Although this woman liked Éowyn in *The Two Towers*, she almost literally held her breath waiting for the Witch King scene in the third film. Éowyn is her favorite character, and a role model from the book, and this fan hoped that the film would treat Éowyn honorably. As Éowyn revealed herself to the Witch King and proclaimed, "I am no man!" the audience cheered.[2] After the screening, I asked the young woman if she was satisfied with the onscreen portrayal of her favorite character. She was, glad that Éowyn "did a good job for us women."

A *Commonweal* article states that "Tolkien always seemed a little theoretical in his presentation of women," but on screen, Éowyn (as well as Arwen) is "specific, mercurial, and commanding." The result is that when Éowyn defeats the Witch King, audiences could feel "battalions of women cheering her on."[3]

Representing all womanhood seems to be Éowyn's fate, whether on the page or screen. She is often either held as a positive role model to represent the strong, assertive woman in a male-dominated world, or denounced because in the book she dresses as a man, Dernhelm, to be able to go to war, thus being perceived as having to renounce her femininity in order to be successful. Éowyn is further penalized by some readers who believe she "sold out" by marrying Faramir and turning into a wife and, presumably, mother.

Unlike other characters in *The Lord of the Rings*, Éowyn faces a burden of being too much or too little of what critics or fans identify as a "real woman." How ironic that this one character is expected to shoulder the weight of all womanhood; many female critics, readers, and filmgoers expect too much from Éowyn, even as they would most likely decry having one real woman serve as the "typical" woman in our or any other society. It is true that Tolkien did not include as many female as male characters; however, the number of characters of a certain gender or race does not indicate an individual character's worth. Conversely, just because there are fewer women does not mean that each female character does not have to represent only a certain "type," usually for political or sociopolitical interpretations of the text.

My interpretation of the text and film used in this chapter is that Éowyn is a strong character but is not created to represent a feminist perspective. She is a hero and can serve as a role model, but Tolkien did not create her to act as a role model for women, nor to serve as the lone representative for a positive or negative type of woman. She, along with the other unsung heroes described in this book, plays a valuable role in the story. Her story within the larger work may resonate with modern readers or filmgoers, not only women, who often face similar familial and social limitations in their effort to live their lives to meet their own, not others', expectations. I do not claim that this interpretation is Tolkien's reason for creating Éowyn; indeed, I know that it is not. However, Éowyn does offer modern readers and filmgoers yet another hero to emulate, one who embodies the characteristics defined in chapter 1 as those of a hero for modern audiences.

Éowyn is an action hero, but not in the sense of most movie action heroes who often serve as judge and executioner of the bad guys. Éowyn determines her destiny by choosing which actions to take; she is prepared for action, warfare in the case of *The Return of the King*, but more importantly, she takes charge and is not afraid to lead. She thinks and acts decisively, even if her opinions are not popular or typical, and she is bold enough to help others act to achieve their objectives as well. Éowyn shows that strength of character is not a male-only trait, and her strength is often illustrated through physical deeds. Éowyn as an action hero is not the typical movie daredevil; she is more of an activist or a catalyst who not only plays out her story according to her own rules, but who sets into motion important changes for other characters, such as Théoden in Jackson's trilogy, Merry in both book and film, and Éomer in Tolkien's trilogy.

In both trilogies, Éowyn directly influences action more than other female characters. Galadriel is a behind-the-scenes initiator of action, in contrast to Gandalf's direct role in guiding the Fellowship. Arwen is a "prize" to be won in both books and films, although her film role becomes more one of seer and protector. Éowyn, however, takes the direct approach. She constantly rails against the "protection" of men (including Théoden, Éomer, and Aragorn) and despises being kept from battle. She is skilled as a warrior but is untested in battle until she rides to war. She even assists the Hobbit Merry Brandybuck, another innocent advised to stay out of the way, in riding to battle. During the Battle of the Pelennor Fields, she finishes off the Witch King of the Nazgûl, who Merry has wounded. Her actions turn the battle as well as inspire others in the Rohirrim, who continue to fight long after she is wounded.

Jackson's Éowyn also serves as a reluctant leader to guide her people to Helm's Deep, even as the men fight wargs and Orcs. On screen, in addition to her commonly accepted female roles as object of love (to Faramir, however briefly shown)[4] or lust (from Grima Wormtongue),[5] nurse to both the possessed Théoden[6] and wounded Théodred,[7] and, in Jackson's *The Two Towers*, surrogate mother to the children who bring word of the Orcs' incursion further into Rohan,[8] and leader and warrior who ultimately takes charge of her destiny. These actions are often brave and assertive, and they lead to Éowyn's role as a hero when she protects her uncle (and king) in battle and ably acts as a warrior on the field.

Éowyn as a Literary Hero

Éowyn's lineage would indicate that she is a classic literary hero, if women could be equally evaluated on many existing scales of literary heroes' development. Éowyn's mother is a princess, Théodwyn, sister to King Théoden. Her father is Éomund, Marshal of the Mark. Upon her parents' deaths, Éowyn and her brother are reared by Théoden, who, as king and uncle, becomes a father figure. Nothing is known of her childhood, but her later actions and attitudes indicate that she has been reared in a warrior tradition. In *The Tolkien Companion*, she is described as "tall and fair, with a graceful step—and a skill with horse and blade to match any Rider of the Mark."[9] That blend of grace and effectiveness in warrior skills marks her as a potential hero long before she travels to the Pelennor. Disguised as the warrior Dernhelm, Éowyn helps kill the Nazgûl king and becomes a battle-tested hero.

Tolkien's description of Éowyn's background more closely matches that of a classic literary hero than his depictions of Merry and Pippin, for example. Éowyn is royalty who has been trained to rule and, if necessary, fight. Because the people of Rohan are known for their horsemanship, Éowyn also has learned to ride well. In terms of a classic literary hero, her background may be expected to lead her into heroic deeds.

However, Éowyn's gender is both a benefit and a problem for her as a heroic character. She may be perceived as Woman, or even Character Whose Gender Allows Her to Kill Witch King, because no living man could kill this fearsome being. Neither is fair to Éowyn as a character, whose reasons for going to battle are not only in response to the decisions of the men in her life to make sure she does not do so. Éowyn must be considered a hero on her own terms, not because of or in spite of her gender.

Éowyn needs to be respected as a multifaceted character who lives up to her own expectations, not those of others. If readers or film audiences consider Éowyn only as a gender stereotype of either the princess waiting to be saved by a handsome prince (or king) or the warrior who dons male clothing and eschews femininity, they miss the point about Éowyn. She is only being herself, and she plays many roles within the story. Some of the roles are more traditionally held by females in medieval-type fantasies; others are more traditionally held by males. Éowyn becomes a hero not because of or in spite of her gender. She is heroic because of her actions and her desire to serve and save others, which she does in many different ways.

Through Éowyn, Tolkien provides a character who has the ability to see the value of others who also have difficulty achieving their goals. She is able to see beyond the surface to understand what others truly need, most likely because she is often frustrated in her own desire to serve others as she sees fit. In understanding those who are not "traditional" in their roles, Éowyn is farther-sighted than Théoden or Éomer, who respect others who are not Men or warriors, but who do not really understand them. For example, although Théoden accepts Merry's service and names him as an esquire of Rohan, he does not truly expect the young Hobbit to serve in battle. Merry himself notes at Théoden's burial that the king was "as a father...for a little while."[10] Théoden feels fatherly in his indulgence of Merry, and indeed enjoys talking with him, but the king takes responsibility for Merry to keep him safe. In a similar way, Théoden most likely has indulged Éowyn's interests in "boy things"—fighting, riding, weaponry— but still believes she should be protected. Similarly, Éomer clearly loves his sister and is protective toward her, especially when Wormtongue makes advances. Nevertheless, Éomer does not even consider her as a potential warrior. Éowyn is foremost his sister, and he cannot really perceive of her in another role.

Éowyn, however, understands someone like Merry, who wants to try to save his cousin Pippin in Minas Tirith, or fight to ensure that ringbearer Frodo can complete the Quest, but is perceived by others as too small or childlike to do what Merry feels that he must do. Éowyn also finds in Faramir an equal partner, someone who has been belittled by his own father and protected by his older brother. Although Théoden is a much kinder surrogate father than Faramir's father, Éowyn knows what it is like to be left behind or underappreciated. She realizes the value of those who are atypical heroes.

Tolkien gives Éowyn a wonderful line as, in disguise as Dernhelm, she asks Merry to accompany her on the road to battle. She repeats a familiar axiom, "Where will wants not, a way opens"—a good way of saying "Where there's a will, there's a way." She also encourages Merry, "Such good will should not be denied."[11] Éowyn recognizes a strong will in others, and when another "outsider" has this will, she assists in helping out. Éowyn's will is just as strong as Théoden's, Aragorn's, or Éomer's, and yet the men's convictions and dedication to their people are encouraged, whereas Éowyn's and Merry's (and even, Éowyn later learns, Faramir's) are frequently considered less important. Éowyn not only has the strength to follow her convictions and serve her people as she has been trained to do, but she also is strong enough to recognize similar desires in others and to help them achieve what turn out to be great deeds.

Tolkien's Éowyn is straightforward and plain speaking. She often seems frustrated and angry when she cannot realize her potential as a warrior. Even when she is mending in the Houses of Healing, she desires to return to battle.[12] She has so often been denied her desires that she expects conflict. When the warden at the Houses of Healing does not release her to follow the other soldiers toward the next battle, she asks to see the steward, or whoever is in charge, in order to gain her release. In this way, she meets Faramir, who can sympathize with her plight but cannot medically release her to return to battle. Instead, he convinces her to remain in Minas

Tirith to heal physically, but in truth, he brings about a greater part in her emotional healing.

In an online interview, Tolkien scholar Thomas Shippey notes that Tolkien's description of Éowyn in the Houses of Healing section "is a careful and sensitive account" of Éowyn's life. She has been left at home while the men leave for war, "trapped with Wormtongue, and watching her uncle fall under his spell. This is a striking and early sensitivity to the theme of female passivity, which people often miss."[13]

Éowyn has faced a lifetime of mixed messages. On one hand, she is taught how to be a warrior, and this is her desire as the best way to serve her people. She is capable of ruling her people. She is given duties to oversee others, and she can take charge. On the other hand, when the time comes for battle, she is left behind to watch after the women and children. She is expected to serve in a passive role while the men must play an active part in national events. Her place in the line of succession comes only after her cousin Théodred and brother Éomer, and she most likely will not rule her people. She has been desired not for herself, but as a trophy of war to be gained by Wormtongue if he successfully undermines Théoden and ensures Rohan's defeat. Aragorn respects her as a potential leader and warrior, but denies her a place at his side as an equal; he cannot love her as a woman, but he can respect her and understand her frustration at being left behind. Tolkien shows Éowyn's dilemma and the contrasting expectations she faces at different times in her life.

In a draft to a reader of *The Lord of the Rings*, Tolkien describes Éowyn as "like many brave women [who are] capable of great military gallantry at a crisis."[14] Faramir is described as a man who may not receive his due as a leader, although he is "evidently personally courageous and decisive, but also modest, fair-minded, and scrupulously just, and very merciful. I think he understood Éowyn very well."[15] They both have a great deal of potential, which has not been allowed to be developed as the characters would like.

Tolkien has Éowyn describe herself in her first meeting with Faramir as one who "cannot lie in sloth, idle, caged."[16] She earlier asks the city's warden if there is something she might do, because in a formerly besieged city, she assumes much must be done. Éowyn is a woman of action; being patient and passive is difficult for her in the best of times and certainly not in wartime. Although Faramir may understand Éowyn's plight, he knows she must heal, physically and emotionally. He gradually wins her trust and friendship, spending several days talking with her before he finally confronts her with his love.

It takes a great deal of persuasion by Faramir before Éowyn understands that another type of life is not only possible, but desirable. Faramir understands exactly who Éowyn is. During their discussions as they come to know each other at the Houses of Healing, Faramir shows his respect for her as a warrior, noting that he, too, knows what it is like to want to serve when he cannot. Faramir recognizes in Éowyn an equal, but it takes time for him to convince her that his love is for her—not as a prize, a soldier, or a future ruler. He loves her for herself.

When Éowyn recognizes her love for Faramir, she understands that her life is not over when she no longer has another battle to fight. She can live in peace and still be an effective woman. She can help others in a new capacity, and she can experience joy and love as well. By the end of *The Return of the King*, Tolkien's Éowyn no longer has to fight to be allowed to be the woman she wants to be. She can be herself and be valued for her merits, without having to keep convincing men of her worth or persuading them of what she needs to do. She can achieve equilibrium and contentment.

By the chapter "Many Partings," Éowyn stands beside Faramir as Éomer, newly crowned king, celebrates her forthcoming marriage.[17] Their union does politically unite Rohan and Gondor; Éowyn is a princess of Rohan, and Faramir a prince of Ithilien. However, Tolkien describes the scene as joyous, and the marriage seems to be based on more than mere politics. Tolkien also asserts Éowyn's power in her future through the way the announcement is made. Éomer announces that "Faramir, Steward of Gondor, and Prince of Ithilien, asks that Éowyn Lady of Rohan should be his wife," and she grants it full willing."[18] Faramir does not ask Éomer for permission to marry Éowyn; he does not tell Éowyn to become his wife; and the marriage is not the result of two kings deciding how best to seal their alliance. Éowyn decides her future and seems joyful about this decision.

Éowyn as a Cinematic Hero

In Jackson's trilogy, Éowyn is both beautiful and deadly. She is determined and knows her own mind. However, she can back up her desire to serve her people by fighting for them with the skills necessary to be an effective warrior. In the meantime, she serves her people in other ways, usually in more traditional roles.

A common view of Éowyn is one that film audiences see twice in the trilogy but first in *The Two Towers*. Éowyn stands outside the Hall of Meduseld, gazing across the plain.[19] She looks like a tragic figure—alone, windswept, serious, yet beautiful. Éowyn is wearing white, and the picture Jackson presents is close to Tolkien's original description of Éowyn as cold and aloof.[20] She watches and waits for the men to return; she is forced to be passive. Her passion is drained, and she is isolated.

However, Éowyn is no princess waiting to be rescued, although early in *The Two Towers* she is tormented by Wormtongue and the evil hold over her uncle, the king. Miranda Otto admits that Éowyn "at first appears to be the classic sort of princess character," but in reality she is an "incredibly tough, fierce, fighting woman with strong ideals."[21] In contrast to being the typical fairy-tale princess, Éowyn has "more backbone than most of those mythic women [that readers or filmgoers] are given in the Western world."[22] Éowyn is literally a lady in waiting; she watches and waits until an opportunity presents itself. Then she launches herself passionately into action and determinedly pursues her course.

In many ways, Jackson shows that Éowyn's life at Edoras is sad and lonely. Éowyn feels loss deeply, but she does not allow grief to overwhelm her. She tends her mortally wounded cousin, Théodred and later mourns his loss.[23] However, she also stands with Éomer to confront their king about Saruman's growing influence on their land.[24] Éowyn is not lost in despair, despite the growing realization that her uncle will do nothing to confront Wormtongue, much less Saruman. When Éomer is banished by Wormtongue, supposedly under King Théoden's direction, Éowyn is truly alone. Yet she later repels Wormtongue's advances with a bitter retort: "Your words are poison."[25] Éowyn may be surrounded by evil forces, and without any current support from her family, but she does not give in to despair. She is tenacious and holds on to hope, even in the darkest times, when she does not know how the future can be changed.

Éowyn cannot reach Théoden, who only seems to hear whatever Wormtongue tells him. Nevertheless, she does not give up. She first tries to make her uncle understand their dire situation when Éomer returns with the wounded Théodred,[26] then, after her brother is banished, again attempts on her own to make Théoden understand.[27] When it becomes clear to her that Théoden will do nothing, she reacts bitterly. For Éowyn, inaction when something needs to be done is wrong.

Despite her disappointment in her uncle, Éowyn moves quickly to protect him when Gandalf begins to remove Saruman's spell.[28] She rushes forward to help him, as Gandalf's "cure" seems to hurt the decrepit old man that Théoden has become. Aragorn holds back Éowyn until the spell is broken, when she pulls away. Éowyn gazes into Théoden's face as he returns to his former self. She is joyful when he recognizes her. Film audiences get the impression that Éowyn's joy is not merely relief that her uncle is back in charge and can now protect her, but that the strong, forceful leader she admires has returned. Even in her weakest moments, Éowyn capably defends herself against Wormtongue in previous scenes. She seems happy that her uncle, not her protector, is once again whole.

Théoden also realizes Éowyn's strength. Hers is the first face greeting him when he returns to himself. He recognizes her—"I know your face"[29]—a line he also uses in *The Return of the King* just before he dies.[30] In that scene, he not only recognizes Éowyn as his niece, but also as a warrior with great courage and ability. In *The Two Towers*, however, Théoden is only beginning to see who Éowyn truly is.

Éowyn may seem full of surprises to Aragorn, too.[31] When the order comes to leave Edoras for the protection of Helm's Deep, Aragorn finds Éowyn testing a blade. His comment, "You have some skill with a blade," is shown true as she effectively parries aside his sword. Éowyn is bitter in this scene as she tells Aragorn that all women in Rohan know how to protect themselves and that she, like so many others, does not fear death. When Aragorn questions what she does fear, she replies quite honestly, "A cage." Having the skills and desire to protect her people as a warrior, but not being permitted to use them, is frustrating and embittering for Éowyn. Although Éowyn may not believe Aragorn at the time, she does one day have the future he sees for her. Aragorn doubts that her fate is to be always left behind, for, after all, she is "a daughter of kings, a shieldmaiden of Rohan." Even if Aragorn does not love Éowyn, he respects her abilities and the qualities he can see in her that will make her a fine leader.

In Jackson's trilogy, Aragorn is the one male character close to her who does not tell her to go home or ignore the meaning of her words. When he expresses surprise that Éowyn is accompanying the men to Dunharrow, where the individual groups of soldiers will be assembled into one large army, Éowyn explains that women of the court traditionally say goodbye to the men at the encampment.[32] However, Aragorn brushes aside a saddle blanket to reveal Éowyn's sword. Neither says anything. Éowyn merely covers the sword again.

Even when Éowyn confronts Aragorn as he leaves to find the Army of the Dead, he does not tell her to go home nor does he rebuke her for questioning the one who will be the high king.[33] Instead, he tells her that he cannot give her what she seeks—presumably a love relationship. He respects her enough to be truthful with her. Éowyn seems to respect directness; she is not a coy romantic. Although she acts shocked and sad at Aragorn's words, she is not the type to fall into permanent despair.

Éowyn seems resigned to her fate to be left behind at this point, not suicidal because she has been jilted by Aragorn. At dawn, Théoden tells Éowyn that she will rule at Edoras if "the battle goes ill," and presumably both he and Éomer are killed.[34] Although this is a vote of confidence in her ability not only to rule successfully but also to have the support of their people to be able to rule, it is not what Éowyn wants to hear. Jackson creates a moving scene between uncle and niece, not king and successor. Théoden gently takes Éowyn's hands and tells her that he does not want her to think only of her duty to her people, or to him, but to be happy again. He wants to see her smile, and he predicts that she will live in happier times. Although not comforted, Éowyn understands the sincerity of her uncle's hopes for her. In many ways, Éowyn has been brought up "like a man. She is capable of doing all of these things that a man can do yet, at this moment, she is being treated as a woman."[35]

Nevertheless, in the next scene, Éowyn lifts Merry onto her horse, and the two are charging ahead with the rest of the Rohirrim.[36] In order to do what Éowyn believes is her duty to fight, she must disobey the direct command of her king, as well as ignore the wishes of her surrogate father. Jackson's Éowyn does not seem angry, selfishly singleminded, or pouty because she cannot get her way—she is an able-bodied soldier who knows that every warrior will be needed to fight, and even then, the army most likely will be outnumbered. It is more likely that there will be no kingdom of Rohan to rule if the battle is lost. As one privy to the goings-on at Edoras, Éowyn understands the need to aid Gondor against Sauron's forces. Jackson shows her standing in the great hall where Théoden and his advisors are talking; she sees Aragorn enter with news that the beacon distress signal has been lighted; she hears her uncle proclaim that Rohan will go to war.[37] Éowyn, probably much more so than the average soldier, knows the importance of the upcoming battle.

Although she may understand King Théoden's necessity to plan for his successor, and her foster father's desire to keep her safe, Éowyn "is internally conflicted. . . . She displays an absolute refusal to watch her country fall down around her while she does nothing."[38] Therefore, Éowyn acts on her own initiative. She disobeys the king, but ultimately this disobedience allows her to perform a heroic act that avenges him. Éowyn is not heroic because she disregards authority; she is a hero because she steps forward to protect another in a moment of crisis and disregards her safety to do so. She is a hero in spite of her previous disobedience.

Before the battle, Éowyn seems just as anxious as Merry.[39] Her eyes are wide open, literally and figuratively, as she waits on the battlefield. She bolsters Merry's courage, and probably her own at the same time, when she assures him that no matter what happens, she will look after him. Ironically, Merry ends up "looking after" Éowyn. When they are separated in battle, she frantically calls his name when the Nazgûl appears. Just when the Witch King finally captures her, Merry stabs the Nazgûl who is strangling Éowyn. This act frees Éowyn to confront the Nazgûl one last time.

Before their fateful meeting with the Witch King, Éowyn directs Merry where to guide the horse as they ride between the legs of the huge mûmakil.[40] Éowyn slashes the legs of the beasts, causing at least one to fall. She acts capably throughout the fight and is creative in bringing down enemies. She also is shown briefly (and more traditionally) in battle, slashing Orcs who surround her and Merry.

During the confrontation with the Witch King, Éowyn keeps her head.[41] Her strength is evident when she beheads the fell beast that the Nazgûl rides. It is a huge, screeching, winged beast, and she slashes through its neck with only two strokes. Considering the weight of a sword and the size and ferocity of the beast, Éowyn must be physically strong and fearless to so easily kill the creature. The Witch King then approaches on foot to kill her. She grabs a shield and avoids being crushed by the Witch King's sword or mace for a time. Only when the shield is shattered and Éowyn wounded does she seem to need any help. Once the Nazgûl is wounded, Éowyn deals the final blow, running her blade through the Nazgûl's helmet and invisible head.

Even though she is wounded, Éowyn comforts the dying Théoden.[42] He recognizes her—in fact, on seeing who has saved him, he looks rather surprised. (The readers of Tolkien's trilogy also may be surprised, as Éowyn does not have the role of comforter to her dying uncle in the book.) Théoden tells Éowyn that he knows he is dying, but she tries to deny it. "I am going to save you," she replies confidently. "You already did," Théoden assures her. That is the only praise Éowyn receives for her heroic deed in Jackson's trilogy, but Miranda Otto's expression shows that Éowyn has received the greatest reward. Although Éowyn does not publicly receive the acclaim she may have sought—at least in Jackson's adaptation—she receives her surrogate father's recognition and acceptance of who she truly is. She has not sought approval for her actions or forgiveness for disobedience. Théoden gives his final blessing to Éowyn, showing that he understands what she has done.

Éowyn's vengeance is "impelled by pity and love" for Théoden, but it has a much larger implication. It is directed "not only to the dead king and father Théoden, or to Rohan and Gondor, but to all of Middle-earth."[43] Even if her bravery cannot save Théoden's life, it does save him from a horrific death (being eaten by the Nazgûl's fell beast) and allows Éowyn best to serve her king. She stands alone against overpowering evil, a valiant move in itself, and she refuses to back down or show fear when faced with such evil. The implications of her courageous act are larger than simple revenge. By ridding Middle-earth of the Witch King, she has destroyed an enemy of great power that could continue to attack on Sauron's behalf. However, Éowyn does not seek such a noble deed; she does what is needed when the moment arises. Her training and desire to be of service blend in one heroic act. In her last moments with Théoden, Éowyn seems at peace with her uncle's acceptance of what she has done and his gratitude to her. Only when Théoden is dead does Éowyn break down in grief.

It is interesting that Jackson allows approximately sixteen seconds to show Éomer's key heroic sequence in battle: Éomer attacks a mûmakil and kills the rider who guides it.[44] Éomer looks wild-eyed with battle lust as he turns his horse to confront the beast, takes aim, and hurls the spear accurately through the rider. Éowyn's heroic sequence takes approximately one minute, forty-seven seconds, from the time that she tells the Nazgûl "I will kill you if you touch him," until the Witch King melts into the dirt.[45] The shot when Éowyn stabs the Nazgûl lasts about four seconds. Jackson gives Éowyn more screen time to show her most important battle deed. Interestingly enough, Éowyn acts much calmer in her attack on the Witch King than Éomer does when attacking the mûmakil; the woman is less "emotional" than the man.

Both Éomer's and Éowyn's definitive moments as warriors are emphasized among the deeds of the many "secondary" characters. (In contrast, for example, Merry's stabbing of the Witch King takes only one second on screen, and many other battle sequences showing the general mayhem on the field involve a series of intercut images that appear so quickly it is difficult to discern one character from another.) Jackson clearly emphasizes Éowyn's heroism with more screen time, including dialogue as well as action.

The final scene in which Éowyn appears is Aragorn's coronation.[46] She is shown standing, smiling, next to Faramir, as they greet the new king. Nothing of Éowyn's post-War life is explained in Jackson's adaptation, but this is not a surprising omission, considering the number of characters and the amount of text that must be simplified for film. In this scene, Éowyn again wears a white dress, as she does in the pivotal scene with Wormtongue in *The Two Towers*. Whereas in that film she seems cold and remote, standing literally on a pedestal high above the city after she fends off her would-be suitor, in *The Return of the King* she has been able to achieve all that she wants to accomplish.[47] Whereas in *The Two Towers* she is being stifled and is forced by circumstances to be relatively powerless, at the coronation scene in the third film, she is in charge of her destiny and has overcome her fear that she will be relegated to the background. Éowyn is still herself—the beautiful woman in white, but she is no longer isolated.

At the conclusion of *The Return of the King*, Éowyn is not alone. She stands with Faramir amid a throng of Aragorn's well-wishers. Her dress is richer, less stark, and the white is embellished with gold. Éowyn, once closed and brittle, has blossomed. It is symbolic for Éowyn, as well as for other characters, that the White Tree of Gondor is shown in full flower in this scene; while it too was once stark, brittle, and cold, it now grows and blossoms, its white petals showering the guests.[48] In this scene, Éowyn, the White Lady of Rohan, seems happy and at ease. She smiles warmly and appears more vibrant, a striking contrast from the figure first revealed in *The Two Towers.*

Tolkien's main points about Éowyn as a hero remain in Jackson's films. Éowyn of course acts heroically on the battlefield and saves her uncle from a more horrible death. She avenges him through her deed, but more importantly, and one aspect shown clearly in Jackson's film, she keeps him from being eaten alive by the fell beast. Éowyn allows Théoden to have a noble death instead of a gruesome one. However, Éowyn also is a strong leader in her own right and is shown caring for the women, children, and old men who are left behind. She may not be allowed to lead in battle, but she is in charge when there are no men, notably Théoden or Éomer, to look after their people. She has the skills and ability, as well as acceptance by their people, to serve as a leader.

Differences between Book and Film Éowyn

As is the fate of many characters in Jackson's adaptation, Éowyn's scenes often differ from the way they appear in Tolkien's trilogy. Some of her speeches are cut up so that one line is given in a different scene on screen and another line from the same speech appears in the final film. However, Jackson also expands some aspects of Éowyn's character. Three scenes highlight some personality differences and character development between Tolkien's trilogy and Jackson's adaptation.

Éowyn's Love Nature

One of the most obvious differences between Tolkien's Éowyn and Jackson's is her increased role as a potential love interest for Aragorn. At least, in Jackson's version, Éowyn suffers a well-documented case of unrequited love. Tolkien does little to develop a true love relationship, but then, male–female love relationships are not an important part of Tolkien's story—even when it comes to the love shared by Aragorn and Arwen. For the most part, that love story is relegated to the appendixes. Jackson does a great deal more to emphasize Éowyn's growing feelings for Aragorn, and the increasing warmth in her demeanor as her love deepens.

Jackson indicates that Éowyn's interest is more than just admiration for a heroic leader, one with the foresight, charisma, and determination to win loyal followers and see the War of the Ring to a successful conclusion, although the respect of a warrior for her captain is part of her admiration for

Aragorn. Éowyn also is shown proclaiming her love in two scenes, each before a large battle. In the extended version of *The Two Towers*, she asks Aragorn to be allowed to fight with him, in short, to act with the others who love him—although it is not clear from her words if she loves him as a leader or as a man.[49] Éowyn seems to include herself with Aragorn's closest friends, Legolas and Gimli, who are standing slightly behind him during this scene. Éowyn also confronts Aragorn before he leaves to journey the Paths of the Dead; she tells him that he cannot leave on the eve of battle.[50] When Aragorn basically asks her to get to the point and explain why she has come to him, Éowyn tremulously asks, "Do you not know?" Aragorn understands that she is not talking about his leaving the company as a leader; he is also leaving her. Éowyn flirts with Aragorn in other scenes, but he always seems careful in his regard for her, or even manages to slip away. For example, during the journey toward Helm's Deep, Éowyn asks Aragorn about his past and his relationship with the woman who gave him the amulet he constantly wears.[51] She tries to get to know him, although she learns that he is still in love with Arwen. (At this point, Aragorn tells Éowyn that Arwen is leaving Middle-earth, but he still seems to be in mourning for the supposed end to this relationship.)

When the Rohirrim, accompanied by members of the Fellowship, arrive at Edoras after the Battle of Helm's Deep and the capture of Isengard, Éowyn brings Aragorn a cup of wine and celebrates his victory.[52] In this scene, more than any other, Éowyn looks regal and beautiful, and so much in love that Théoden tells her that he is happy for her, for Aragorn is a good man. No one seems to notice that Aragorn does not reciprocate her feelings. Throughout much of two films, Aragorn does not indicate more than a platonic concern for Éowyn, and his final "rejection" of her does not seem to motivate her to turn to death in battle as the only way to soothe her pain. Because Éowyn has been adamant to go to war all along, this final refusal seems just one more loss that Éowyn must overcome. She does not act like a woman who goes to war only because she has lost her true love. If that were the case, Jackson's Éowyn should not bounce back quite so quickly by the coronation scene, when she appears smiling and very much part of a couple. With the elimination of the Houses of Healing sequence in the theatrical version of *The Return of the King*, Éowyn's love for Aragorn seems to be superficial at best, for audiences do not see how or when she begins to love Faramir, only that they seem to be a happy couple by the time of Aragorn's coronation.

Jackson's script includes many of the same words as Tolkien's text, but the meanings have been changed to emphasize Éowyn's romantic love for Aragorn. Tolkien brings Aragorn to Éowyn in order to bring her news after Théoden and Éomer have departed toward Minas Tirith.[53] When Éowyn learns of Aragorn's plans to follow the Paths of the Dead, she advises him not to go because the errand will most likely kill him. Aragorn explains why it is safe for him to travel these paths, and he further tells her that he would not go on a suicide mission. Éowyn's next strategy is to beg to go with him, but again Aragorn refuses, noting that she has been commanded to stay behind with her people, and her duty is to look after them. Even if he could ask King Théoden for her company on this dangerous journey, Théoden and Éomer are not coming back in time. Éowyn then gives the "cage" speech about fearing a life of being always left behind. She accuses Aragorn of really telling her "you are a woman, and your part is in the house."[54] Aragorn insists that she does not have a role to play in gathering the Army of the Dead, to which Éowyn replies that neither do the men who follow Aragorn. "They only go because they would not be parted from thee—because they love thee."[55]

Before Aragorn departs the next morning, Éowyn again pleads to go with him, and is again refused. Tolkien describes her watching Aragorn leave, "still as a figure carven in stone, her hands clenched," only "stumbling as one who is blind" after the riders are out of sight.[56] Tolkien does not write specifically that she was blind with tears or grief; perhaps she was angry, frustrated, and defeated in her desire for this opportunity to join the battle, not necessarily to join Aragorn.

Jackson takes these words and splits Éowyn's important speeches across several shorter scenes in two films, making Éowyn's love seem to build for Aragorn over time. Tolkien's use of the same lines highlights a disagreement between Éowyn and Aragorn and underscores Éowyn's frustration at always being left behind. Whereas Jackson's films change Éowyn's interactions with Aragorn from initially confrontational (e.g., the sword-wielding scene in *The Two Towers*, when she laments a possible future in a "cage")[57] to infatuated (e.g., also in *The Two Towers*, when she embraces Aragorn after the Battle of Helm's Deep)[58] to shyly adoring (e.g., when she presents him with a cup of wine in *The Return of the King*)[59] to desperate (e.g., when she confronts Aragorn before he journeys to find the Army of the Dead).[60] The words may be the same, but Jackson's adaptation develops Éowyn's emotional responses to Aragorn the man as well as the future king.

Tolkien acknowledges Éowyn's attraction to Aragorn, but a fine summary of her complex response to him comes from Faramir, not Éowyn. He understands Éowyn's refusal to join her brother at Cormallen immediately after the war is ended, although Faramir questions whether she stays in Minas Tirith to remain with him—or to avoid Aragorn. When Éowyn realizes that Faramir's love for her is real, and she loves him in return, she recognizes that she also has changed: "I will be a shieldmaiden no longer, nor vie with the great Riders, nor take joy only in the songs of slaying.

I will be a healer, and love all things that grow. . . . No longer do I desire to be a queen."[61] The things she loved in the past, in the time that now passes away, much as the Third Age is passing away, are her duty to the people of Rohan, which she felt she could best serve as a warrior, and her love of men who lead nobly and well in battle—Théoden, and then Aragorn.

When Éowyn looks at Faramir, she sees understanding and strength not only of a warrior, for she recognizes that Faramir would be an effective soldier, but also of a peacetime leader in Ithilien. She accepts a new role for herself in which she can best serve as a healer; her love relationship also can grow over time, not merely be framed by the fortunes of war. In Tolkien's books, Éowyn recognizes a longer lasting love than the immediate attraction to a charismatic, fearless leader, a lord to whom she can offer service and for whom she can fight. Tolkien explains that "Éowyn's love interest in Aragorn is ultimately tied to her desire for power and that her realizing this forces her to see her true feelings towards both Faramir and her earlier shieldmaiden tendencies."[62] With Faramir, Éowyn discovers a new role for herself as a partner to Faramir and a nurturing presence in their new homeland.

Jackson's depiction of Éowyn is necessarily more brief to fit the constraints of time and the number of characters in the trilogy. Her important battle deeds are shown, most notably in killing the Witch King, but her further development as a character is not a necessary part of the final film. The love relationship begins and ends with Éowyn seeking to accompany Aragorn into battle or being allowed to fight with him. Her reasons for seeming to fall in love with Faramir are not shown in the theatrical version, and the only accommodation to Tolkien's "happy ending" for Éowyn and Faramir is made by showing the two standing contentedly next to each other during Aragorn's coronation. Faramir tilts his head toward her as they both acknowledge the new king, but they have no dialogue. Only proximity and expression show that they are, indeed, a couple.

Film audiences may like to see more of a romance and, indeed, Jackson may have included more romantic elements to appeal to female filmgoers who may not enjoy the battle sequences as much as male viewers do. Éowyn's heroics in the plot do not depend on her emotional relationships. Éowyn as a character, not specifically a hero, may be more appealing to modern film audiences if she becomes more involved with the leading Man.

The Houses of Healing

Jackson's theatrical version of *The Return of the King* does not include scenes of Aragorn healing Faramir, Éowyn, and Merry in the Houses of Healing, a significant chapter in Tolkien's book. In the book, Éowyn is physically healed by Aragorn, but her emotional healing is not complete until she develops a relationship with Faramir.

Éowyn's ability to heal and to move toward the future is an important part of her heroic development. She is not merely a battle veteran or a hero. If so, she might become an embittered hero because she is not well enough to fight in the Battle of Cormallen, which would greatly diminish her effectiveness as a hero, either in Tolkien's story or for modern times. A hero who can only truly live in times of crisis, whose battle deeds are the only reason for life, and in whose reflected glory the future seems bleak is not a good role model for our time, or any other. However, a hero who finds the best way to serve others and can help people in whatever way is needed at the time is one worth emulation and greater respect.

Éowyn becomes this type of hero by knowing when she needs to fight in order to protect others and when she can best help others heal. Tolkien illustrates how Éowyn is able to move from wartime into peacetime and to continue to be a hero to her (new) people. Her selfless interest in protecting and helping others turns into the willingness to help others become whole. Aragorn is able to begin her physical healing; he deals with the external Éowyn, only what can be seen from the outside. Faramir, on the other hand, is able to begin her emotional healing; he deals with the internal Éowyn, which he is able to see and value. The Houses of Healing scenes show the growth and healing in Éowyn and make her later decision to wed Faramir understandable. It also provides a fitting way to end her infatuation with Aragorn as he heals her and allows her to go toward a new life.

Female Stereotypes

The theatrical versions of Jackson's films show Éowyn in more than one type of role. She nurtures the ill, wounded, or homeless, but she also dons armor and handles a sword well. She smiles shyly at Aragorn with love in her eyes, but she also says what she thinks in no uncertain tone. As with other characters, such as the Hobbits, in Jackson's trilogy, the division of what is exclusively male or female is not emphasized. However, one scene in the extended version of *The Two Towers* can be voted most likely to rankle women.[63]

On the road to Helm's Deep, the people of Rohan stop to make camp. Éowyn brings a kettle of soup to feed the men. She first approaches Gimli, who takes a whiff and politely declines the dinner. Éowyn then reaches Aragorn, who accepts a bowl. The stuff she ladles into the bowl looks unappetizing, and the lumps within the broth are unidentifiable. Still, Aragorn, ever the gentleman, thanks her. He tries a sip when Éowyn turns away, and then begins to pour the rest on the ground. Suddenly Éowyn remembers a question she has for Aragorn and returns to him, to see the soup apparently half eaten. She watches him choke down a mouthful, and he lies that the soup is good. Éowyn's face lights up, and she asks "Really?" as if craving his praise for her culinary abilities. Aragorn tries to be polite but noncommittal, and he quickly refuses a second helping.

Turning Éowyn's ability, or rather inability, to cook into a joke belittles the character that Jackson has so carefully built with the rest of the films. It turns her into one of two stereotypes: the "businesswoman" who is good at men's work but cannot manage to cook (or take care of a home) or the naive young homemaker who tries desperately to please her man but fails to have the proper skills. This scene is out of character from all other scenes involving Éowyn, and the brief departure into Éowyn as comic relief makes audiences laugh *at* her, not *with* her. It is an unfortunate departure not only from Tolkien's depiction of the character but also from Jackson's usual interpretation of her.

In a magazine interview, Miranda Otto explains that some scenes initially filmed but cut from the theatrical release are "lighter" moments, but that a later decision, based more on Tolkien's presentation of Éowyn, is that "she's not that sort of character. She's very much this strong and somewhat stubborn woman."[64] Audiences interested in a consistent, if serious, portrayal throughout all scenes may wish that the decision also had been made to delete the soup scene from the extended version of the film.

Loss, Feminism, and Éowyn

Éowyn, perhaps more than any character save Frodo at the end of *The Return of the King*, suffers loss. Théoden explains to Aragorn that she lost her father at the hands of the Orcs and shortly thereafter lost her mother to grief.[65] As the foster daughter of Théoden, her uncle, she learns to act as a shieldmaiden. She is accomplished with sword and, as any member of a horse-revering culture, rides well. Probably as a result of shared interests, as well as being the surviving female member of a royal family, Éowyn feels close to her uncle, brother, and cousin Théodred. No doubt her bond by shared interests as well as blood makes the loss of Théodred even harder to bear. That he dies as the result of an Orc attack must be difficult for Éowyn on many levels. Her grief is clearly shown during Théodred's burial (in the extended version of *The Two Towers*) when she sings a dirge as the body is carried into the cairn.

For audiences in the early 2000s who frequently see the scope of loss from battles and terrorist actions as reported on Internet and televised news, Éowyn's series of losses is more understandable. For Éowyn, as well as survivors of tragedies and families who have lost loved ones to an international conflict, grief is always near and finding a way to live with loss is an ongoing ordeal. That Éowyn manages to find love and to live more than a life of grief or revenge also indicates her stature as a hero for modern times.

However, death is not the only source of her losses. For a long time, Éowyn loses Théoden to Wormtongue's and Saruman's influence. Théoden does not recognize Éowyn, who also loses her status with the king as well as any sense of his protection and love. As a further result of Wormtongue's corrupting influence, Éomer is banished from Rohan. Thus, Éowyn loses her brother and is left bereft of her family for a time.

The fear of an even more personal loss rules much of Éowyn's behavior. She is in danger of losing herself. Wormtongue backs Éowyn into a corner so that she is vulnerable without her family. He openly lusts for Éowyn, and she is faced with the dilemma of losing herself in an arranged, loveless marriage to the evil Wormtongue or running the risk of physical death, as there is no one else to protect or provide for her. In either scenario, she loses herself.

This dilemma is resolved when Gandalf saves Théoden, who then banishes Wormtongue from Rohan. Nevertheless, Éowyn next faces loss of self through her relationships with powerful men who, in one fashion or another, love her and want to protect her, but end up stifling her.

Théoden feels paternal love for Éowyn. He respects her as a leader and puts her in charge of the women, old men, and children at Helm's Deep. Théoden tells her to rule after him if he dies in battle, but he does not consider her as a potential soldier during real warfare. Although he presumably did not protest at her training with weapons, he wants to shield her from battle. Théoden wants Éowyn to be happy in more traditional ways— such as surviving him to continue the family line and to rule in his stead. He thinks he knows what is best for her, and he expects her to obey his wishes not only because he is her king but because he is her uncle/father figure.

Aragorn shows compassionate love toward Éowyn. He cannot give himself to her, but he respects her. In an abstract way he wants what is best for her, too, because they share common interests. However, this abstract love is not enough on which to base a real relationship; it is more the compassion and concern (at least on Aragorn's part) of a comrade. Aragorn expects Éowyn to remain behind, but he does not trouble with her once he becomes committed to his own course of action.

Éomer offers a sibling's love and protection. He supports his sister and cares for her, but in the big brother way of wanting to protect her from danger. He does not consider her an equal; for Éomer, his sister may be old enough to speak freely with him, but he expects her to obey him and their uncle.

Éowyn risks losing the love and protection of each of these men by acting on her own desires. She does not do what the men in her life expect her to do; she determines her own course of action. Éowyn shows that she has a strong personality by speaking openly to these men who are her superiors in family and cultural status; she is not hesitant to voice her opinions. However, once Éowyn has been "put in her place" by each of these men, who for their own reasons do not want her to accompany the army to battle, she decides what she will do to fulfill her obligations to her people.

Éowyn's heroic impulse is to do what is necessary for protecting her people. Her only objective is to serve her people honorably, and she is resigned to the overwhelming odds against returning from battle. Éowyn is not heroic because she defies men, or authority, to do as she pleases. Neither are her actions selfishly based in the need for honor or glory, although those were earlier desires in her fantasy of being heroic. Instead, she chooses to serve in the way she has been trained—to fulfill the expectations she set for herself when she gained skills with weapons. Miranda Otto says that Éowyn "joins the battle because that's who she is. It's her will, and she can't suppress that.... Her determination is to be the person she is."[67] Éowyn is being true to herself by deciding to go to battle in whatever way is possible. She is a pragmatist who turns her wishes into reality.

Éowyn acts bravely in following her own counsel to (1) assist Merry in going to war, (2) fight alongside the Rohirrim, (3) protect her king/uncle, and (4) kill a fearsome enemy as part of this protection. She steps up to act heroically in battle and makes the most of several situations to help turn the battle toward the Rohirrim's and Gondorians' favor. Bravery is facing herself and her fears and then acting not selfishly to get her own way, but to serve as she was trained to do.

Once the battle is over, in Tolkien's *The Return of the King*, Éowyn attracts the attention, and later gains the love, of Faramir.[68] As both heal in Minas Tirith's Houses of Healing, Faramir is drawn to Éowyn's strength. He gradually wins her affection, although it is a difficult struggle for Éowyn only wishes to return to the war. Her physical weakness prevents her from continuing the fight, but her will most definitely has not been weakened by her encounter with the Witch King or the loss of Théoden. Only when Éowyn learns that the war has been won with the destruction of the Ring does she begin to accept Faramir's love. Éowyn begins to look forward and to perceive a time when she will not need to don armor as the best way to serve her people.

At that point, Éowyn moves toward a peacetime role. She has found a partner, not a lord, in Faramir. They understand each other and in many ways are much alike. When Éowyn agrees to marry Faramir, she has not lost herself in the relationship; she has found an outlet not only for self-fulfillment but for joy.

Éowyn may seem more feminine in this new role, at least by outward appearances, but she does not give up herself. She does not have to dress like a man or act like a warrior at this time; she can be herself and still dress like a princess; she can become a partner in marriage. As one author summarizes a discussion of Middle-earth's female characters, "perhaps Tolkien is showing... that all types of femininity are valid."[69] Éowyn does not accept or reject being a woman at different points in the story; she is always true in meeting what she believes is her duty to her people and to herself. In this way, Éowyn represents Tolkien's theme of loss and the strength of its power to effect change.

Much of Middle-earth is destroyed by Sauron's (and Saruman's) actions, but the lands are renewed after the war. The Shire, for example, must be rebuilt after the ugly structures built by Sharkey's men are torn down, and the beauty of the Hobbits' former homes must be restored. Trees and flowers are planted, and in the year following the destruction (aided in part by Galadriel's gift of special soil), the Shire blossoms again. Families are healed with the birth of especially beautiful children.[70] Tolkien shows, in the Shire and elsewhere, that life goes on, and even where loss is great, change can take place. The survivors must look forward to make places and people better in the future.

So it is with Éowyn. She has survived the loss of many members in her family, she has been wounded in battle, she has seen warfare up close, she has overcome frustration and disappointment as well as grief. Yet she can move forward in a new role as a healer; she can build a future with Faramir; she can find happiness and fulfillment in a new world. W. A. Senior writes that Tolkien's success as an author of epic fantasy is largely because of "the depth of... loss and his constant reaffirmation of its power and effect" in a story that is forward looking, "away from a destructive past and toward a healing future."[71] Éowyn's strength as a character is her ability not only to survive loss, but to find the best way—for her—to keep moving forward and making a positive contribution to her society. That she is able to overcome great loss and adversity helps make her a hero.

Éowyn and a Modern Definition of *Hero*

In chapter 1, an outline of the characteristics defining a modern hero, for film or book, lists these five items:

1. She acts on her convictions.

Éowyn is strong willed and frequently speaks her mind. Everyone around her knows exactly what she thinks and what she believes her role should be. However, Éowyn does more than speak forcefully; she backs up her talk with action, even if that is not popular (and in fact could be treasonous, if her disobedience had not turned out as well as the situation would allow).

Éowyn shows her convictions in small ways, too, especially in Jackson's *The Return of the King*. When she takes Merry with her to war, she does not treat him as a mere tagalong, what Théoden called "a burden" who would slow the warrior who carried him to battle.[72] Instead he sits before her (instead of riding behind her, as Tolkien describes) and takes the reins to guide them as Éowyn assaults the mûmakil. She has promised Merry before the battle that she will look after him, and when they are toppled from their horse, Éowyn frantically calls for Merry, from whom she has been separated. In the chaos of battle, amid dead and dying bodies large and small, Éowyn might be expected to forget her promise and to look first to herself. Instead, she looks around for Merry and is distraught not to see him nearby. Even under duress, Éowyn intends to keep her promises.

Éowyn is a woman of her word, and she backs up her word with action. She is a determined woman and an honorable hero for modern times.

2. She plans strategies and carries them out successfully, even if this strategy is planned on the run. She is a thinking hero who may have to plan spontaneously as a crisis occurs or think on her feet during a crisis.

"Where will wants not, a way opens" is the key to Éowyn's personality. To be successful as a woman and a sometimes surrogate leader in place of Théoden, Éowyn must have the ability to plan ahead and then see that her plans are carried out, whether she directs others or completes the tasks herself. Éowyn is a practical planner in both situations. When she directs the people of Rohan to safe refuge at Helm's Deep, she must follow her uncle's orders, but she also has to make sure that his plan of retreat to the fortress is successful.[73] In Jackson's *The Two Towers*, Éowyn is shown telling the frightened people to stay together as they flee toward Helm's Deep, although her heart clearly is with the warriors heading off to fight the warg riders. Once the refugees are safely within the gates, she begins directing the disposition of supplies and takes charge until Théoden arrives.

The extended version of *The Two Towers* shows Éowyn begging Aragorn to let her join him in battle, to fight alongside the others who also love Aragorn and would follow his leadership to whatever end. Aragorn tells her that he cannot make this decision and clearly bows to the King of Rohan's wish that Éowyn go to the caves with the women and children. Éowyn seems to learn from this experience, however.

When the Rohirrim are called to fight in *The Return of the King*, Éowyn brings her sword (and apparently also her armor) to Dunharrow.[74] When the army rides off, she does not ask permission this time, but makes the choice herself to go to war. Éowyn could not have planned how she would react in battle, but her earlier development of battle skills and her determination to protect her people by serving as a warrior allow her to act heroically when the moment comes for her to step forward. Éowyn's "plan" for herself is to fight for her people, and she makes sure that she does so.

> 3. She offers to sacrifice herself, if necessary, for the cause.

When Éowyn first rides to war, she is not suicidal, but she understands that she is going to sacrifice herself for the cause. At this point, she believes she has little to live for, and perhaps an honorable death is the best she can achieve. On a theoretical level, Éowyn understands the nature of sacrifice, but it becomes real only when she comes face to face with an overwhelming number of Orcs, and later Haradrim, waiting to kill her people. Yet, when the Witch King threatens Théoden, who cannot fight any longer for himself, she quickly places herself between her uncle and the Nazgûl. Éowyn does not seem to want to become a martyr, but she is willing to die to protect those she loves. Tolkien and Jackson illustrate this part of her heroic personality in *The Return of the King*.

> 4. She grows as a character, showing under extreme circumstances the heroic qualities that always have been part of her makeup, but have not been recognized until these qualities are needed.

Recognition is the key word here, and then it should refer to recognition by others. Éowyn always believes she has the ability not necessarily to act heroically, although in her dreams of valor on the battlefield she probably wants to be recognized for her brave deeds, but to act nobly on behalf of her people. Her training and skills prepare her to serve as a warrior, but her ability to serve in this capacity has never been seriously recognized by men.

Éowyn also grows as a character who sees beyond her desire to fight for those she loves; this part of her story is mentioned in Tolkien's appendixes and only alluded to in Jackson's final film. By then, Éowyn has learned what war truly is like, and her illusions of the grandeur of battle most likely have been shattered. A realistic Éowyn is not bitter or remorseful. Instead, she takes her experiences to move forward and to serve in other ways as a leader and healer. Her ability to move forward, not to live in the past or become mired in mourning, illustrates her personal growth and shows an important way that heroes can help society move forward after a tragic event.

> 5. She embodies the values of love of family and home, which provide the impetus for her to act to protect the people and places she loves.

This element is clearly shown in Jackson's latter two films, as Éowyn is shown tending the wounded Théodred and ailing Théoden.[75] She also feeds and looks after the children bearing the message of the Orcs' invasion further into Rohan, as well as leads the people to and directs the organization of supplies in Helm's Deep. After Théoden has been mortally wounded during the Battle of the Pelennor Fields, Éowyn stays with her uncle, both to give and receive comfort, as he dies.[76]

In addition to her capacity to nurture those who are in need, Éowyn's entire sense of service to her people is based on her ability to defend them as a warrior. Even though she has to sneak into the army to be able to fight for her country, she does so. Éowyn's sense of "family" extends beyond her immediate kin to the larger "family" of the people of Rohan, to whom she feels great responsibility. This love of family, people, and Rohan motivates Éowyn not only to immediate acts of valor in battle, but to an ongoing life of service. In Tolkien's trilogy, Éowyn continues this life of service post-war, as she enters into a new relationship with Faramir and the people of Gondor.

Éowyn's ability to use her skills to the best of her ability to aid others makes her heroic and especially appropriate as a role model for modern audiences. She is a character with whom women may relate. As Miranda Otto explains, "she takes on a male exterior and gets to live out that side, which is another thing that modern women can relate to—they've gone out into the world in that way, too."[77] She places herself out in the world to confront its ills and to protect others. Although she does not denigrate the women who are left behind, that role is not for her. It is not what she is trained to do, and it is not part of her nature to be content out of the action. She is an action hero who refuses to stand in the shadows when she has the resources to help others, whether it be a specific act such as protecting and avenging Théoden or a more general activity such as guiding her people to safety. She overcomes her fear to act effectively and honorably, and her actions are true to her nature and sense of what is right.

Éowyn is not a martyr who only feels obligated by duty to serve others; the desire to help others—although she often questions the best way she is permitted to help—is an important part of her personality, and all her actions are based on this desire. Although Éowyn initially tells Aragorn that she also looks for valor and renown as a warrior, after she has found both in battle, she is content to find a more peaceful way to serve her people post-war. She grows as a character to incorporate all aspects of her personality into a life of service; by helping others, she best fulfills herself.

5

Galadriel and Arwen as Inspirational Heroes

Galadriel and Arwen are usually perceived as minor characters in J. R. R. Tolkien's trilogy. They appear seldom, and when they do, their beauty is often the subject of comment. Gimli, for one, becomes so enamored of Galadriel that he does what no other Dwarf would have dreamed doing: he vows to serve this lady, and he does so throughout the Quest.[1] In *The Return of the King*, Éomer and Gimli discuss who is more beautiful, Galadriel or Arwen.[2] However, these Elven beauties offer much more than a striking appearance; they motivate other characters to be able to complete the Quest, and their choices influence the direction that Middle-earth takes after the Elves' influence diminishes.

Both Galadriel and Arwen are visionaries. They have a vision for Middle-earth, and in Arwen's case, specifically for Aragorn's future role in it. However, they also are able to interpret and, apparently, send visions to others. Their mystic qualities help make them inspirational heroes. They inspire others to great deeds, and their practical activities behind the scenes further the plot, both in Tolkien's trilogy and in Peter Jackson's.

Jackson's trilogy emphasizes the visions of Galadriel and Arwen and the female Elves' behind-the-scenes roles that end up determining the fate of Middle-earth almost as much as Frodo's and Gollum's disposal of the One Ring. These Elves not only envision the future, but act on these visions to sway the outcome of events. Jackson's trilogy includes scenes not in Tolkien's books that highlight these visions. However, through *The Silmarillion* as well as *The Lord of the Rings*, Tolkien provides a rich history of the Elves and describes Galadriel in particular as a powerful leader. Although Arwen's story in *The Lord of the Rings* is brief, her love for Aragorn is a crucial part of his life and an influential factor in his ascension to the throne.

Galadriel as a Literary Hero in *The Silmarillion* and *The Lord of the Rings*

In simplest terms, Galadriel is a daughter of Finarfin, who is a descendant of the Valar, and Galadriel herself is one of the Eldar, one of the "first" Elves, whose lineage goes back only a few generations to the creation story, according to *The Silmarillion*.[3] Galadriel is exiled in Middle-earth, perhaps more of a matter of bad timing than anything else. In a letter dated August 4, 1973, Tolkien writes that Galadriel is not banished to Middle-earth because she has done some evil deed; she is "an enemy of Feanor," who started a rebellion among the Elves against the Valar and whose rebellion in Middle-earth causes the Valar to forbid those who left Valinor from returning. Galadriel goes to Middle-earth on her own instead of as part of the rebellious group of Elves, and Tolkien emphasizes that her reasons are "legitimate, and she would have been permitted to depart, but for the misfortune that before she set out the revolt of Feanor broke out."[4] When emigration to Valinor ends as a result, Galadriel is forced to remain in Middle-earth.

However, she does well in her new home. She is a ringbearer of one of the rings of power. She, along with her spouse Celeborn, leads the Elves in Lothlórien. This is where the Fellowship finds her after they leave Moria and seek sanctuary in the safe haven of Lothlórien.[5] Galadriel has been described as one "whose life span extends back to the start of the First Age," her knowledge and "wisdom unexcelled" by that of other Elves.[6]

Although Galadriel is a recognized leader whose lineage is most noble, she is not a typical literary hero. She "rules" the Elves, although Tolkien does not call her a queen.[7] The label of "saint" sometimes is given to Galadriel because of Gimli's devotion to her, which has been interpreted as the same type of devotion others have to Mary in the Catholic religion, but Tolkien denies this connection.[8] In many ways, Galadriel defies easy classification. She is less mystical than spiritual, for she often inspires other characters to go beyond what they think they can do; however, she is not spiritual in the sense of being like a saint. Her behind-the-scenes actions not only are heroic for their results, but she also motivates other characters into helping others or acting heroically on their own.

In *The Lord of the Rings*, Tolkien creates a fully formed character who already has, quite literally, the wisdom of the ages. She understands the nature of evil, and she works to assist the Fellowship on the Quest, even as she realizes that the coming dominion of Men dooms the power of the Elves. Her part in the Quest story is only an interlude in her long life, but Galadriel is heroic throughout the War of the Ring in her ability to assist others through her use of visions and her choice of gifts.

Unlike many other characters discussed in this book, Galadriel does not have to grow or change much in order to act heroically. She could choose to stay out of the brewing troubles in Middle-earth and hide in Lothlórien to await the outcome of the War of the Ring. She could fade away in Middle-earth or beg pardon from the Valar in order to return home. Yet she chooses to intervene on behalf of the Fellowship, and thus of the races living in Middle-earth who fight Sauron, although she knows that, even if the "good guys" win, she will lose her power. The ring of power she has guarded for many years will be useless, and with the return of the King of Gondor, Men will become the prominent race in Middle-earth. Nevertheless, Galadriel chooses to help the Fellowship and offers her counsel, as well as other gifts, to improve their chances for success.

Tolkien shows that, for all her wisdom and age, Galadriel still must challenge herself on the question of ultimate power. Although she has wielded a certain amount of power as a ringbearer and Elven leader, Galadriel does not know for certain what she would do if handed the opportunity for ultimate power, which the One Ring can provide. If she would have had to go to war for it, she probably would not have done so; open conflict is something she seems to recognize, but does not actively participate in herself, once she lives in Lothlórien. However, Frodo provides Galadriel with a very easy way of gaining ultimate power—he offers to hand her the Ring. Galadriel's only obstacle is herself, and she finds within herself the strength to turn down this opportunity. She seems relieved and happy, if physically diminished, when she tells Frodo that she has passed her test and is able to remain herself.[9]

Galadriel is no stranger to power. She has seen its effects on Elves and Men throughout the ages. "Power in the works of Tolkien is often to be found in the hands of a woman," and Galadriel's power in Lothlórien "far eclipses" that of her husband.[10] Because she is familiar with it, power is both a temptation and a curse to be avoided. In Jackson's *The Fellowship of the Ring*, Galadriel reminds Frodo that to bear one of the rings of power "is to be alone."[11] She understands Frodo's burden, but she does not want to take it. Galadriel knows all too well the effects that such power can have over one who attempts to wield it; the power does not truly tempt her, and she can remain who she is. Galadriel is a positive, helpful force who understands the nature of self-sacrifice and freely gives up her one chance for complete power, even though she knows that her life will drastically change because of her choice.

In this way, Galadriel is very much a modern hero who is often tempted by more power, even when she is powerful already. Modern heroes may be tempted by fame or money, or the possibility of gaining even more fame or money, for example, to sell their story to be made into a television movie. They may be tempted by the lure of more profits to do something questionable in their business dealings. Even heroes who have the best of intentions as they grasp more power may find themselves constantly fighting to use that power wisely or ethically.

Galadriel's choices, including self-sacrifice and the use of her talents to assist the Fellowship, make her a hero for modern times, albeit in ways different from the other unsung heroes described in this book.

Arwen's History in Tolkien's Work

Arwen also is difficult to categorize using any of the previously discussed definitions of a classic literary hero. She is the daughter of Elrond, whose house rules Imladris (called only Rivendell in Jackson's films); her mother is Celebrian, the daughter of Celeborn and Galadriel. She is reared for part of her long youth in Lothlórien, although she later returns to her father's home.[12,13] What is known about Arwen's nature, as Tolkien created it, can be learned from a few brief passages in *The Fellowship of the Ring* and *The Return of the King*.

When the representatives of Middle-earth meet for a feast before the Council of Elrond, Frodo first sees Arwen and is amazed by her loveliness. Tolkien explains that Arwen recently has returned to Elrond's house after spending many years in Lothlórien with Galadriel.[14] Arwen does not speak during this scene; in fact, she is only mentioned because Frodo sees her. Arwen is mentioned twice more in this chapter, once as she walks with Elrond and a second time as she sits near him and also talks with Aragorn. Again, Arwen is only mentioned in a report of what Frodo observes; again, Frodo is nearly overwhelmed by her beauty and piercing gaze.[15] She possibly stands with other members of Elrond's household when the Fellowship departs from Rivendell, but Tolkien does not specifically mention her.[16]

In Tolkien's tale, Arwen does not play a part in the reforging of Aragorn's sword, although this becomes one of her greatest acts in Jackson's trilogy. (Aragorn's ancestor Elendil originally used the sword, and a shard of the broken sword is used by Isildur to sever the Ring from Sauron's hand during an early war against Sauron. This sword is called Narsil, and when reforged, is renamed Andúril. The reforged sword then is used by Aragorn during the War of the Ring.)[17]

Even Arwen's wedding to Aragorn is given only limited space at the end of a chapter in *The Return of the King*. Elrond, accompanied by Elves from throughout Middle-earth (including Galadriel and Celeborn), brings Arwen to Aragorn and simply gives her to him; the pair are then wed. Frodo once more is awed by Arwen's beauty and tells Gandalf that the marriage is a fitting conclusion. He uses the metaphor of day and night both being blessed now, a reference to Arwen Undómiel, the Evenstar, whose dark and somewhat mysterious beauty seems a fine counterpoint to Aragorn's kingly persona.[18] Arwen weds Aragorn on Midsummer's Day, a time when the earth is in full bloom and with the promise of growth; this particular date is especially fitting for Arwen's union, because she is at the height of her beauty and power. All she has wanted for Aragorn has been achieved, and Elrond recognizes this fulfillment by giving her in marriage. From this point, Arwen's beauty will begin to wane as she ages and eventually dies, as do all mortals. Her joining with Aragorn after a long, arduous path toward the fulfillment of his destiny is the pinnacle of her power and joy, when all those she loves are together in one place to celebrate.

Arwen finally speaks in the chapter "Many Partings," when she explains to Frodo that Bilbo, who is living at Rivendell and does not attend the wedding festivities, has aged rapidly now that he no longer lives under the Ring's protection. More importantly, she provides Frodo with an amulet—a jewel to help him through difficult times when the darkness overcomes him—and through her grace makes it possible for him to take her place on the ship to Valinor, if he so desires.[19] Arwen's gift, the kindest granted in the entire trilogy, is the greatest action that Arwen takes in Tolkien's tale, and it is fitting that her dialogue with Frodo comes at this time. Arwen's gift aids Frodo after the Quest, just as Galadriel's gifts aid him during it. In this way, Arwen carries on the tradition of understanding exactly what is needed and providing it. Through this dialogue, Tolkien also shows that Arwen clearly understands her own choice to remain in Middle-earth, one she calls "the sweet and the bitter."[20]

Arwen is given much more dialogue in appendix A,[21] as her story is told in more detail. Tolkien describes Aragorn's first meeting with Arwen and the way in which he falls in love with her. Arwen seems at times bemused by Aragorn, who at first is surprised to realize that she is a great deal older than he is, although she looks like a young maiden. He also comes to understand that she has more wisdom and experience than he. Of course, Elrond is not terribly excited to learn that his foster son has fallen in love with his daughter. Even separation does not stop the beginnings of this love.

During a later meeting in Lothlórien, where Arwen once again lives, she and Aragorn have time together to get to know each other. They pledge themselves to each other, appropriately at Midsummer, a fact that again does little to please Elrond. Once Arwen makes her choice to remain in Middle-earth, Elrond despairs; he does not want to lose his child, because he plans eventually to return to Valinor and does not want to be forever parted from his only daughter. Speaking as a loving, but strict father/foster father, Elrond tells Aragorn that Arwen will only marry him once he is king; Elrond does not want Arwen's life to be wasted in Middle-earth. When Aragorn becomes high king, Elrond honors his "agreement" with Aragorn and gives his blessing to Arwen's union with him.

Throughout this section of the appendixes, the majority of dialogue belongs to Arwen and Aragorn, who meet, get to know each other, and realize the sacrifice of Arwen's choice to live a mortal life. Tolkien's Arwen is firm in her commitment to Aragorn; she makes her choice freely and clearly understands the consequences of her decision. In this brief section, Arwen indeed seems to be a wise, worldly Elf who determines her own fate and is willing to embrace both the joy and the sorrow resulting from this choice. She is more than a beautiful background player or a prize that Aragorn receives at the end of his long labors. She has a deep understanding of others, and she uses her knowledge to support and love Aragorn, but also to help Frodo through what she understands will be painful days ahead. She seems wise and compassionate, not merely window dressing or a passive beauty. These qualities make her heroic in Tolkien's trilogy, for Arwen is steadfast in her loyalty to and love of Aragorn, even though this devotion costs her immortality. Hers is a difficult choice, not a romantic reaction. Arwen understands the price of her loyalty, but she also believes that her support of Aragorn is necessary for his ultimate ascension as king.

Unlike in fairy tales, or even to some extent Jackson's trilogy, the beautiful princess is not "saved" by her prince/king; she does not improve her station in life by being "won" by her male companion. If anything, Aragorn is lucky to have been deemed worthy of Arwen's love. He has to prove himself to her father and achieve a position of power and respect before Arwen is "allowed" to make the sacrifice to stay with him. Tolkien's trilogy, even with its limited descriptions of Arwen, creates a union of equals who realize and value what they have in each other.

The Link between Arwen and Luthien

A quick summary of the story of Luthien and Beren is necessary so that *The Lord of the Rings'* readers and, in particular, film audiences can appreciate the link between Arwen and Luthien. In *The Silmarillion*, Tolkien tells a story about an immortal and a Man who fall in love, but theirs is a relationship full of peril.[22] Beren, a Man wandering in exile, discovers Luthien. Although Beren is the son of a prominent leader, he is nevertheless outclassed socially by Luthien, the daughter of Melian and Thingol; Melian is one of the Valar, and Thingol, a great Elven king.

Beren falls in love with Luthien at first sight. She sings gloriously and is beautiful beyond anything he has ever seen. However, when Luthien is discovered with Beren, and he is brought before Thingol, Luthien's father vehemently objects to their love. He separates the two, eventually imprisoning Luthien so that she will not run off to Beren. Thingol sets an impossible Quest for Beren: he must retrieve one of the Silmarils, currently in a crown worn by the powerful Morgoth, and give it to Thingol. (Luthien, of course, cleverly manages to escape so that she may help Beren with his Quest.)

During this Quest, Beren faces many obstacles and tests. He is imprisoned by Sauron until Luthien, through her cunning and magic, frees him. Together, Beren and Luthien enter Morgoth's fortress, and while Luthien distracts Morgoth, Beren takes a Silmaril from the crown. Even then, their journey is not smooth, as they are chased and Beren maimed before he can bring the Silmaril to Thingol. Eventually, Beren completes the Quest, and Thingol sees how true his love is for Luthien, and hers for him. However, Beren has been mortally wounded, and Luthien cannot bear to lose him. She begs for his life to be restored, winning the pity of the Valar. Luthien must choose to give up her immortal life in order to be with her lover. She agrees, and although she is united with a resurrected Beren, she suffers the fate of all mortals and eventually dies.

In the few scenes in which Arwen appears in Tolkien's trilogy, she is compared with Luthien, most often because she shares Luthien's incredible beauty and resembles her physically, with similar dark hair and pale skin. When Frodo first sees Arwen, he remembers that she has been described as looking like Luthien.[23] In the Hall of Fire, the Fellowship later listens to the lay of Beren and Luthien, furthering the comparison.[24] After her marriage, Arwen mentions to Frodo that she has made the choice of Luthien.[25] In appendix A, Tolkien tells how Aragorn "mistakes" Arwen for Luthien when he first sees her. He has been singing the lay when he first spies Arwen, then calls her "Tinuviel," and almost immediately places himself in the role of Beren.[26]

Even Jackson's trilogy makes a brief allusion to Beren and Luthien. Before the Hobbits and Aragorn (Strider) arrive in Rivendell, Frodo catches Aragorn singing in Elvish one night when he thinks the Hobbits are asleep. Frodo understands a bit of the lay, but he asks Aragorn to explain the tale fully. Aragorn wistfully describes the story of a beautiful Elf who falls in love with a Man. When Frodo asks what becomes of her, Aragorn replies sadly, "She died," and then effectively ends the conversation by suggesting Frodo rest.[27] Audiences understand that Aragorn is aware of the comparison between Beren's love story and his own, and the thought of Arwen's death because of her love for him pains him.

For Tolkien, the difficult romance and undying love between Luthien and Beren is a crucial part of the story. In a letter, Tolkien explains that "the tale of Arwen and Aragorn [is] the most important of the Appendices; it is part of the essential story." The story does not easily fit within the structure of the story, which Tolkien calls "hobbit-centric," and so it is placed in the appendixes.[28] Modern readers may be more familiar with appended materials being considered secondary or of peripheral importance to the body of a text; however, Tolkien's appendixes are very much important additional sources in order better to understand characters, places, and events. That Arwen's main story is relegated to appendix A does not diminish its importance. The relationship between Arwen and Aragorn often parallels that of Luthien and Beren, and an understanding of Luthien's story can provide insight into Arwen's choice to remain in Middle-earth.

Similarities between Arwen and Luthien

Arwen is similar to Luthien in several ways: each believes in her lover and the power of true love; envisions a specific future and plans actions to make that future happen; chooses mortality in order to remain with her lover; rules her own life, despite her father's wishes; protects her lover during his Quest; is renowned for her beauty and is considered to be a great "prize."

Arwen, like Luthien, easily could have given up such a difficult relationship. Each, after all, is the daughter of a ruler, is an Elf with an incredibly long lifespan compared to that of a mortal Man, and has a wealth of prior experience and wisdom on which to draw. Arwen's position gives her "access to the greatest Elven minds of her age. . . . She would have heard first-hand accounts of Elvish sorcery, warfare, and scholarship."[29] However, both Arwen and Luthien recognize love and believe in the power of true love. Otherwise, why would they choose such a difficult path when undoubtedly they have many suitors from whom to select throughout their long lives? Logically, they understand much about the world; emotionally, they value love for a mortal Man over every other consideration.

Arwen, like Luthien, faces obstacles created by her father to slow down, if not end, the relationship. The Quest set for Beren at first may seem more perilous than Aragorn's; Beren must return one of the Silmarils to Thingol. As a mere mortal, Beren lacks the powers of other races and can easily be killed. Only through Luthien's continued assistance and support does

Beren ultimately succeed, although it costs him his life (which is returned because of Luthien). Aragorn does not have to go on the Quest to win Arwen's hand, but Elrond (in Tolkien's trilogy) makes him aware that he must become king in order to wed Arwen.[30] Aragorn must have a social status to match Arwen's within her culture. To do so requires him to overcome Sauron, as well as the many other obstacles he faces during the War of the Ring and to retake the throne of Gondor. Throughout the series of tasks and obstacles that become part of the larger Quest to attain his destined role as king, Aragorn receives the support and assistance of Arwen.

Luthien and Arwen believe in the Men they have chosen, and once they are committed to love these Men, they do whatever it takes to encourage, support, and ultimately ensure they succeed. They do not wait to see how a Quest turns out; they actively work on behalf of their future mates. In Jackson's trilogy, Arwen's role is more pronounced, and she is shown as everything from a warrior to a sacrificial victim as she does her part to ensure that Aragorn succeeds and eventually becomes king.

Luthien goes so far as to grow her hair so that she can use it in her escape from the tower where her father imprisons her; she often sings to distract or bewitch others to help Beren during his Quest; she accepts the condition that she become mortal so that she and Beren are not parted by death. Although Tolkien does not describe so many situations in which Arwen becomes involved in the Quest, she is shown consistently as being devoted to Aragorn. When they are reunited in Lothlórien after a long separation, Arwen pledges her life to Aragorn and tells him that she foresees greatness for him. This pledge takes place before the realities of the Quest are manifested.[31] Galadriel passes on to Aragorn a jewel, the Elfstone, which comes from Arwen, as he prepares to leave Lothlórien early in the Quest.[32]

In Jackson's trilogy, Arwen does everything she can to further the Quest. She wanders in the Nazgûl-infested countryside until she finds Aragorn.[33] She tells Aragorn in no uncertain terms that she is better suited than he in taking Frodo to Rivendell, and she later draws her sword in order to defend Frodo and confront the Nazgûl as she carries the injured Frodo to Rivendell. As representatives from Middle-earth gather for Elrond's Council, Arwen encourages Aragorn, who is seen doubting himself as he reverently touches the broken sword used by Isildur, which is enshrined at Rivendell. She is the one to remind him softly, but forcefully, of his future role.[34] In Jackson's *The Return of the King*, Arwen urges Elrond to have the sword reforged and to take it to Aragorn. She determines that "it is time" and sets the process in motion.[35] In these and other ways, as described in the following sections, Arwen not only supports Aragorn but, once she has made her decision to place her future with his, she uses her knowledge and skills to ensure that Aragorn fulfills his destiny to become king.

Arwen and Luthien support and protect their chosen Men despite the wishes of their fathers. Luthien's father is especially outraged that a mere Man would seek to join with Luthien, despite the obvious love between them. He uses his considerable power to keep the lovers separated, to the point of imprisoning his daughter and sending her beloved to almost certain death. As Luthien's mother warns her husband, his actions do nothing more, in the end, than to separate him from his daughter. Luthien never receives her father's blessing for her choice, and she openly rebels against his wishes. Luthien clearly knows her own mind and decides what she wants for her life, to the obvious anger and displeasure of her father. Not only does Thingol lose his daughter because of her mortality, but he also emotionally loses her the moment that he sets an impossible Quest for Beren.

Although Elrond does not go to such extremes to separate Arwen and Aragorn, he takes Aragorn aside and explains to him the vast difference in experience and "class" between the two. He places the condition that Aragorn must achieve his destiny before he may wed Arwen, which seems to be a moot point as Arwen clearly knows her mind and has pledged herself to Aragorn. However, Arwen's relationship with her father is much closer than Luthien's to Thingol, and undoubtedly both Arwen and Aragorn (whose foster father is Elrond) value Elrond's blessing. In Jackson's *The Return of the King*, Arwen angrily confronts Elrond after she has a vision of her possible future as Aragorn's wife and mother to their son; she accuses him of withholding information from her.[36] Although the bond between the two is not severed, it is strained in this scene, although Arwen has her way and, a few scenes later, is directing Elrond to reforge the sword for Aragorn. Elrond complies, and in the final scene in which the two are shown, he happily brings Arwen to Aragorn so they may be married.

An obvious similarity between Arwen and Luthien is the choice each makes to live a mortal life in order to remain with her love. For Arwen, this means forsaking a future with her family—including her mother, who long ago sailed across the seas. For Luthien, the choice is more immediate. Beren is already dead when Luthien is offered the chance for his resurrection at the price of her mortality. She would rather have a shorter life than to be separated permanently from Beren. Arwen's choice does not "save" Aragorn from death, but it does allow them to share several years as wife and husband before he succumbs to old age.

The superficial similarity between Arwen and Luthien is their beauty, but this is the least important part of a comparison. Both are known and coveted for their beauty. Luthien's beauty draws many potential suitors, whereas Arwen's has the power to enthrall not only Aragorn, but Frodo and later Éomer. Tolkien describes Luthien and Arwen as being dark-haired beauties whose loveliness is almost unbelievable. However, these Elves are much more than just beautiful creatures to be won by the appropriate mate; their appearance is only part of their strength and allure. They also are determined females who know what they want and go about ensuring that their vision of the future has the opportunity to unfold as they wish.

Differences between Arwen and Luthien

The similarities outweigh their differences, but Luthien and Arwen are not interchangeable, nor is Arwen just a replica of Luthien in a later time. In Tolkien's story, Luthien is younger when she falls in love, and she is more openly rebellious to her father. In fact, she never receives his blessing and seems content to leave their broken relationship un-mended. On the other hand, Arwen maintains a strong relationship with her father and receives his blessing for her marriage. She is older and does not run after Aragorn; she uses her knowledge to help him, but she does not accompany him during the Quest. "The hair-cutting, the fleeing, the father-defying, the breaking-and-entering" found in Luthien's story are not anywhere in Arwen's tale in *The Lord of the Rings*.[37] (Tolkien's Arwen thus differs from actress Liv Tyler's Arwen, who is more of a warrior princess early in *The Fellowship of the Ring*[38] and whose visions bring her to Aragorn at different points in *The Two Towers*[39] and *The Return of the King*.[40])

Luthien also benefits from her mother's intervention in the growing rift between her and her father. Melian counsels Thingol that his actions only tear apart his relationship with his daughter, which he will regret; of course, Thingol does not listen to Melian, but she nevertheless has the insight her husband lacks.[41] Arwen's mother is not available to counsel her daughter or to advise Elrond; Celebrian lives in Valinor. Although Galadriel, in Tolkien's trilogy, sometimes seems to be a surrogate mother who helps bring Aragorn and Arwen together, in Jackson's trilogy, Arwen does not have the benefit of any close female family member to help her. Tolkien at least mentions that Galadriel provides fine clothing and, in effect, "cleans up" Aragorn before he sees Arwen after many years in Lothlórien; Galadriel seems to be assisting in getting the two together.[42] Jackson's Arwen is left to her own devices, but she seems more than confident and capable in her love relationship with Aragorn.

Both Luthien and Arwen are strong female characters whose person-alities may not be understood fully with only a reading of *The Lord of the Rings* or a viewing of Jackson's trilogy. Their lives parallel each other, and their strengths of character makes their choice for a mortal life seem sweetly tragic. Tolkien indicates that true love is not without peril or loss, but it is worth all the sacrifice nonetheless.

Galadriel and Arwen as Cinematic Heroes

The strongest images of Galadriel and Arwen are those that show them as visionaries, either in the mystic sense of having or explaining visions or in the practical sense of making events happen to further their interests in Middle-earth. Each character sees, gives, and discusses visions. The impact motivates other (male) characters to action and influences the outcome of the Quest. In addition, the gifts that these Elves bestow on members of the Fellowship show Galadriel's and Arwen's prescience in understanding what is needed to achieve their vision of a Middle-earth free from Sauron's evil.

The Elves' Telepathic and Visionary Gifts

Both Galadriel and Arwen have similar "supernatural" gifts that seem very natural to Elves. Galadriel speaks to others' minds and seems to have the ability to read them, as well. She appears in a vision once, but her more active role is to communicate with others to motivate them to greater acts of bravery (and risk). Galadriel is persuasive through her communication skills, both aloud and telepathically, and she uses these skills to great advantage. Arwen is shown both sending dreams/visions to Aragorn, with whom she has the closest spiritual/love connection, and seeing visions. Although her gifts are used primarily to motivate Aragorn to different actions or to revive him so that he can continue on the Quest, because Aragorn is an important leader, Arwen's ability to influence him also changes the course of Middle-earth history.

Galadriel's Visions and Telepathic Communication

Galadriel's strength as a visionary is emphasized throughout the films. In Jackson's *The Two Towers*, Galadriel seems to talk with Elrond telepathically.[43] Jackson shows Galadriel, presumably still in Lothlórien, speaking aloud her concern about the upcoming battle at Helm's Deep. She tells Elrond, who is in Rivendell, that Frodo is starting to understand that the Quest will consume him, and the fate of Middle-earth may hinge on the Elves' involvement in battle.

In a scene shortly thereafter, a contingent of Elves arrives at Helm's Deep. Haldir, from Lothlórien, leads them and asks Théoden if the Elves may join forces with Men.[44] The implication is that Elves from Rivendell and Lothlórien arrive in time to help turn the battle to Men's favor. Galadriel's ability to "speak" with Elrond and his ability to get the message show a heightened form of communication. Galadriel also tells Elrond that she knows that he has "seen" the status of the Quest.[45] The interaction between Galadriel and Elrond, although they are depicted on screen as standing in different locations, shows that both of these Elvish leaders have visions and can communicate telepathically.

Galadriel's ability to communicate with others by speaking to their minds is emphasized in each film as well. Jackson first illustrates this communication with voiceovers during the scene in which the Fellowship first meet Galadriel, who sends her thoughts into the minds of the travelers.[46] For example, she not only welcomes Frodo but reminds him that he carries evil in the form of the Ring. Galadriel also reads minds. She explains aloud what has happened to Gandalf before anyone tells her what has befallen him in Moria. Boromir is visibly upset after his encounter with Galadriel. (He later confides to Aragorn that Galadriel seems to know his fears for Gondor and that he has heard Galadriel's voice in his head.) After discerning the thoughts of the Fellowship, Galadriel says aloud that the Quest is "balanced on the edge of a knife"—with a pause to glare meaningfully at Boromir—but that "hope remains while the company is true," giving a friendlier, but rather meaningful look to Sam.

In the extended version of *The Fellowship of the Ring*, a voiceover of Galadriel comforts Pippin with the assurance that he will be able to act courageously when the time for bravery comes.[47] Pippin might simply be remembering her words, but the implication is that Galadriel can know what each member of the Fellowship needs to hear, and she also knows each person's thoughts regarding the Quest. The "inner messages" that Galadriel sends foreshadow events that the audience will see later in the trilogy; these scenes also emphasize Galadriel's power and provide useful counsel uniquely suited to the different members of the Fellowship. Even without her mirror, Galadriel seems to earn the title of "sorcerer" given in Tolkien's trilogy[48] and is called a "sorceress" and an "Elf-witch" by Gimli on film as the Fellowship enters Lothlórien.[49]

Galadriel's visions also prompt action in Middle-earth and revive Frodo when he is most in doubt about his ability to succeed. Galadriel offers only Frodo a look into her mirror in Jackson's trilogy,[50] although both Frodo and Sam glimpse a possible, and horrific, future in Tolkien's work.[51] Jackson shows Frodo's vision as dark; the intercut images are black and white and shown so quickly that the audience does not have time to interpret each one. Most notably, an enslaved Sam, cringing under a whip as he dares lift his head, makes an impression. Audiences thus understand why Frodo decides to continue the Quest—the consequences of his failure seem ominous. At the conclusion of this vision, Galadriel knowingly tells Frodo that she also has seen similar visions. Frodo does not even need to describe what he has seen.

Galadriel, along with few others, such as Gandalf, understands the necessity of the Quest. Just like Frodo's vision in the mirror, success or failure, good or evil, seems as black and white as the images Frodo has seen. By allowing Frodo to see firsthand a possible future for Middle-earth—one that includes a burning, slavery-ridden Shire—Galadriel instills in Frodo the fear of such a future and the urgency of his mission. If Frodo doubts the necessity of the Quest, especially after Gandalf has been lost in Moria, his doubts are likely dispelled by what he has seen in the mirror.

Jackson also integrates Galadriel into *The Return of the King* through another vision sequence.[52] When Frodo collapses outside Shelob's cavernous lair, he laments sending Sam away (another scene unique to Jackson's trilogy) and realizes just how alone he is to complete the journey. As he falls, he envisions himself in a beautiful, flowering field, and a smiling Galadriel offers him a hand to pull himself up. Just as the phial of starlight earlier has helped to drive away Shelob and light Frodo's way, Galadriel in glowing white dress, almost shimmering on screen in the sunlight, also lights the way and revives Frodo. This symbolic act pulls Frodo to his feet in the real world, giving him the renewed ability to move on with the Quest.

Arwen's Visions

Arwen also knows of her father's visions and seems to have inherited this gift. In *The Return of the King*, Jackson shows the audience Arwen's vision as she travels to the Grey Havens.[53] Arwen pauses on the trail, oblivious to the Elves around her, as she "watches" her young son running to Aragorn. When she sees the amulet the child wears—the jewel she has given Aragorn—she understands that the child is hers and Aragorn's. Arwen angrily returns to Rivendell to confront Elrond. She accuses her father of withholding that knowledge from her, and he declares that this possible future is almost lost. Neither doubts the ability to see the future, or at least one possible version of it. They only question which version will take place. Elrond clearly admits that he is a seer, just as Arwen is shown to be.

Arwen also displays the ability to give visions to others. Partly to beef up Arwen's role in *The Two Towers* and to remind audiences of the romance between Aragorn and Arwen (who are separated throughout this film), Aragorn has a vision of Arwen when he most needs to be revived.[54] Aragorn has just survived being dragged off a cliff into a river, and when he washes ashore, he looks more dead than alive. Audiences see Arwen appear on screen—as if in Aragorn's dream/vision—to kiss and comfort him. This vision revives him, and he is able to return to Helm's Deep as a renewed leader.

In *The Return of the King*, as Aragorn sleeps in a tent at Dunharrow, he again dreams of Arwen.[55] In this vision/dream, Arwen is weak and pale, her life force dwindling as she wishes she could see Aragorn one more time. Aragorn wakes violently from this horrifying dream, only to be summoned to Théoden's tent, where Elrond awaits him. Elrond confirms that Arwen is indeed dying, and her life can only be saved if Sauron is destroyed. This nightmare of a vision motivates Aragorn to accept the reforged sword, Andúril, from Elrond and to seek the Army of the Dead, who later sway the Battle of the Pelennor Fields into Men's favor.

Unlike Arwen, who has waking visions, Aragorn is "given" dreams or visions while he is unconscious or asleep. Jackson's filming of these dream/vision sequences implies that Arwen sends the information to Aragorn at a time when he both needs immediate help and is in a receptive mental state to receive the information. Men might typically disregard visions as not being "real"; Aragorn receives the dreams/visions when his logical mind cannot override the information. Although Aragorn has long lived around Elves (as he mentions casually in the extended version of *The Two Towers*), he also is a Man, and in particular a man of action, used to relying on his skills and ability to interpret what he sees and hears in the physical world.[56] In contrast, Jackson shows the Elves sending telepathic messages and seeing visions in the waking world, indicating that Elves, including Arwen, accept visions more readily as a part of their reality.

Arwen's visions empower Aragorn and motivate him to action. In *The Two Towers*, after receiving his dream/vision, Aragorn is able to travel to Helm's Deep and alert Théoden that a massive army of Orcs approaches. In *The Return of the King*, Aragorn accepts his destiny as the returning King of Gondor and heeds Elrond's counsel. Although Arwen does not directly influence Aragorn through her physical presence, the visions he has of her prompt him to act. In an interview, Liv Tyler summarizes her character as a "symbol of endless hope, belief, and encouragement."[57] Her actions behind the scenes are based on her complete faith in Aragorn and her commitment to their love.

Her belief prompts her to act on his behalf and to encourage her father and her future husband to accomplish greater deeds. In Jackson's trilogy, Elrond seems almost hesitant to reforge the sword, for example, but because of Arwen's urging, and his love for his daughter, he does as she asks and then takes the reforged sword to Aragorn at Dunharrow.[58] In the cinematic trilogy, Aragorn doubts himself and seems more a modern Western man than Tolkien's future king, who always accepts his destiny. Arwen expresses her confidence in Aragorn and encourages him to continue—as he views the shards of Isildur's sword[59] and during a respite at Rivendell, when he questions whether he should go on the Quest.[60]

Even when Arwen is not present in a scene, her influence encourages Aragorn. Elrond seems to be an emissary on behalf of Arwen as he presents

Andúril to Aragorn at Dunharrow. When Aragorn balks at seeking the Army of the Dead, Elrond uses Arwen's failing health to motivate Aragorn to take the Paths of the Dead.[61] Arwen's constant vision of Aragorn as King of Gondor, fulfilling his destiny as Isildur's heir, keeps the action going and, especially in Jackson's trilogy, makes her a more dynamic force with which to be reckoned.

The Elves' Heightened Senses

Elves in some leading capacity, such as Galadriel, Elrond, and Arwen, seem to have some ability to sense information in ways different from other races in Middle-earth. Whether that is an ability common to all Elves, just to those in hereditary leadership roles, or only to certain families is not clear.

Legolas, for example, also has the ability to sense more than Men can, even if he is never shown having visions, and no other character discusses visions with him. In Jackson's *The Return of the King*, Aragorn finds Legolas outside the halls of Meduseld in Edoras after a victory celebration. Legolas eerily comments that the starry night is too still and the "eye of the enemy"—presumably Sauron—is moving closer. A moment later, Legolas exclaims that the enemy has invaded the castle and bolts inside, where he and Aragorn discover Pippin under the influence of the palantír.[62]

Legolas seems to know what is happening without seeing or hearing the event, and Aragorn does not seem surprised by his friend's knowledge. Perhaps the gift of foreknowledge—or the ability to see visions or sense information in ways others cannot—is given to all ruling Elves. After all, Legolas is a prince in Mirkwood, Galadriel rules Lothlórien, and Elrond, Rivendell. As Elrond's daughter, Arwen is a high-ranking Elf.

Ultimately, the source of this visionary power is not important in the films; the ways in which it is used are significant. Whereas Legolas is involved in the daily action—primarily warfare—and uses any heightened senses only peripherally, Galadriel uses her visionary power in every one of her scenes in the films. Although Arwen does not use her visionary ability to this extent, as Jackson's trilogy progresses, she more actively protects Aragorn and acts on her visions, even as she knows that by doing so, she endangers her life.

Inspirational Gifts

Both Galadriel and Arwen are excellent gift-givers, knowing exactly what each character needs to succeed in the Quest. Again, Galadriel's focus is on the Fellowship and the larger Quest, whereas Arwen's gifts, at least in Jackson's trilogy, favor only Aragorn. These gifts may seem strange or misleading when they are first given, but they have an important role in helping each character successfully continue the Quest or overcome an evil influence.

Galadriel's Gifts

In Tolkien's *The Fellowship of the Ring*, a lengthy section details the gifts that Galadriel gives to members of the Fellowship before they continue the Quest. Jackson's version shortens the gift-giving scene but shows the variety of gifts that usually seem well suited to the recipient.[63] Galadriel provides Merry and Pippin with weapons appropriate to their size, thus giving Merry a special "dagger" instead of a Westernesse sword gained from the Barrowdowns with which to bring down the Witch King.[64] It is unclear whether Merry gets back this special dagger when the weapon apparently is taken by the Orcs who capture him. Jackson's version makes no mention of the unique qualities of the weapon that Merry uses, only that, because he is a Hobbit, he can help to kill the Witch King. In fact, Tolkien only explains that Galadriel gives Merry and Pippin silver belts, not weapons; Jackson's trilogy shows the gifts of both daggers and belts.

Sam receives rope, which seems to disconcert him in light of the gifts just provided Merry and Pippin. In Jackson's trilogy, this gift seems meaningless; in fact, the rope is seldom seen or used. Sam is able to tie a lead to Gollum, but the rope serves mostly as a way to abuse Gollum and does not seem like a positive use of Galadriel's gift.[65] In the extended version of *The Two Towers*, Sam and Frodo use the rope to descend a particularly imposing cliff face.[66] Sam laments the loss of the "real Elvish rope" because he knows how to tie a secure knot and should be unable to free the rope with merely a tug from the bottom of the cliff. Nevertheless, the rope mysteriously unties itself and falls into his hand. "Real Elvish rope," Frodo grins as the pair continues their journey. Galadriel's gift to Sam, in the cinematic version, is more of a sight gag than a source of help along the Quest.

Frodo's gift is more helpful, as shown in Jackson's trilogy. Frodo is given a phial of light, which provides helpful in *The Return of the King* not only to light his way but for both Frodo and Sam to stave off Shelob, who is frightened by the power of this light.[67]

The extended version of *The Fellowship of the Ring* allows more interaction between Galadriel and Gimli.[68] Audiences see that Gimli is hesitant to ask for a golden hair from Galadriel's long locks, but Galadriel joyfully grants this request, earning her Gimli's devotion. In the theatrical version, audiences only learn of Galadriel's gift when Legolas later asks Gimli what he received. The healing effect of Galadriel's gift to mend the longstanding rift between Dwarves and Elves is lost in the theatrical version of the film, and the power of Galadriel's ability to mediate the dispute and help establish a bond between Legolas and Gimli is diminished in the cinematic versions. (A fuller description of the importance of Galadriel to Gimli is provided in chapter 6.)

Not all gifts are shown in Jackson's trilogy. In Tolkien's *The Fellowship of the Ring*, Galadriel bestows an important gift on Sam, who then shares it with the rest of the Shire once it again has been secured. Tolkien describes Galadriel's gift of earth from her orchard.[69] This soil eventually is spread across the Shire to heal the land and bring back new life. It is a powerful gift, one that results in the lush rebirth of many parts of the Shire. Galadriel knows the importance of rebirth, and she sees in Sam a gardener who most likely will not horde this treasure for his own garden but will use the gift wisely. Galadriel's ability to see beyond the present turmoil and help heal the land is another example of her "vision" for Middle-earth and the healing of its races.

Tolkien also provides Aragorn with a brooch from Galadriel (the equivalent of the amulet that Arwen gives him in Jackson's trilogy). Technically, the gift comes from Arwen through Galadriel to Aragorn, as Galadriel explains that the Elfstone has passed from Galadriel, to her daughter Celebrian, to her daughter Arwen, and now to Aragorn. Although the jewel does not have magical powers, it nonetheless makes Aragorn seem more kingly in the eyes of the Fellowship, and Aragorn stands taller while wearing this gift.[70]

A standard gift to all members of the Fellowship is a cloak. In Jackson's trilogy, the garment takes on special significance in many scenes. In *The Two Towers*, for example, Pippin drops the clasp from his cape so that Aragorn might find it; the brooch fastening the cloak helps Aragorn, Legolas, and Gimli know that they are on the right track and that Merry and Pippin are still alive, even though they have been captured.[71] Later in the film, Sam becomes trapped in a rockslide and is in danger of being seen by the Haradrim force entering the Black Gate. Frodo quickly drapes his cape over Sam and himself, making them appear like a large bolder rather than two frightened Hobbits. The disguise works, and Sam and Frodo are saved because of the "magic" cloak.

Jackson's filming also provides a glimpse into the fine qualities of the Elven capes. As Gimli jogs behind Legolas and Aragorn early in *The Two Towers*, the sunlight shines through the finely woven cloth, making it seem almost translucent. In close-ups of characters wearing the cloaks, however, the cloth looks more like a heavier wool. The filming supports Tolkien's description of the cloaks as being light enough to keep the wearer cool, but heavy enough to keep him warm. Although the cloaks do not contain magic (which Pippin directly asks), they are described as keeping the wearer out of the sight of an enemy; they are protective in the sense of stealth, but they are not made to be worn as armor.[72]

Many critics commend Galadriel's choice of gifts, which illustrate her vision in understanding not only the needs of each member of the Fellowship, but the upcoming perils on the Quest as well. The gifts seem "almost as Christian grace in material form," as the gifts help the Fellowship "physically or spiritually at times of crisis."[73] These gifts follow the lines of other gifts given to literary heroes and are similar to those that the "Homeric queens give Odysseus" on his journey—food, drink, clothing, and counsel among them.[74] Galadriel's gifts make "the successful completion of the quest possible—for without Galadriel's aid Frodo would never have been able to reach Mount Doom."[75] Although Jackson's trilogy deemphasizes or changes some gifts and their importance, in *The Two Towers* and *The Return of the King*, Jackson shows the special role that some gifts, most notably Frodo's phial and the cloaks, play in saving Frodo and therefore ensuring that the Quest continues.

Galadriel's gifts supplement her visionary qualities and provide unique assistance to the Fellowship. Although Galadriel does not go along on the journey, she nevertheless remains keenly interested in it, especially in Jackson's trilogy. Her ongoing presence throughout the Quest is a guiding force that shapes the Quest and helps ensure its success. Galadriel does not act in battle hero fashion. She is not a warrior, but she acts behind the scenes to monitor what is happening and to become involved when necessary. Her heroism is the choice to get involved and to ensure a good start to the members of the Fellowship, who at this part of the story do not know how perilous the journey will become.

Arwen's Gifts

Jackson's trilogy also implies a connection between the amulet of the Evenstar that Arwen gives Aragorn in *The Fellowship of the Ring* and her life force, a connection unique to the films.[76] In addition to providing Aragorn with visions that strengthen and inspire him, Arwen gives a tangible expression of her love toward and belief in Aragorn. In the first film, the amulet only seems to be a token of her love, although Aragorn tries to return the amulet before he leaves Rivendell. At that time, perceptive audience members may wonder if the jewel is more than just a symbol of Arwen's love and her willingness to wait for Aragorn until he returns from what certainly will be a devastating war. Arwen's assertion that the amulet is hers to give to whomever she chooses seems to mean something more. Perhaps "giving herself" also implies that she gives him her virginity, and in reality with this gift she also places her life in his hands. The jewel seems to represent Arwen's formal choice to forgo the voyage across the seas in favor of a mortal life in Middle-earth.

Tolkien's trilogy describes Arwen's choice but does not link it to a protective amulet given to Aragorn. Instead, Tolkien's Arwen gives Frodo a jewel to wear to help him fend off the lingering darkness and illness after the Quest; she also provides Frodo with the grace to be able to travel to the Undying Lands in her place.[77] In Jackson's trilogy, no mention is made of the reason(s) why Frodo is allowed to travel with the Elves from the Grey Havens, and only Aragorn (and later the vision of Aragorn's son) is shown wearing an amulet given by Arwen.

Arwen must be supernaturally powerful if she can channel her protection and life energy into the amulet that Aragorn wears. The jewel becomes more than a memento of their love; it becomes a means to bring Aragorn successfully through numerous battles and, Arwen hopes, into his role as king. As Galadriel notes in the extended version of *The Fellowship of the Ring*, she can give Aragorn no better gift than that provided by Arwen.[78]

Once Aragorn wears the amulet that Arwen insists he keep, even if he still wants to end their relationship and have her leave Middle-earth for a safer life, Aragorn is seldom shown without the jewel. A telling example of the amulet's power occurs in *The Two Towers*.[79] When an Orc snatches the amulet from Aragorn during battle, he falls off a cliff and appears to have been killed. The tragedy is not a direct result of his losing the amulet, but Aragorn does seem to run out of luck the moment that the amulet is removed.

Legolas takes back the amulet from the dying Orc. When Legolas joyfully greets the returned Aragorn at Helm's Deep, the Elf immediately gives the amulet to Aragorn. He is moved and gratefully clasps Legolas's hand. In the next scene with the future king, a powerful Aragorn bursts through the heavy wooden doors of the king's hall to tell Théoden of the approaching army.[80] Aragorn, who only a few scenes before seems nearly dead, appears strong and forceful once he once again wears the amulet.

Arwen's life force through the jewel of the Evenstar invigorates Aragorn; she seems to share her life with him, and she becomes visibly drained when Aragorn prepares to head into what could well be a suicidal battle on the Pelennor. In *The Return of the King*, Arwen is dying as the evil forces tip the odds into their favor.[81] Elrond tells Aragorn at Dunharrow that Arwen's life is bound to the fate of the "good guys"; if the Quest fails, Arwen dies. This information is especially distressing to Aragorn because he has just awakened from a nightmare in which Arwen is dying and the amulet falls and shatters on the floor. Jackson provides a close-up of the amulet, which is now dull; previously it has been lustrous and vibrant. The image mirrors a previous scene in which Arwen tells Elrond that she no longer has the option of taking the ship to Valinor. She has made the choice for a mortal life, and her life force appears to be weakened drastically. Jackson lights Arwen darkly, and her makeup is paler. In particular, her formerly ruby lips are pale and dull.

The possible loss of Arwen's life, as shown through the waning power of the amulet and his dream/vision, motivates Aragorn to accept Andúril from Elrond—and his role as a future king. Audiences are left with the impression that Aragorn does not fear his own death, but he wants Arwen to survive, even if he cannot be with her. Her self-sacrifice motivates him first to convince the Army of the Dead to fight for him, at Ithilien and the Pelennor; it also inspires him to overcome any doubts he has about fulfilling the role of high king and being effective in the coming confrontation with Sauron. Arwen's amulet is a powerful tool to protect and inspire Aragorn throughout the Quest.

Portrayals of Galadriel and Arwen in Book and Film

In addition to the comparisons made between Tolkien's and Jackson's trilogies in the previous section, Galadriel and Arwen differ from their transition from book to film in two ways. First, the lack of back story for either character isolates them and makes them seem more like "generic" Elves than high-born, wise, and ancient beings who share a powerful family connection. In particular, Arwen seems young, her youth misleading for audiences who may not understand that in Tolkien's world, Arwen has greater experience and knowledge than the far younger Aragorn. Second, and more important, Arwen is portrayed inconsistently in the films. Of course, as she is mostly a character described in Tolkien's appendixes, Jackson adds many scenes not found in the books to feature Arwen and incorporate her into each film in his trilogy. However, the added scenes often create a fluctuating perception of Arwen as an aggressive or a passive hero.

The Lack of a Back Story

Jackson's trilogy provides no back story for either character, and indeed, none is needed for audiences to understand the visionary roles of these characters. However, because the relationship between Galadriel and Arwen is never clearly expressed, many audience members unfamiliar with Tolkien's trilogy may not understand that the two are related as grandmother–granddaughter, or that Galadriel and Aragorn have met previous to their encounter in Lothlórien during the Quest. The relationship between Galadriel and Elrond also is not specified as that of mother- and son-in-law; in fact, Celebrian, Galadriel's daughter, Elrond's wife, and Arwen's mother, is not mentioned—a detail not needed to understand the film's plot. Nevertheless, a lack of understanding of these genealogical details somewhat undermines the strength of these Elven characters.

Other than the obvious physical connection that they are all Elves (visible to audiences because of these characters' pointed ears and flowing tresses), filmgoers most likely have no sense that Galadriel or Arwen is incredibly ancient in human terms of measuring longevity, and they have seen much of Middle-earth's history, which may have helped to make them wise. Their experience is vast, and they are in many ways more attuned to Middle-earth than are Men, Dwarves, or Hobbits. The lack of back story for Galadriel in particular isolates her from other characters; she is not only physically removed from other characters by being shown only in Loth-lórien, instead of the more often featured Rivendell, but she does not travel, as do Arwen and Elrond, at least in the film version of the story.

A strange dichotomy works in the films. Galadriel appears in more scenes and is shown in each of the three films, so her overall role is larger than that in the books. On the other hand, because she is bound to Lothlórien, filmgoers are much more aware that Galadriel is remote and isolated from the Rivendell Elves and the Fellowship. She is at once both more involved in the Quest and remote from the interactions with other characters who are not in Lothlórien. In Tolkien's trilogy, Galadriel appears seldom, but her appearances take on more weight because she is seen less often, but the scenes in which she is described are longer and more detailed. In Jackson's trilogy, Galadriel is an ongoing, more omniscient presence, which enhances audiences' perception of her as a visionary and more mystical character. For example, her voice narrates the history section early in *The Fellowship of the Ring*, creating the (correct) impression that Gala-driel knows firsthand what happened.[82] The shift is not a negative one, but, like other shifts in characterization in the filmed trilogy, it creates a dif-ferent impression of Galadriel.

The lack of a back story creates a different mood for Galadriel's por-trayal, although actress Cate Blanchett looks as audiences might expect Galadriel to be—ethereal, genteel, quietly amused at times, forceful at others, but always seeming to be all-knowing, as if she can see right through a character. In appearance, the flowing blond hair, white gown, and care-fully graceful step also make Galadriel seem appropriately beautiful and removed from mere mortals.

Of course, Tolkien's back story for Galadriel is provided in much more detail in *The Silmarillion*, and readers interested in learning more about the Galadriel shown in *The Lord of the Rings* can turn to the later-published (but chronologically previous) book to discover how Galadriel came to be a leader in Lothlórien and a ringbearer herself. Audiences who have never read *The Lord of the Rings*, much less *The Silmarillion*, do not know just how strong a political leader Galadriel has been or that she lives in exile in Middle-earth.

Galadriel appears only as a ruler in Lothlórien, one who has some personal connection to Aragorn and who knows of Arwen. The extended version of *The Fellowship of the Rings* emphasizes this familiarity as Galadriel gives her blessing to Aragorn and discusses Arwen's future.[83] However, the family connection is not specified. Audiences only need to understand that Galadriel is powerful, seemingly in charge at Lothlórien, and the owner of a mirror that is both compelling and fearsome. Galadriel's true strength and long knowledge of Middle-earth are only hinted in Jackson's trilogy.

Tolkien's histories of the races of Middle-earth are legendary. Readers of the lay of Beren and Luthien, from *The Silmarillion*, or those who are familiar with Tolkien's *The Lord of the Rings*, especially the appendixes, should realize that Arwen comes from a long line of powerful leaders. The females in her family include Luthien and Galadriel, and her father also is a visionary leader. Her ability not only to have and send information telepathically or mystically, but her will in choosing to use this ability to further what she believes is necessary, make her a heroic character. Much is implied through Tolkien's histories about Arwen's background; the author explains that Arwen chooses to live a shorter lifespan in Middle-earth rather than abandon her love, Aragorn. Jackson takes the "outline" provided in Tolkien's trilogy and embellishes it with additional scenes and dialogue.

Jackson takes much greater license with Arwen than with Galadriel and gives Arwen much more to do. In fact, during the early days of filming, Arwen is involved even more in the action; she originally is scheduled for a more dynamic role as a warrior at Helm's Deep. Some fans seemed upset at this direction for Arwen, and the rumored fighting Elf princess caused quite a stir.[84] Even Liv Tyler explains that she had difficulty in understanding what her character would be doing.[85] As Tyler notes in an interview published in 2004, "In the original scripts, Arwen fought with the elves at Helm's Deep. She was along for the whole trip," a change from what finally transpires in *The Two Towers*.[86] Tyler further comments that she used her frustration over the conflicting directions for Arwen to help her portray Arwen's frustration at being left out of the action. Although many possible actions and interpretations of Arwen are considered, in the end, she remains at Rivendell throughout most of the Quest, only venturing to Minas Tirith once the War of the Ring is over. Éowyn remains the only female who consistently desires to fight in hand-to-hand combat in the finished films.

Nevertheless, Arwen appears in all three films and is given much more to do in Jackson's trilogy. She becomes a stronger motivating force in the films, and the love story between Arwen and Aragorn is given more detail. Audiences may find it difficult to believe that Arwen has lived for hundreds of years; in appearance, she seems far younger than Aragorn. Because Arwen also is given no back story in the filmed trilogy, her skills and knowledge may seem surprising in one so young. Unlike in Jackson's version, in which Arwen often seems merely dainty and lovestruck, she is a strong, determined Elf who has the power to make her visions come true.

Because no back story is given for either Galadriel or Arwen in the filmed trilogy, each seems disconnected from the other, as well as from their lineage to other Elves and strong females. Each stands alone as a strong female character working behind the scenes rather than in the day-to-day action of the male characters, primarily Men. Nevertheless, each character uses her power to act as a behind-the-scenes visionary hero.

Arwen's Expanded, but Inconsistent Role

Arwen truly becomes a character involved directly in the action in Jackson's films. She is portrayed as a warrior princess in *Fellowship of the Ring*, dutiful daughter and faithful lover in *The Two Towers*, and ascending queen in *Return of the King*. Although she appears in but a few scenes in Tolkien's trilogy, the author provides enough details of her relationship with Aragorn that Jackson could reasonably expand Arwen's role in each of his three films. However, perhaps because she in many ways is a new creation for the films, in some scenes, audiences receive a very different picture of Arwen than in others. The characterization is uneven, which can leave filmgoers confused as to the "true" nature of Arwen.

Tolkien's Arwen, for example, never appears on horseback with a sword in her hand. This depiction, especially before the release of the first film, has been a concern for fans of the books. Arwen as a warrior appears in only one sequence, as she (not Tolkien's Glorfindel) outdistances the Nazgûl to bring Frodo safely to Rivendell. Not only does Arwen accomplish this important task, but when she is first introduced to film audiences, she places her sword against Aragorn's throat and wonders aloud at his ability to be caught unguarded.[87] In this scene, Arwen seems well skilled with a sword and is an aggressive hero who goes looking for Aragorn and the Hobbits. She is confident that she is better suited than Aragorn to rush Frodo to her father's care.

In later scenes in *The Fellowship of the Ring*, Arwen does not appear as such a warrior princess, but she is still forceful in her support of Aragorn. She reminds him that he can fulfill his destiny, and she is very much going to be a part of his future, despite his fears for her life, not to mention her happiness.

By *The Two Towers* and throughout most of *The Return of the King*, Arwen and Aragorn are separated. Jackson brings the two together through vision/dream scenes, which is a practical way of keeping Arwen in each film while not further changing Tolkien's plot. However, because Arwen has no battle scenes or rescues to perform alongside Aragorn, she loses her warrior persona. Instead, Arwen often seems weepy and beautiful, her expressive eyes conveying her love for Aragorn.

Even in *The Fellowship of the Ring*, as the Fellowship leaves Rivendell to begin the Quest, Arwen tearfully watches Aragorn depart; this does not seem to be the same character who, just a few scenes previous, is an independent warrior.[88] In *The Two Towers*, Arwen weeps as Elrond harshly describes her future if she chooses to remain in Middle-earth.[89] She realizes the great loss she faces. If she remains, she may lose Aragorn to death in battle, and even if this does not occur, she surely will lose him to death within a short time, as Elves measure it. If she remains, she also will lose her father. If she leaves, she certainly loses Aragorn, who cannot join her in Valinor. Unlike Tolkien's Arwen, who seems more composed and certain of her decision, even as she recognizes the losses she will suffer, Jackson's Arwen is more emotional in realizing the consequences of her choice.

The cinematic trilogy relies on visual and aural elements instead of text to tell the story, and what audiences see is what they get. Arwen looks younger than Aragorn, but the reverse is true. She is centuries older and has the wisdom of long years of experience, as well as more formal education. Arwen is not a young Elf blinded by love; she is mature and well knows the ramifications of her choice of a partner. Of all the many Elves, as well as Men or those of other races whom she has met, Arwen chooses Aragorn. She is more than just a believer in the man; she understands what a powerful role he can play in Middle-earth. In Jackson's trilogy, Arwen is often counseled against her choice, as if she does not realize the implications of her decision. She seems younger than her book counterpart and than Aragorn, whereas Aragorn is really the much younger partner who must make sure that he can be worthy of Arwen's devotion.

In Jackson's trilogy, Arwen makes the decision to remain in Middle-earth with Aragorn, and thus to become mortal, on her own, as does Arwen in Tolkien's trilogy. However, the cinematic Arwen seems more modern; hers is a choice of love, and she alone can make it. When Aragorn accepts her love, the two become a couple and, audiences assume, will someday marry, provided both partners survive the war. In Tolkien's story, Elrond explains the great differences between Arwen's social standing and age and Aragorn's, and conditions are placed on Aragorn to prove his worthiness of marrying Arwen. Although Elrond cannot force Arwen not to make her choice to remain in Middle-earth, he has more authority over her marriage. In Jackson's adaptation, Elrond really has nothing to do with Arwen's marriage. He might approve or not, but the decision is hers and Aragorn's.

Elrond may try to influence Aragorn by explaining how difficult it might be for her to stay in Middle-earth, but Arwen ultimately determines what she will do and whom she will marry.

Nevertheless, in Jackson's *The Two Towers*, Arwen is shown leaving Rivendell, apparently at the persuasion of her father. There is no doubt that Arwen loves her father and wants to please him. Although she does not look happy as she turns one more time to Elrond, she still rides away. This is another example of an inconsistency in Arwen's behavior. At times, she is adamant about staying in Middle-earth, while in other scenes she seems to acquiesce to others' wishes for her to leave for Valinor.

In *The Return of the King*, Arwen is well along the journey to the Grey Havens when she has a vision that motivates her to return to Rivendell.[90] Arwen's determination to remain in Middle-earth, no matter what, seems lessened in Jackson's trilogy. Only in *The Return of the King*, when Arwen tells Elrond to reforge the sword, does Arwen seem at ease with her decision again. Once more she is the Arwen from *The Fellowship of the Ring*, who adamantly tells Aragorn that her choice is made.

By the time the sword is reforged, Arwen's life force is being drained, which is shown in *The Return of the King* through changes in her makeup, now paler and duller.[91] Gone is the robust Elf of renowned vibrant beauty. In her place is a wistful Arwen, often left lounging on a divan. Only Aragorn's success can "save" her from imminent death, as her fate is now linked to the fate of the One Ring. This departure from Tolkien's depiction of Arwen makes her sacrifice more immediate and real to filmgoers, but it also diminishes Arwen's strength as a forceful female character. Although Jackson finds ways to insert Arwen into more scenes in the trilogy, the inconsistencies in her portrayal sometimes undermine her effectiveness as a forceful female character. Tom Shippey suggests that the insertion of scenes and dialogue, such as Arwen's inclusion in The Flight to the Ford, is most likely a case of "bowing to popular taste" and "a moment for female viewers to place themselves in the story."[92] Although Arwen becomes a "real character" involved in more action scenes, she is not a continually strong presence, and her shift from aggressor to victim sometimes is disconcerting.

Galadriel and Arwen as Heroes for a Modern Age

As outlined in chapter 1, these two unsung heroes meet the elements defining a literary and cinematic hero for a more modern time:

1. They act on their convictions.

Both Galadriel and Arwen recognize that the choices they make will irrevocably change their lives, and possibly not for the better. Galadriel knows that she will lose power, as the ring she carries will no longer allow her to protect the Elves in Lothlórien. She will "diminish" in her words and sail to the Undying Lands. Arwen faces a probably sadder future: a long life without her beloved husband, even if they are able to have many years of joy together.

Galadriel's conviction to help the other inhabitants of Middle-earth against a great evil allows her to guide the Fellowship, and in Jackson's trilogy, prompt Elrond to become involved so that Men, in particular, have a greater advantage against Sauron. Arwen's involvement is more personal; she promotes Aragorn in all that she does, and by doing so helps Sauron to be overcome, the One Ring to be destroyed, and a just ruler to come to the throne of Gondor. Everything these Elves do is based on their belief in the rightness of their course of action.

2. They plan strategies and carry them out successfully.

Arwen and Galadriel are visionaries who act on what they want to happen for Middle-earth (and especially for Aragorn). Their actions are carefully considered, and they put into motion events that lead to a successful conclusion to the War of the Ring. Through their visions and gifts, Galadriel and Arwen work behind the scenes to effect change and have a powerful impact on events in Middle-earth. They use their wisdom and experience from their long lives to help them guide others in the Quest.

Unlike other characters who have to think on their feet or make decisions quickly while on the run, Galadriel and Arwen rely on years of experience and knowledge of history to be able to direct their and others' future activities. Some actions may need to be more timely than others, but Galadriel and Arwen have more time to put their plans into motion and then to guide or persuade others to take actions at the appropriate times.

3. They offer to sacrifice themselves, if necessary, for the cause.

Galadriel's sacrifice is her loss of power as a ringbearer and a leader in Lothlórien. However, she also is allowed to return to her former home in recognition of her assistance in defeating Sauron. (Galadriel's "pardon" is described in Tolkien's works but is not included in Jackson's trilogy. However, Galadriel's loss of power is evident in both trilogies.)

Arwen's sacrifice is more apparent, as she gives up the possibility of a long, seemingly immortal, life and the opportunity to live in peace with her family in Valinor. Although she also receives a reward in the form of a presumably happy marriage to Aragorn and the birth of a son, she is aware of the price for this happiness. In Jackson's *The Return of the King*, Arwen's sacrifice is shown clearly by her growing weakness and impending death; what she is giving up, with no promise of Aragorn's success at that point in the story, is obvious to audiences.

> 4. They grow as characters, showing under extreme circumstances the heroic qualities that always have been part of their makeup, but have not been recognized until these qualities are needed.

This point is less well defined for these characters. Galadriel faces a point of personal growth and change when she meets the challenge provided by Frodo: Should she take the One Ring and become a terrifying but beautiful ruler over Middle-earth? Galadriel recognizes this temptation, but she turns down the offer of power. This final test is the pinnacle of her growth and is heroic in the sense that she chooses not to take ultimate power and remake the world the way she wants. She chooses to fight evil on her own terms and understands the way that ultimate power can corrupt even someone with the best intentions. However, Galadriel has been recognized already for her leadership qualities and does not dramatically change, beyond this one test, during *The Lord of the Rings*.

Arwen also does not change dramatically throughout the story, but in Jackson's trilogy she becomes more involved in the behind-the-scenes action. She is an inspirational hero who motivates others and who recognizes heroic qualities in them. For example, in Jackson's trilogy, Arwen unswervingly encourages Aragorn and helps him overcome self-doubt that he can succeed in refusing the lure of the Ring and eventually become king. Both Galadriel and Arwen are effective in seeing what others need in order to succeed, and then providing them with the materials or encouragement so that they fulfill their heroic potential.

> 5. They embody the values of love of family and home, which provide the impetus for them to act to protect the people and places they love.

Galadriel's protection is offered more to the "good guys" in Middle-earth than specifically to her family; her love and devotion are broader in scope. She sees the future for Middle-earth if Sauron is allowed to have the One Ring, and she fights against that evil, not specifically for herself or her family, but for the general good.

Arwen, however, is clearly motivated by her love for her family, and it is a source of conflict for her. She has a close relationship with her father, illustrated particularly well in Jackson's trilogy, but she also loves Aragorn completely. Although she can never fully resolve this conflict, she shows her love for both her father and future husband in several scenes, and she is happiest (in book and film) when she can wed Aragorn with Elrond's blessing. Arwen's love for individuals is extended to Frodo, who receives her merciful offer to help him heal. Arwen understands what these characters need, and her compassion and love motivate her to help them in different ways so that they can accomplish what they need to do, and also receive a measure of peace.

Both Galadriel and Arwen are inspirational heroes who work behind the scenes to encourage, provide counsel and gifts, and motivate other characters to perform their own heroic deeds. Although these Elves often seem removed physically from the action, their powerful presence is felt throughout and beyond the Quest. Their visionary activities make them heroic characters, without whose intervention the Quest may have been lost or, at least, the future of Middle-earth drastically altered.

6

Legolas and Gimli as Intercultural Heroes

Neither Legolas nor Gimli may be a surprise as battle-ready heroes in J. R. R. Tolkien's and Peter Jackson's trilogies. Both seem capable of using weapons well; they seem more battle ready than most of the other unsung heroes discussed in previous chapters. In Jackson's trilogy, both warriors are shown many times in combat, and their wartime heroics are certainly one aspect of their success as heroes for current film audiences. However, these characters are heroes in a modern sense for yet another reason: their close friendship.

The bond between Legolas and Gimli represents a special kind of heroism: conquering fears and prejudices within oneself and one's culture and then sharing one's insights with others who may not yet have overcome their own biases. This friendship is a great example of the cliché "opposites attract." In this case, the opposites at first are repelled by each other, but over time, they form an enduring bond that survives a lifetime. Thematically, the friendship between Legolas and Gimli "affords Tolkien countless opportunities for comparing elf and dwarf nature."[1]

The long history of Dwarves and Elves is well described in Tolkien's *The Silmarillion*. In brief, unlike the Elves, who are the chosen and first-created children of the Valar, the Dwarves are created in secret by Aule, who then offers to destroy his creation when they are discovered. Although the Dwarves are spared from this destruction, they are kept hidden, and Elves have dominion. Dwarves are "second-class" creations, not fully formed and not as perfect as Elves. Whereas the Elves are beautiful and joyful,[2] Dwarves are "stone-hard, stubborn, fast in friendship and in enmity."[3] They are not as beautiful as Elves, and they have different types of skills. The ways in which the two races are created and the initial "value" of each cause the first rift between Elves and Dwarves.

Even a superficial comparison between Elves' and Dwarves' physical characteristics also shows that the two differ greatly. The first obvious difference is one in height, as Elves are more akin to Men and thus taller than Dwarves, who are taller than Hobbits, but not by that much. Elves are close to the natural world; "the beauties Tolkien associates with trees— grace, beauty, delight, longevity—he bestows on elves."[4] Whereas Elves appear more ethereal, in physical build, Dwarves are stockier and have been described as the "humanized forms of mineral qualities: hard, grim, enduring, unyielding."[5] The Dwarves "provide a counterpoint to the elegance and nobility of Elves."[6]

There is also the lifespan difference. Although Dwarves live a long time, they cannot claim the longevity of Elves, who, quite possibly, can survive so long as to seem immortal.[7] Both can die, such as in battle, but Elves more likely than not will normally outlive Dwarves. Their common ground is their very long memory; culturally/racially, each group can remember a great deal—good and bad—about the other.

Additional obvious differences are their preferred places to live and the ways they perceive the world. Dwarves work and live beneath the earth and value the metals and minerals found within it. By trade they are craftsmen who work well with their hands and are skilled with metalworking and jewels. Bilbo's gift from the Dwarf Thorin of a mithril shirt is a fine example of both the mining skills of the Dwarves, who retrieve the valuable mithril from deep within the mountains, and their craftsmanship, to create such a lightweight, carefully made garment.[8]

Elves live not only with the earth, understanding many of its secrets, but their homes often are closer to the sky. (This is true of the Wood-elves, of whom Legolas of Mirkwood is a part.) The Elves in Lothlórien, for example, build their homes in trees and create a vast world within the forest. They do not destroy the trees in order to make their homes; they build within nature to live with and among the trees.[9]

These differences point to larger gaps between the cultures. Dwarves seem grounded; they live within the mountains and build their cities of stone. Their world feels "heavier" because of the materials with which they build. A Dwarf's step is steady and measured; in Jackson's *The Two Towers*, Gimli has trouble keeping up with Aragorn and Legolas as they pursue the Orcs on foot. However, he keeps jogging along, not fast but steadily. This is a good illustration of the Dwarves' steady, solid trek through life.[10] Dwarves are pragmatic and build things to last. They mine and work with their hands; they get dirty. Dwarves, "while not beautiful in themselves . . . [appreciate] beauty and [are] capable of great depths of feeling."[11] They are effective representatives of living in the day-to-day world. Practical and efficient, they value what they can do with their hands, complete tasks a step at a time, plod methodically through the world, and carve their culture into and from rock.

As Gimli explains to Legolas as they depart from Lothlórien, Dwarves value experience. Although Legolas suggests that the memory of Galadriel will always be sweet, Gimli believes that the most important moment of his life has already passed. Because he cannot be content with only a memory, this knowledge makes him melancholy. Current experiences and the here and now are more valuable than a memory of the experience. The way that Dwarves perceive life differs greatly from that of the Elves.[12]

The world of the Dwarves' opposites, the Elves, feels "lighter" because they live above the earth. They wake the trees and teach them to speak. Although they build, they seem "above" getting dirty or working primarily with their hands. Their culture seems to be built upon thought and memory. They value what they can remember of the world, its long history, and what they know. Although they sometimes get involved in the affairs of other cultures, such as their involvement with Aragorn's ancestor Isildur in an old battle against evil, they seem aloof and often removed from the day-to-day workings of Middle-earth.[13] They value what they remember, which is a glorious past, and toward the end of the Third Age, they understand that they are gradually fading only to become a memory.

Such differences would seem difficult to bridge even if Elves and Dwarves want to make that effort, and for much of their history, they do not. When a culture or race is considered by others—or itself—as superior to another, the gap between the two is even more difficult to span.

In the personal history between the houses of Thranduil (Legolas's father) and Glóin (Gimli's father), no love has been lost, either. Thranduil imprisons Glóin, a fact not likely to go unrecalled by Legolas or Gimli. During the Council of Elrond, Tolkien has Glóin interrupt Legolas's telling of the Elves' treatment of Gollum. Glóin has witnessed the Elves' "hospitality" first hand when, as a member of the Dwarf contingent led by Thorin, the Elves capture and hold him for several days. Glóin may wonder how long the Dwarves would have been held captive if Bilbo had not helped them to escape.[14] When Glóin says, " 'You were less tender to me,' he means of course not the opposite but the obverse, 'You were more cruel to me.' "[15] Glóin does not forget, nor does he mind reminding everyone else at the Council, including Legolas, of the ways the Elves have dealt with the Dwarves. Gollum has been mistreated by many races in Middle-earth and is not anyone's favorite to warrant special treatment. Glóin wants the members of the Council to understand that, nevertheless, Gollum's treatment by the Elves is better than what the Dwarves receive.

Finding common ground against this backdrop is certainly challenging, and when Legolas and Gimli are first introduced to readers in Tolkien's *The Fellowship of the Ring*, neither seems capable of surpassing old prejudices and anger, although during the Council itself, Gimli is surprisingly quiet.[16] Tom Shippey notes that "Gimli is the only named person in the Council who does not speak, perhaps out of dwarvish deference to his father."[17] Jackson's version creates a different first impression of Gimli during a scene in *The Fellowship of the Ring*, in which the representatives to the Council of Elrond loudly argue over what should be done with the Ring.[18] Gimli shouts over the din, "I will be dead before I see the ring in the hands of an Elf!" and "Never trust an Elf!" Even before he and Legolas become part of the Fellowship, Gimli shows the ingrained mistrust and suspicion that exist between the Dwarves and the Elves.

Becoming friends is not a heroic act per se. However, reaching out to another who has been one's enemy, then taking the time to learn about not only that person but his or her culture, and in the process becoming close friends, is an act undertaken by heroes. To overcome such diverse interests and backgrounds, as well as the emotions accompanying these, requires a heroic effort. Legolas and Gimli, throughout the course of the Quest, begin to make this effort and eventually reap the personal benefits of their close association. However, their post-Quest years are equally important, as they show that their bond comes not only from comradeship in fighting a common enemy, but also from the true appreciation one has for the other, and consequently, for the other's culture and race.

Legolas and Gimli as Literary Heroes

Unlike the Hobbits, whose heroic development is much more of a journey into self-awareness through initiation into new experiences, both good and bad, or even unlike Éowyn, whose knowledge of war is more theoretical than practical prior to the Battle of the Pelennor Fields, Legolas and Gimli seem well accustomed to weapons and how to use them. They appear to be seasoned, or at least highly trained, warriors by the time they join the Fellowship.

During the War of the Ring, Legolas and Gimli develop first an effective partnership and later a personal bond. Their friendship is first of its kind between Dwarves and Elves, and it shows to the rest of Middle-earth the ability of different races to appreciate and understand each other. If an Elf and a Dwarf not only can work together in wartime but also allow their friendship to flourish in peacetime, then the other races of Middle-earth surely can do the same.

Legolas and Gimli successfully pass three "tests"; these allow the characters to develop as intercultural heroes. To bridge the gap between races and cultures, the hero must be able to do three tasks: (1) be open to mediation, (2) value the differences between the cultures or races while maintaining his/her cultural or racial identity, and (3) be willing to let go of past grievances, no matter how offensive or debilitating they have been. Gradually throughout *The Lord of the Rings*, Legolas and Gimli pass each of these tests. Their development is not speedy; change does not take place immediately. However, when the change is wrought, it is permanent and ensures that their relationship will not only survive, but thrive.

Mediation as the First Step toward Friendship

As the Fellowship begins its journey, Legolas and Gimli often snipe at each other and seem diametrically opposed. Early in the Quest, Gandalf first cannot find the entryway into the mountain so the Fellowship can pass through the mines of Moria, and then later he cannot remember the password to enter. Gimli is eager to show everyone, but especially Legolas, what hospitality is all about; perhaps the Elves can learn what hospitality to strangers, even enemies, really means once they participate in the Dwarves' feasts. When Gandalf cannot locate the entrance, Gimli comments that the doors are invisible, and if the ones who made them forget the password or location, no one can find them.[19] In Jackson's *The Fellowship of the Ring*, this comment provides Legolas with the opportunity to reply, "Why does that not surprise me?"[20] His tone indicates all too clearly that he thinks the Dwarves have a rather poor system, most likely symptomatic of other Dwarf inadequacies as well.

Tolkien, however, does not use this line as another opportunity for Legolas to interject a negative comment about Dwarves. Instead, Tolkien provides both Legolas and Gimli with a chance to needle each other. The Fellowship wanders for a day as Gandalf searches for the entrance; they hike through rough terrain, and Gimli often takes the lead in the search for landmarks. When Gandalf finally locates the precise spot where the doors should be, he mildly comments that the landmark of the holly bush was planted in happier times when all races, including the Dwarves and the Elves, got on well with each other. Gimli replies, " 'It was not the fault of the dwarves that the friendship waned,'" to which Legolas immediately pipes up, " 'I have not heard it was the fault of the elves.' "[21] Gandalf stops the argument before it can truly begin and asks Legolas and Gimli to work together, if only for Gandalf's sake, as he needs both of them to assist him on the journey. At this point in the story, neither Legolas nor Gimli backs down from an argument, and each stubbornly maintains his prejudices against the other. Gandalf is one of the mediators at this stage of the Quest; he intervenes to keep harmony within the Fellowship, and he is careful to point out that each side in the historic dispute has been wrong. He does not play favorites, and his intervention emphasizes that neither Dwarves nor Elves are completely wrong, but neither is one race completely right. Both sides have their faults.

Tolkien exacerbates the friction between these characters in a later chapter when the Elves of Lothlórien greet the Fellowship.[22] At first Legolas hesitates even to mention to Haldir, the head of the welcoming party, that a member of their group is a Dwarf. When Legolas finally explains this to Haldir, Gimli is denied entrance into the Elves' realm. Frodo and Aragorn next mediate between the Dwarf and the Elves. Frodo quickly intercedes; he tells Haldir that Gimli is trustworthy and a friend to Elrond. At this point, Haldir agrees to let Gimli pass, but only if Aragorn and Legolas act as guards, and only if Gimli later is blindfolded. The Fellowship travels quietly with the Lothlórien Elves until they arrive near the Elves' homes. At this point, by law Gimli needs to be blindfolded. Of course, Gimli vehemently protests. Aragorn finally suggests that everyone in the Fellowship be blindfolded if Gimli must be, a statement that immediately rankles Legolas. After all, he is distant kin to these Elves and should be treated well. For the first time, Legolas grumbles that everyone here has a common enemy. At some level he begins to concede some common ground with Gimli. Aragorn ends the dispute when he insists that, as he is the leader of the group, his word is final. Thus, the entire Fellowship is treated equally and led blindfolded the rest of the way into the Elves' homeland.

With the chapters "Lothlórien" and "Farewell to Lórien," Tolkien describes Galadriel's role as a final mediator to bring together the Dwarves and the Elves. As a leading representative of the Elves and a leader in Lothlórien, Galadriel has the ability to understand Gimli's animosity toward Elves and the power to make a strong statement of friendship on their behalf.

Galadriel is the most effective mediator. Only an Elf truly can represent the Elves or show by example what Elves are like, just as only a Dwarf truly can represent the Dwarves.

Before Gimli meets Galadriel, his "fears about [her] and the woods of Lothlórien show how the dwarves have demonized the Lórien elves and, by extension, elves in general."[23] However, when Gimli sees Galadriel face to face, his fears and suspicions dissipate, and he "immediately falls under Galadriel's spell, his heart won by her empathy for dwarvish homesickness for Khazad-dûm, her own sense of exile from the Undying Lands echoing the dwarves' sense of exile from their homeland."[24] Gimli stands in awe of Galadriel's beauty, and his sincere appreciation of beauty—a common trait in Dwarves, who value the beauty of the gems of the earth—wins him the respect of other Elves, especially Legolas. Galadriel takes the first step in welcoming Gimli to Lothlórien, and she later generously grants his request for her golden hair by gifting him with three hairs that he vows to enshrine if he returns home. Gimli allows Galadriel and Legolas to see his softer side when he wonders at Galadriel's beauty; he becomes vulnerable in front of his former enemies.

Through Galadriel's mediation, Legolas and Gimli personally are able to find common ground and thus are able to explore more ways that Elves and Dwarves culturally may be able to find common ground. Legolas begins to see that Gimli, and by extension the Dwarves, can appreciate beauty just as much as the Elves do and can express their wonder and awe of nature in gentler terms than their normally aggressive, blunt speech. For his part, Gimli learns that the Elves are beautiful, not only physically, but emotionally and culturally, and he respects what they can offer and have provided Middle-earth. Gimli pledges himself to Galadriel's service. His request shows that Gimli now values the "gold" of interaction with Galadriel more than the gold or other minerals of the earth. By the time Legolas and Gimli depart Lothlórien, riding together in a boat as they begin the journey anew, they are forming a partnership. Each tries "to persuade the other of the beauty of his way of life. The goal is no longer mutual denigration but mutual enlightenment."[25]

With Galadriel's mediation and the exchange of gifts (i.e., a token of beauty, given personally by Galadriel, and Gimli's undying loyalty and pledge of service to Galadriel), a truce has been established at least between the Lothlórien Elves and Legolas (a Mirkwood Elf) and one Dwarf. It is a small start on the way to repairing the rift between Elves and Dwarves, but it is an effective one. When Legolas and Gimli become friends, they also become an example of the ways that Elves and Dwarves can successfully work together. This example continues not only throughout the War of the Ring, but post-Quest through the rebuilding of Middle-earth and later, when Legolas succumbs to the sea longing and heads across the sea to the West, Gimli chooses to accompany him and is allowed to enter the Elves' sacred land. What may seem to be a small act of kindness and under-standing between Galadriel and Gimli has far-reaching effects throughout Middle-earth.

Gimli is heroic in honoring his commitment to Galadriel, and thus to other Elves, even though this undoubtedly makes him an outsider to his own people. Yet he does not back down or break off his friendship with Legolas, even when they are no longer fighting a common enemy. Legolas also chooses to continue the friendship and dares to do what has never before taken place—bring a Dwarf to the hallowed ground of the Elves.

Only the ringbearers previously have been granted this honor, and then only under special conditions. Gandalf most likely vouches for Bilbo and Sam, and their crossing must have the blessing of Elrond and Galadriel, who travel with Bilbo to Valinor and who know that Gandalf promises Sam the same journey later in life. Frodo is allowed to sail by the grace of Arwen, who has chosen mortality and given up her right to this journey. For Legolas to choose to bring the former enemy of the Elves into their sacred homeland is a heroic endeavor.

Value Cultural Differences

Once Gimli and Legolas begin to develop their friendship after they leave Lothlórien, their rivalry becomes more teasing. They establish a new bond, which develops throughout *The Two Towers* and *The Return of the King*. The friends handle situations differently, but true to their natures. Their diverse approaches strengthen their teamwork; each provides something unique to the friendship.

For example, Gimli is usually quicker to anger than Legolas. When Éomer first encounters Aragorn, Gimli, and Legolas in Rohan, Éomer makes disparaging comments about Galadriel, who he considers to be a cunning witch. If the trio is favored by her, as Aragorn has said, then Éomer figures that the little group also may be sorcerers with evil intent. Gimli naturally takes offense at this slander of Galadriel and immediately grips his axe. Gimli and Éomer trade insults for a moment before Legolas joins in by notching an arrow in his bow, but Legolas seems to respond more to the immediate threat to Gimli than to the general denouncement of Galadriel.[26]

Gimli's more explosive nature is emphasized during a similar scene in Jackson's *The Two Towers*. On screen, Éomer makes a more general comment about a "white Wizard" who travels around the countryside, although the implication is still made that the Wizard is up to no good. However, Galadriel is never mentioned, and Éomer refers to the Wizard as "he" and "an old man." The audience can assume that the "white Wizard" either refers to Saruman, who is always shown in white robes, or (for readers of the book) foreshadows Gandalf the White, who is shortly thereafter reunited with Aragorn, Legolas, and Gimli in Fangorn Forest.[27] Gimli's anger, therefore, seems misplaced when he grips his axe and challenges Éomer. Legolas, as in the book, defends Gimli, and the effect is that the friendship is shown stronger on screen. Gimli also appears to be more temperamental than his companions. Such seems to be the nature of Dwarves.

After the Battle of Helm's Deep, Gimli explains to Legolas the importance of the Glittering Caves and Men's misuse of them only for storage and refuge in times of trouble. " 'My good Legolas, do you know that the caverns of Helm's Deep are vast and beautiful? There would be an endless pilgrimage of Dwarves, merely to gaze at them, if such things were known to be,' " Gimli exclaims.[28] When Gimli mentions that Dwarves would pay gold even to view such caves, Legolas retorts amiably that he would pay a fortune not to have to see them, or to be let out if he happened into the caves. After Gimli continues expressing his wonder at the caves' beauty, Legolas hopes that Gimli may return in peacetime to see the caves again, but he cautions his friend not to tell other Dwarves, who would destroy the underground beauty through mining. Gimli contradicts this assumption by explaining " 'No dwarf could be unmoved by such loveliness,' "[29] and provides the analogy that Dwarves could no more destroy such underground beauty than Elves could destroy a forest.

Although the Dwarves and Elves value different sources of beauty, they both enjoy and revere it. Gimli explains the differences in cultural values, but concludes by finding common ground. From Gimli's analogy, Legolas can understand what the caves would mean to the Dwarves, but he also understands that Gimli can appreciate beauty just as much as an Elf can. This type of discovery takes place in many conversations in the books.

In Jackson's version of *The Return of the King*, the comparisons between Dwarves and Elves are not as numerous, and the dialogue between the characters is less frequent and briefer. However, some scenes show Gimli's or Legolas's understanding of the cultural differences between them and prompt them to bridge these differences.

One such scene takes place as Legolas, Gimli, and Aragorn travel to find the Army of the Dead. After Aragorn boldly marches through the entryway into the mountain where the army resides, Legolas hesitates only a moment before following. Although there has been no prior scene to indicate that Legolas would not normally choose to go beneath ground, he still does not seem terribly excited at the prospect. Nevertheless, he follows Aragorn without hesitation. Gimli, who normally feels at home in a cave, stands outside the entry. "An Elf will go underground where a Dwarf dare not?" he exclaims in frightened wonder.[30] He finally overcomes his fear and belatedly follows his companions.

Only his love for Aragorn and Legolas (and probably his sense of competitive pride with the latter) could prompt him to enter a place he fears. Gimli seldom is afraid of anything and at other times, notably during the Battle of Helm's Deep when he literally leaps into action, seems almost suicidally without fear. John Rhys-Davies, who portrays Gimli, comments that Gimli would rather "fight against overwhelming numbers rather than run. If he has a weakness, . . . it's spooky things."[31] Overcoming the fear of the unknown and the supernatural Army of the Dead are difficult for him, but if Legolas can overcome his dislike of caves, then Gimli can overcome his own fear.

Throughout the battles of *The Two Towers* and *The Return of the King*, the friends maintain a macabre rivalry in seeing who can kill the greatest number of Orcs. This "game" is not typical activity for Elves, even those in battle. As Michael Martinez asks in one article about Legolas, "Can anyone picture Elrond counting coup on Orcs in the midst of a very serious struggle over the future of Rohan?"[32] Perhaps because he is a relatively young Elf, but more likely because he wants to show Gimli that an Elf can be just as effective a warrior as a Dwarf—or that he can "better" his friend in friendly competition—Legolas counts enthusiastically and keeps a running tally throughout the battle.

In Tolkien's description of this battle, the Men are in danger of losing the battle when Gimli appears to have been lost. When Gimli finds Legolas after the battle ends, Legolas is relieved to see his friend in one piece. Gimli has been wounded and wears a bandage about his head. When Gimli proudly announces his total, Legolas declares Gimli the winner, having killed one more Orc. " 'But I do not grudge you the game, so glad am I to see you on your legs!' " Legolas adds.[33]

Readers may get the impression that Legolas lets Gimli win, partly out of relief at seeing his friend alive and relatively unscathed. In contrast, in Jackson's extended version of *The Two Towers*, Legolas has come up one Orc short in the competition.[34] A smug Gimli sits atop a dead Orc. As he cleans the gore from his axe, Gimli proudly announces his total and con-descendingly consoles Legolas that his total is not bad for a "pointy-eared Elvish princeling." Feeling his honor as a warrior impugned, Legolas lets fly an arrow that lands in the already-dead Orc; not coincidentally, the arrow also lands between Gimli's legs. In a game of male one-upsmanship, Gimli teases Legolas about his masculine prowess, and Legolas replies with a shot quite close to Gimli's groin. As filmed, the competition takes on a more modern tone as the two smugly try to prove their superior masculinity.

Jackson also plays up this rivalry and the coup-counting game in *The Return of the King*.[35] When Aragorn and his friends arrive on the Corsair ships and enter the Battle of the Pelennor Fields, Gimli first announces "There's plenty for the both of us" when he sees the overwhelming number of approaching Orcs and then exclaims "May the best Dwarf win." Their cultural differences in fighting methods are put aside as both the Elf's bow and the Dwarf's axe, as well as the warriors who wield them, are highly effective. Instead, the competition becomes a matter of pride, rather than a competition to determine which race has better warriors.

Ability to Let Go of Past Grievances

In *The Two Towers* and *The Return of the King*, Legolas and Gimli appear to have let go of past grievances and solidified their friendship. Jackson's *The Return of the King* includes a lovely line that illustrates how far the friendship has come. When Legolas and Gimli face what most likely will be their deaths at Cormallen, Gimli becomes sentimental, musing that "I never thought I'd die fighting side by side with an Elf." Unlike the former mean-spirited taunts and later gentler jests about Elves, this comment is spoken softly. Gimli does not turn to look at Legolas, but Legolas smiles down on his friend. "What about side by side with a friend?" Legolas asks lightly, at which point Gimli gazes directly at his friend and agrees that he could do that.[36] This gentle sentiment before battle indicates the openness between the two characters, so that neither has to hide his true feelings in front of the other. It becomes a significant moment, too, in that the friends take time to acknowledge their close bond.

For a gruff Dwarf renowned for his ferocity and courage, this soft side is again a more modern interpretation of what it means to be male. Jackson's adaptation shows that "real Dwarves" do have a gentle side they are not ashamed to show to those close to them, and this sentiment does not detract from Gimli's heroic persona in battle. It does, however, enhance his relevance as a hero for modern times, one who is not just a fearless warrior, but who also is a caring, thoughtful character.

Gimli and Éomer, in Tolkien's *The Return of the King*, also end their old feud. During his first encounter with Gimli, Éomer denounces Galadriel, and Gimli threatens Éomer in order to defend Galadriel's honor. In post-war Minas Tirith, Éomer has the opportunity to see Galadriel and Arwen and afterward calls Gimli to him. In a humorous section (at least humorous as far as Tolkien's writing goes), Éomer tells Gimli that he still does not believe that Galadriel is the fairest of all, and so Gimli replies that he needs to get his axe in order to uphold Galadriel's honor. However, Éomer then amends his statement by saying that he would have thought Galadriel fair, but on seeing Arwen, now believes that she is the fairest he has ever seen. Éomer adds that he could get his sword to uphold her honor if Gimli disagrees. Gimli agrees to call a draw; he prefers the "morning," the golden beauty of Galadriel, whereas Éomer prefers "evening," the dark-haired beauty of Arwen Evenstar.[37]

Although both warriors have battled in the same army to defend Middle-earth, and the old feud now is only in jest, this scene shows how Gimli, representative of Dwarves, no longer has a quarrel not only with Éomer, but with Men. Personal disagreements as well as territorial and intercultural disputes are being settled in the dawning age of peace.

Once the Fellowship disbands, Legolas visits the Glittering Caves with Gimli to fulfill a promise made during the War of the Ring. The beauty of the caves renders Legolas speechless, and Gimli is more eloquent in describing their glory. In this way, the Dwarf and the Elf exchange roles, because Elves are noted for being more poetic, and Dwarf speech is harsher. (Galadriel first comments that Gimli is not articulate in Lothlórien in expressing his wish for a gift from her, but she notes that the sentiment behind the wish is what is important.)[38] Especially in Tolkien's trilogy, Legolas and Gimli are heroes who take the time to learn more about each other and to share information about their respective cultures. They bridge a racial and an intercultural gap to show that even former enemies can become friends once they overcome their prejudices and begin to work together toward a more tolerant future.

Cinematic Interpretations of Legolas and Gimli

Jackson's trilogy, of course, includes fewer Gimli–Legolas scenes than do the books. Such is the nature of a film adaptation. However, the film characters differ in two principal ways to how they are portrayed in the book, in addition to structural differences in the telling of the story. Legolas on film is often portrayed as a Superelf, and Gimli is more emotional on camera than in print. Finally, Jackson has restructured Aragorn's coronation scene in such a way that emphasizes Legolas's and Gimli's importance to Aragorn.

Orlando Bloom, who portrays Legolas, explains that he envisions the Elf as "a cat.... Cats never look stiff or heavy. They are graceful and poised, but always switched on."[39] Indeed, Legolas's grace, especially under fire, makes the special effects sequences more visually effective, but they also separate him from all other characters, including Elves. Only Legolas, with his Superelfin style, can hop nimbly onto a cave troll or leap gracefully to avoid being smashed by the huge chain the troll wields.[40] Only Legolas can glide on a shield down a stone staircase[41] or scale a charging mûmakil.[42] The special effects make Legolas seem to have super powers, with his grace and agility far surpassing that of other characters.

Although these special-effects feats may make Legolas seem less realistic on film, they also endear him to audiences. Young men, in particular, may identify with Legolas's "coolness factor." Legolas performs the best "stunts" and seems like an extreme sports enthusiast: he climbs, swings, skateboards, leaps. He is a man's type of Elf—Legolas is a key player in the fight sequences and is courageous as well as "cool." Legolas even handles weapons with style. As he gives his weapons to Théoden's guards before first entering the Golden Hall, he skillfully spins the knives as he hands them over.[43] In addition, he carries an astonishingly high number of weapons. True, Legolas is a handsome Elf with beautiful blond hair and refined features, but he also is daring and deadly in action.

Those fine features of Orlando Bloom also make Legolas a favorite character for young women, who see him as a romantic Elf. The huge surge in Bloom's popularity owes a great deal to the fans who idolize Legolas because he is good looking and athletic, as well as being a memorable character. The casting of Bloom as Legolas balances what young filmgoers want to see in their heroes—a good-looking character who is cool as well as effective. Orlando Bloom brings a special quality to the role, one that attracts male and female filmgoers.

The heroic feats in battle are only performed by Legolas; even those who are well-skilled in battle, such as Gimli, Aragorn, or Éomer, do not overcome enemies so spectacularly, and apparently without breaking a sweat. The special effects are visually interesting, but they break the "reality" of the battle scenes. Superelf is fun to watch, but because his actions are so far beyond what any other warrior is shown doing, audiences are made more aware that Legolas's actions are clearly computerized stunts that no "real" character could do. Even in a fantasy, in which belief may be suspended more readily, Legolas's scenes stretch believability. They provide filmgoers with visually spectacular action, as well as the set up in *The Return of the King* for one of Gimli's most humorous lines. After Legolas wipes out not only all the Haradrim riding the mûmakil, but the huge beast itself, and then lightly jumps to the ground as the beast crashes, Gimli grumbles, "That still only counts as one!" The tag line for the coup-counting game is funny to audiences, but it is definitely a modern interruption into an otherwise grim battle scene.[44]

Jackson's Gimli also has differences from his book counterpart. Cinematic Gimli is much more openly emotional than Tolkien's character, and his ability to broadcast his emotions so plainly makes him a broader character than that portrayed in the books. In some scenes, for example, Gimli is tearful. When the Fellowship discovers that the Dwarves living in Khazad-dûm (or Moria) have been killed and that Balin, Gimli's relative and leader of these Dwarves, is dead, Gimli wails with grief.[45] This reaction is much more vocal than Tolkien's description that Gimli simply raised his hood to cover his face.[46] In the cinematic *The Fellowship of the Ring*, after the remaining members of the Fellowship emerge into the light, Gimli weeps, and Boromir comforts him. Legolas stands alone, as if in shock, but Gimli is nearly inconsolable in his grief.

In *The Two Towers*, Legolas, Gimli, and Aragorn are told that Merry and Pippin are dead, having been mistakenly killed when the Rohirrim attack the Orcs.[47] Legolas silently reaches out and squeezes Gimli's shoulder as Gimli bows his head in despair. Later in this film, when presumed-dead Aragorn returns to Helm's Deep, Gimli pushes aside the crowd to hug Aragorn, although he also says that he should kill him for causing the Dwarf such concern.[48] Near the conclusion of *The Return of the King*, Gimli wipes away a tear of joy as he watches Merry and Pippin cavort with a newly healed Frodo.[49]

The characters are successful (at least most of the time) with audiences because they are different from what filmgoers may have expected. Elves in the trilogy often seem ethereal and subdued. Legolas fits that description at times, but he also has outbursts and is an active warrior. He even has a sense of humor. In some ways, Legolas defies audiences' preconceived ideas of an Elf—and so Legolas must seem to Gimli. In the same way, Dwarves may be stereotyped as gruff and coarse or only interested in the earth's riches. Gimli can have those traits, but he also can be surprisingly sentimental. Jackson's Legolas and Gimli are not what audiences, or the characters themselves, may have anticipated, which makes them more interesting to each other and to audiences.

Another difference in characterization allows Gimli to serve as comic relief at times. Gimli's emotional responses sometimes seem over the top, such as in the scene in Moria when the Balrog approaches. In the film, Gimli's eyes become incredibly large, and his mouth forms a perfect O of surprise.[50] The reaction is larger than that of other characters. At other times, Gimli's dialogue is better suited for broader comic relief. When the Fellowship must leap from one crumbling column to another to escape the Balrog, Gimli refuses to be thrown across the chasm, exclaiming that "Nobody tosses a Dwarf!" in a modern reference to dwarf-tossing. Gimli nearly falls as he completes the jump under his own power and is only saved when Legolas pulls him up by the beard. Gimli's "Not the beard!" line is a further bit of humor interjected into an otherwise serious scene. The dwarf-tossing joke is mentioned one more time, in *The Two Towers*,[51] when Gimli asks Aragorn to toss him across a chasm so that he can fight the Orcs attempting to batter their way into the castle. Gimli hesitatingly tells Aragorn not to mention the toss to Legolas, presumably so he would not lose any "masculinity points" in his ongoing competition with the Elf. In scenes like these, through physical and spoken humor, Gimli's character comes across as more whimsical than he does in Tolkien's trilogy.

Although Tolkien does not dwell on the emotional aspects of what could be highly dramatic scenes, his words explain the depth of feeling Gimli has toward the Hobbits. Gimli, after all, is the one who discovers Pippin's body beneath the dead troll after the Battle of Cormallen.[52] Later, when Pippin has recovered sufficiently to celebrate a reunion with Frodo and Sam, Gimli reminds Pippin to turn in early, as he is still healing and has only been out of bed for a single day. He notes fondly that he has been worried about Pippin as he cautions the young Hobbit to look after himself. Tolkien's Gimli is less demonstrative although still concerned; Jackson's version is "larger" emotionally.

A major difference between the books and the films occurs in the coronation scene.[53] Gimli and Legolas both present the most important coronation "gifts" to Aragorn: his crown and his bride. (Although I hesitate to consider Arwen as an "object," in this scene she does seem very much like a prize who has been won and is being awarded to the "best Man.") Through their place in the ceremony, Gimli and Legolas are shown in important roles. Pragmatically, their roles allow them, as well as others in the Fellowship, to be featured briefly in the "farewell" scene in which all characters are together one last time. It would not be fitting for Gimli or Legolas only to be seen in the crowd (as Faramir, Éowyn, and Éomer are); their larger roles in the Fellowship and greater number of scenes in the films mean that they have to be featured more prominently in the last group scene. However, the roles they play in the ceremony also indicate their importance to Aragorn and also the solidarity among Men, Elves, and Dwarves.

At the beginning of the ceremony, Gimli holds the crown, which is taken by Gandalf to be placed on Aragorn's head. This is different from the book, in which Aragorn asks that both Frodo, as ringbearer, and Gandalf assist in the coronation.[54] In the film, Gimli stands before the people, freeing Frodo to stand with the rest of the Hobbits, who are later recognized by Aragorn for their importance in saving Middle-earth.[55] Legolas leads the contingent of Elves who, seemingly to Aragorn's surprise, have arrived to present Arwen as a bride. Legolas addresses Aragorn in Elvish, then smiles and stands back while Arwen is revealed. Thus, Gimli and Legolas symbolically lead Aragorn into his two greatest roles—as king and as husband/bridegroom.

The Importance of Multiculturalism in Modern Heroism

Two points need to be made about the importance of multiculturalism in a discussion of modern heroes: heroes come from any background or any culture, and characters serving as modern role models/heroes should respect those from cultures different from their own. Tolkien's heroes, in the form of Legolas and Gimli, do so, and Jackson's adaptation, although altering the characters for film, holds true to this friendship.

Tolkien has been called racist by some critics and fans, especially in the case of the darker Haradrim and the dark-skinned, slanted-eyed Orcs.

The "bad guys" have different physical traits from the "good guys." Tolkien has been accused of cultural and social class bias as well, especially in the master–servant relationship between Frodo and Sam, and Sam's common speech. As mentioned in chapter 4, Tolkien further has been labeled sexist, partly because male characters far outnumber female. Tolkien's treatment of many different peoples may not be perfect for any one group and should be analyzed in detail by critics interpreting different aspects of *The Lord of the Rings*. I do not think that Tolkien set out to write against any one group of characters in order to discriminate against nationality, race, class, gender, or ethnicity. For this chapter, I acknowledge these concerns but do not focus on the research pro or con about racism, in particular, in the text.

Based on Tolkien's history of Middle-earth, the likelihood of a close, enduring friendship between Legolas and Gimli is highly unlikely. Each is initially aware of the other's cultural biases, as well as the many other differences that make up an individual's preferences and outlook on life. Until each is willing to appreciate the other's background and ideas and build on common ground, ethnocentricity could very well keep the two characters separated. Therefore, to learn in Tolkien's appendixes that the two are such close friends that they end up sailing away together, readers see just how large a cultural gap has been bridged and how far personal friendship can come in helping once-enemies overcome their cultural conditioning. In Jackson's trilogy, the "friendship" line just before the Battle of Cormallen signals the depth of Legolas and Gimli's friendship. Through this friendship "Tolkien shows . . . an example of how tolerance is possible between people from widely divergent and naturally mistrustful backgrounds."[56]

The Necessity of Facing Change

Legolas and Gimli are successful intercultural heroes because they are willing to change. At the end of the Third Age, every culture, every race is facing important changes, and the way that each responds to changes beyond their control speaks a great deal about their longevity in Middle-earth.

One possible response to a rapidly changing world is to live in the past and to refuse to participate in the world being created. This response is not escapism, because the emerging world and its many changes are acknowledged. However, people choosing this response just do not want to be a part of the new world or do not believe they have a place within it. Such is the response of most Elves, who realize they have no future in Middle-earth in the Fourth Age. The ones who remain live in a past that is being forgotten; their culture fades.

Another response is to leave the new world and return to another. For example, people in our time move to remote locations to leave behind the problems of traffic congestion, or return to a way of life not requiring wired, much less wireless, technology. The Elves who leave Middle-earth to return to Valinor (e.g., Elrond, Galadriel, Celeborn) are examples of those who choose this response. Frodo, although not representative of an entire culture or race, also responds this way. He has been too badly wounded by the end of the Third Age to see his place in the future, and so he retires where he will not have to participate in the changes coming with the Fourth Age.

A third response is to be innovative and encourage changes, preferably for the benefit of others. Being a catalyst for change that improves lives—or at least trying to bring about such change—without harming others is a risky choice. There is no guarantee that what is meant to be a positive change may not, in the future, have negative consequences that cannot be foreseen. For example, until a new technology becomes commonplace, all the ramifications of this technology cannot be known. In recent Western history, the past hundred years has introduced a number of new technologies. For example, automobiles create new industries and products as well as enhance personal travel. However, automation started in the automobile industry spread to other businesses, leading to fewer factory jobs, noise and air pollution from so many vehicles on the roads, and time lost through traffic congestion. These problems are a few downsides that might not have been anticipated in the early 1900s.

Although the changes promised by King Elessar are not necessarily technological, this response is typical of Men, who often believe in progress brought about by rebuilding. Aragorn/Elessar promises a time of peace, in which races and cultures work together. Indeed, this is the situation in Ithilien, where Faramir of Gondor is a prince, Éowyn of Rohan is a princess, Gimli assists in the rebuilding of the city, and Legolas starts one of the last colonies of Elves. Progress also includes rebuilding the cities destroyed by war and reestablishing Gondor as a place of culture and beauty. In the Shire, Sam also is an agent for change when he busily replants trees and shares Galadriel's gift of the special soil to encourage new plants to grow. However, Tolkien also removes the problems of rapid technological changes in the Shire brought about by Sharkey—the factories and ugly buildings are torn down and proper Hobbit homes restored. Being a catalyst for changes and choosing to promote healing may be an idealistic choice.

A final response to change is to gather power to try to remake change as one person or a few people see fit. The lure of power to effect the type of changes wanted by a small group often begins as the previously discussed desire to do good, but, as Tolkien shows with the stories of Saruman and

Sauron, power is addictive. Trying to control what happens by controlling all the variables involved within world change is impossible; not even the strongest leader can control everything. Dictatorships are one example of this response to power. Sauron tries to control Middle-earth's future by creating the One Ring. Saruman's desire for power leads him to create armies to do his bidding directly, although he is seemingly under the control of Sauron. Even Gandalf realizes that he would be tempted to misuse the power provided by the One Ring, even if he wants to do great good by wielding such power. Tolkien acknowledges this response to change by showing the nature of power and the ways that even good people can too easily become ensnared by it.

Entire cultures may respond to change in these ways, but individuals also have their own choices to make as to the ways they respond to global change. In Tolkien's *The Return of the King*, Legolas and Gimli, for example, individually choose to help rebuild Middle-earth; however, they also change personally. Legolas remains open to new experiences and makes good his wartime promise to Gimli to accompany him to the Glittering Caves.[57] Although an Elf is not comfortable underground, he remains open to seeing the beauty of the jeweled caves by choosing to see the world through Gimli's eyes. Gimli gives up a secluded life with Dwarves in their hidden mountain cities by choosing to participate aboveground in Middle-earth society. He even chooses to spend the remainder of his life completely away from Dwarves and in the company of Elves when he accompanies Legolas across the sea.[58]

Neither Legolas nor Gimli ever gives up who he is. Legolas does not become more Dwarflike in his perception of the world, although he understands what Gimli values and why he does so. Gimli uses his skills as a craftsman to help rebuild, and he enjoys sharing what he perceives as beautiful with Legolas. Gimli prizes his friendship with Legolas above all other, but he does not want to be an Elf.

Everyone can change, but it is a difficult, lengthy procedure, and often it is easier just to abandon this process. As an Elf, who already is millennia old by the War of the Ring, Legolas should be most resistant to change, even without the socialization to mistrust and dislike Dwarves. Gimli also is long-lived and aggressive by nature; it is not typical for him to show a gentler side when he normally is gruff and combative. "Legolas and Gimli are the two characters for whom change is least likely, given that one is an Elf, whose very nature is unchanging, and the other a Dwarf, his being crafted from enduring stone."[59] Yet Tolkien uses these two characters as representatives of their races to show that even in such extreme cases, personal friendship and cultural/racial respect are possible.

"By the time of the War of the Ring, the Elves no longer look forward."[60] Tolkien describes the Fellowship's vision of Galadriel as she wishes them farewell from Lothlórien. Although the Fellowship's boats are moving on the river, it seems as if they are stilled and "Lórien [is] slipping backward . . . sailing on to a forgotten shore."[61] Perhaps because of their ability to let go of the past and look forward to a new future, Legolas and Gimli seem active much longer in Middle-earth than others of their races. The Elves dwindle as a people, fading from Middle-earth. Those who remain live across the sea and are no longer seen by the peoples of Middle-earth. The Dwarves also decline over time, and although some cities remain for a time, they do not have their former glory. Yet even during the War of the Ring, Legolas plans to travel with Gimli after the war, and both choose to travel together toward an unknown future when they sail across the sea.

Michael Swanwick summarizes two possible responses to the end of an age: to hold on or to let go. He notes that the people who choose to hold on to what they have, to "try to seize the power to ward off change are corrupted by despair."[62] It is impossible to stop change. Spending all one's time trying to control change is fruitless. However, those people who choose to let go also choose "to suffer and make sacrifices, to toil selflessly and honorably, and then to surrender their authority over what remains, ultimately gain the satisfaction of knowing that the world has a future worth passing on" to future generations.[63]

Gimli and Legolas choose the latter path. During the Quest, they let go of past prejudices and begin to consider each other first as individuals, and then as members of a different race that is worthy of their attention and respect. In the Fourth Age, they toil to make a better future for others in this new world, but their work, and their choice to live and work together, instead of returning to their own peoples, undoubtedly is a costly decision. Gimli's final decision to make one last journey with Legolas must be difficult for "one who still must love the things of Earth." Nevertheless, Gimli "chooses in the end not to be parted from the two souls he most loves, Legolas and Galadriel."[64] By letting go of the past, Legolas and Gimli do suffer loss; however, they also participate in the future and reap new rewards from their continuing friendship.

Many people living in the late twentieth and early twenty-first centuries may feel like they, too, are living at the end of an age and facing an uncertain future. Like Tolkien's characters, individually and as members of a culture, they must choose how to respond to such rapid global changes within their lifetimes. Tolkien faced such changes, and readers learn his response to change as they journey through Middle-earth along with his characters. The changes faced and choices made by Legolas and Gimli make them especially applicable heroes for modern times. Although they also are battle veterans and serve ably as warriors, their true heroism comes when they face their own prejudices and misconceptions about a former enemy and learn to find common ground with a new friend.

Legolas and Gimli and a Modern Definition of *Hero*

Chapter 1's outline of the characteristics defining a modern hero, for film or book, includes the following five items. In addition to their roles as intercultural heroes, Legolas and Gimli also can be defined as heroes for modern times through these items.

1. They act on their convictions.

Once Legolas and Gimli become part of the Fellowship, they never turn back and are committed to completing the Quest. Even when the Fellowship has been torn apart, they readily follow Aragorn and overcome all types of hardships to complete many smaller missions as part of the larger Quest. They relentlessly follow the Orcs who capture Merry and Pippin and do not rest until they know that the Hobbits are free. They then follow Gandalf the White's counsel and participate in many major battles in Rohan and Gondor. They continue to rebuild Middle-earth after the war and deepen their relationships with other races. Once they are individually convinced of the path they should take, they do not veer from this path.

The best "conviction" of these two is that their friendship is worthwhile, and it becomes the most important factor in their lives. Once Aragorn becomes king, Gimli could return to the remaining Dwarves and become more isolated with his people, as could Legolas. Instead, Legolas brings Elves to Ithilien, for example. Legolas and Gimli could simply remember their comradeship during the War of the Ring, but not continue to develop their bond. As an Elf, Legolas might be content with a memory of their friendship, but he chooses to maintain the relationship; perhaps this shows a shift in his values to prefer current experience instead of cherished memory. Gimli chooses to accompany Legolas across the seas, and Legolas must be very much committed to the friendship in order to gain that privilege for his friend. The greatest commitment of Legolas and Gimli is to their friendship, and it serves as a shining example of the ways that diverse peoples can work together and love each other.

2. They plan strategies and carry them out successfully, even if this strategy is planned on the run. They are thinking heroes who may have to plan spontaneously as a crisis occurs or think on their feet during a crisis.

The only "strategy" that Legolas and Gimli seem to follow is this: Stick to Aragorn. They do not blindly follow him, but they are loyal to him and follow the course that he, in consultation with Gandalf, sets. This allegiance to their friend and leader takes them into danger throughout most of the trilogies, but they do not waver in their desire to follow Aragorn into any situation. They may individually despair for a moment, but they never seriously consider abandoning Aragorn.

In battle, both characters certainly have to think on their feet. The result often is a move that could be self-sacrificing but ends up saving another character. They both are quick witted in battle and fearless in putting themselves forward as the battle changes so that they can be most effective as warriors.

Tolkien also describes some promises that Gimli and Legolas make to each other, such as Legolas's promise to return to the Glittering Caves and Gimli's promise to accompany Legolas into the forests once the Quest is completed. Although these promises are made during wartime, the partners fulfill their promises to each other once it is over. They could have chosen to write off their promises as ones made to a friend during dire wartime conditions, but they honor their word and use their post-Quest experiences to deepen their friendship and learn more about the other's culture. Their loyalty to others and commitment to fulfilling what they have promised are heroic qualities.

   3. They offer to sacrifice themselves, if necessary, for the cause.

Self-sacrifice is almost a certainty in the many battles in which Gimli and Legolas take part. Orlando Bloom describes Elves as beings with "great physical and mental strength . . . powerful, full-blooded people."[65] John Rhys-Davies explains that Gimli is a great warrior with "eagerness to accept what would appear to be a suicidal mission" but really indicates his "courage and the strength of his heart."[66] These descriptions are apt especially in the battle scenes, in which both Legolas and Gimli appear fearless and willing to fight, and, if necessary, to die, for their friends.

Here are only a few examples from Jackson's *The Two Towers*. Gimli leaps from a parapet to defend and fight with Aragorn when the wall is breached at Helm's Deep; he jumps into action and charges an over-powering force in order to help Aragorn return to safety.[67] Gimli later accompanies Aragorn without hesitation to stave off another overpowering force so that Théoden's men can bolster the door and keep Orcs from entering the castle from the main gate.[68]

In *The Return of the King*, Gimli and Legolas are powerless against the Army of the Dead. Aragorn, as the rightful King of Gondor, is the only one whose weapons can "kill" the dead soldiers, and he is the only one the Army must obey. Still, Legolas and Gimli back up Aragorn when he confronts the Army. Although Legolas's arrow sails harmlessly through the specter, Aragorn's sword is effective in confronting the King of the Dead.[69] During the last battle, at Cormallen, Aragorn is about to be killed by a troll. Jackson shows a distraught Legolas vainly attempting to get to Aragorn's side, oblivious to the rest of the battle around him.[70]

These are only a few brief instances of Legolas and Gimli offering, by word or most often, by action, to give their lives in order to save their comrades, in particular, Aragorn. Their fearlessness in battle and their willingness to die not only for the larger cause of saving Middle-earth but also for their friends, certainly make them heroes.

> 4. They grow as characters, showing under extreme circumstances the heroic qualities that always have been part of their makeup, but have not been recognized until these qualities are needed.

The many examples, in books and films, of Gimli's and Legolas's individual and collective heroics in battle show that they are warrior-heroes. However, their gentleness with each other under duress may not be expected. Gimli and Legolas are not sentimental characters, yet their concern for each other is heightened when they know they may die in battle. Gimli's awe of and devotion to Galadriel is another example of the vulnerability that heroes may show, a trait that does not make them weak but makes them more fully "human." Gimli and Legolas could have been mere fighting "machines" who almost glibly fight ferociously and, during the course of a given battle, save lives of their comrades as well as take lives of their enemies. Their wartime actions are expected of first-class warriors, and they are effective fighters, to say the least.

However, what makes them memorable heroes is their ability also to show tenderness with each other and the members of the Fellowship, as well as with special others such as Galadriel. The quality to open up to another and show a gentler side of personality may not be expected from a cool, aloof Elf or a stubborn, gruff Dwarf, but both characters reveal a softer side at several points in the story.

> 5. They embody the values of love of family and home, which provide the impetus for them to act to protect the people and places they love.

Although Gimli and Legolas first join the Fellowship as representatives of their races and cultures to help determine the fate of Middle-earth, they eventually come to realize that their "home" goes beyond their places of origin. "Home" becomes a place beside a dearest friend, so that wherever one goes, so does the other. Tolkien often describes Legolas and Gimli as riding together, or, in the end, sailing away together; their friendship is so close that one does not lead and the other follow—they travel together. Jackson most often shows Gimli riding with Legolas, and in scenes when they are not required to ride, the two are seldom apart. The two stand side by side in battle, and they defend each other on and off the battlefield.

However, their love is not limited to this one dear friendship. Both Gimli and Legolas demonstrate time and again their loyalty to Aragorn, and they often put themselves in harm's way to accompany him. For example, in the cinematic *The Return of the King*, Aragorn tells them to stay behind when he leaves to travel the Paths of the Dead. Gimli and Legolas both comment that he does not know them well if he thinks he can slip off without them; the pair refuses to abandon Aragorn, even if they otherwise would have continued with Théoden into battle.[71] They are united as a team to help Aragorn; they work together as a cohesive unit.

Their devotion to the other members of the Fellowship is only slightly less, and Gimli in particular feels kindly toward the Hobbits. In an interview, John Rhys-Davies explains that Gimli "feels toward the hobbits as a grown man feels toward children. His job is to protect them."[72] Gimli takes his job seriously, and throughout the books and films looks after the Hobbits when he travels with them.

"Family," especially among intercultural or multicultural relationships, takes on a broader meaning, and the extension of Legolas's and Gimli's "family" and "home" across the many races and cultures allows their characters to develop beyond battle heroics into a fuller, deeper maturity. Although they could be considered heroes for their battle deeds alone, they become memorable characters because they go beyond what is expected of them to develop abiding friendships.

In these ways, Gimli and Legolas show that being intercultural heroes includes considering other races of Middle-earth, not just blood relatives, as part of their extended families. Their friends become more than just comrades-in-arms, although that is a powerful bonding force. Their ability to form close friendships and to improve race and intercultural relations, more than any other single factor, establishes them as heroes for a modern age.

7

The Changing Social Definitions of Heroes

*T*he *Lord of the Rings* provides readers and film audiences with an entertaining classic tale, an epic that can become a resonating myth across Western cultures. It also provides "human," everyday characters who can be role models for youths and adults, at whatever stage of their psychological, spiritual, and physical development. Many characters are important as heroes because they can inspire readers and audiences to be better people individually; they stand up for what they value, such as friendship, love, and loyalty; and they offer hope for the success of collective action. In short, they give readers and film audiences many paths by which to surpass their everyday circumstances and limitations to do great things. "Great" might be as simple as standing up to a schoolyard bully. It might be as profound as leading a nation toward peaceful goals after a powerful struggle. "Heroics" may take place in a single moment of self-sacrifice or a lifetime of devotion and service.

At a recent Popular Culture Association/American Culture Association conference session about J. R. R. Tolkien's and Peter Jackson's trilogies, a member of the audience brought up a comment he had heard from an interview with actor Viggo Mortensen (Aragorn in Jackson's films). The actor reportedly commented that perhaps the value of the trilogy would be that audiences might be moved to act on the values represented in the films. Presumably, friendship, loyalty, love, service, and so on were the values he meant. Perhaps this will become so. Perhaps readers and film audiences will remember some themes in Tolkien's work and be motivated to make some small change in their lives.

This concept of using Tolkien's works as inspiration for personal growth was reiterated by one of the founders of TheOneRingNet (TORN), a fan-supported Web site that provides information and sponsored special events, such as an Oscar party, related to the trilogy. Once the final film was released theatrically and the award season over, many passionate fans looked for something to fill their time. After all, they had spent several years following the development of the films and participating in a variety of fan-related activities. In an editorial posted on TORN in April 2004, fans were encouraged to use what they learned about Middle-earth and Tolkien to improve their lives or to share their talents with others.[1]

Similarly, a fourth-grade student in Utah used his love of Tolkien's books to improve his reading skills, as well as to learn life lessons. He won a writing contest by explaining how much Tolkien's *The Lord of the Rings* meant in his life. He wrote of friendship, love, and the ability to overcome fear. What is especially interesting is that the boy once had difficulty learning to read, but his interest in the books helped him stick with reading.[2] The idea of applying Tolkien's themes to improving one's life seems especially appealing to fans of the books and films, who often have supported causes favored by the leading actors in Jackson's trilogy or used Tolkien's works to motivate them toward greater goals.

Nathan Hunt's recent exploration of fandom, and in particular, knowledge of trivia, shows that something as "simple" as fandom can have cultural implications as well as social relevance for the fans involved. Knowing trivia, for example, allows fans to "claim special access to, and knowledge of, specific texts and groups of texts and, in so doing, to make claim to ownership of them."[3] Tolkien's fandom knows a lot about the books and films, as well as trivia about their creation. They most certainly seem to have claimed "ownership" of Tolkien's works and applied their knowledge to everyday life.

The values inherent in Tolkien's trilogy and translated in altered ways on film should have a continuing impact on individuals, although the popular furor for all things Tolkien may subside again after the release of the final DVD or the fiftieth anniversary of the publication of *The Lord of the Rings*. Interest in *The Lord of the Rings* seems to be cyclical. At certain points in history, when fantasy seems especially more palatable than reality in world events, interest in Tolkien's epic should again increase. As well, if Jackson's films are shown periodically as special events, whether in theaters or on home screens (similar to the annual showings of the fantasy *The Wizard of Oz* or the biblical epic *The Ten Commandments* in the United States), there should be renewed interested in the story.

The values espoused by Tolkien's heroic characters have been subverted to different causes during the past fifty years. Tolkien was not a hippie in any sense of the word; in fact, he was much closer to the establishment against which the hippie social movement peacefully resisted.

Nevertheless, during the 1960s in the United States, hippies and other young adults who were not so extreme in their lifestyle embraced what they saw as the crucial values in *The Lord of the Rings*: rejecting corporate power as an evil and embracing agrarian values and a simple, back-to-nature lifestyle. Although Tolkien's work is not an allegory for any particular period in the past or the current century, it nonetheless speaks to people who are looking for change in their lives and who are dissatisfied with the political or social climate.

Tolkien fandom reached one peak in the 1960s, when "the fan above the age of 25 was exceptional."[4] (This is quite a contrast to the ages I observed during the marathon showing of Jackson's trilogy in December 2003 at an Orlando, Florida, cinema; grandparents, adults, and their adolescent children all stood in line equally eager to see the final film. Most likely, fans who were twenty-five or younger in the mid-1960s still may be Tolkien fans forty years later, with the upcoming generations discovering the tale along the way.) As a member of the American Tolkien Society writes of the 1960s, the "American Dream was crumbling; even the college education which had been held out as a blank check in the 1950s no longer carried the assurance of a job. American youth sought a refuge."[5] Those looking for a better way of life and seeking solace in an epic about the triumph of good and a return to peace flocked to Tolkien and made his words their guidelines. "Frodo lives" was a battle cry on college campuses and communes in the United States during this time. The peaceful nature of the Hobbits—along with their quiet, community-oriented Shire life—made them seem heroic in the chaotic United States of the mid- to late 1960s.

Now, fast forward to the early 2000s. The list of world problems seems neverending—the September 11, 2001, attacks in the United States, fears of terrorism worldwide, ongoing wars and genocide in several countries, global trade initiatives and protests against the World Trade Organization, political infighting and scandals in more than one nation, a shaky U.S. economy amid fears about job losses (especially through outsourcing), the Iraqi War. It does not seem surprising that Jackson's trilogy provides a similar "refuge" for young filmgoers dissatisfied with the current state of life and satisfies a desire to find heroes who overcome their own terrible problems to emerge victorious. These heroes return to their former lives wiser and more appreciative of simple virtues; they do not glorify power and only threaten violence when no other action seems effective (as in the scouring of the Shire).

Add to that interest in a fantasy tale the power of well-made films with spectacular, including some never-before-seen visual effects, and Jackson's trilogy helped propel Tolkien's works back into a very bright spotlight. As *Newsweek* proclaimed just prior to the release of *The Return of the King*, "heretical as it may sound, many audience members are as hungry for Jackson's vision as they are for Tolkien's."[6] Although Jackson's films undoubtedly would have been acclaimed without this particular sociopolitical climate of the early 2000s, Tolkien's themes may be especially appropriate for readers to remember or for film fans to investigate at this time in Western culture, as the need for heroes continues. The heroic characters, and the values they espouse, seem to have a continuing broad appeal.

Otherness and the Recognition of Heroic Qualities

People who feel dispossessed or outside the cultural norm may gravitate toward Tolkien's themes. Thomas Shippey, a former colleague of Tolkien's and himself a professor and author of critical works about Tolkien's writings and influences, says that the multiple-plot structure of Tolkien's *The Lord of the Rings* makes each character "feel lonely and isolated, while in the broader view . . . everyone's story is a part of everyone else's: much more like reality."[7] Realizing one's *otherness* from the societal norm, while recognizing that a single life does have an impact on others, is an important growth arc not only for Tolkien's unsung heroes but for audiences/readers as well.

Although *Otherness* can take many forms, it is often based on gender, age, race, or religion, or on personal preferences, genetics, or lifestyles, for example. Feeling outside the mainstream can be based on anything, but the result is the same—the person perceived as Other is different from typical members of the dominant group and lacks one or more of the desired or common characteristics; that group has some type of power over the Other, making acceptance by the group desirable. The unsung heroes discussed in this book all are Others in some way, but they learn to value their difference from the dominant group to accomplish important, often life-saving tasks and to assert their unique place within the group.

This sense of Otherness does not have to be considered negative, either to the individual or to society. It is this very Otherness that is what helps develop each *Lord of the Rings* character's heroic potential and often leads the character to step forward and become a hero. Readers and filmgoers who also feel they are Other or outside the recognized norm of society may identify with these previously unsung characters and their ability to act heroically in a crisis. They may find in themselves the qualities and values that inspire heroism.

For the Hobbits, the most obvious source of Otherness is their size. Throughout both trilogies, Merry and Pippin (because they spend the greatest amount of time in the company of Men, Orcs, and Wizards) are often defined and categorized by their size. They are too small to be perceived useful, except occasionally by Gandalf who, in Jackson's *The Return of the King*, for example, prefers Pippin's small size for tasks like climbing to the beacon at Minas Tirith.[8] Smallness and the ability not to be readily seen come in handy for such specific deeds. Most of the time, though, smallness is not a desired quality, especially not among the Rohirrim preparing for war.

In Jackson's version, Éomer chides Éowyn for encouraging Merry to prepare as any other warrior.[9] When Éowyn retorts that Merry's heart is as big as any other warrior's and he should be allowed to fight for his loved ones, Éomer jokes that "I do not doubt his heart, only the reach of his arm." Ironically, Merry's reach is long enough to wound the Nazgûl attacking Éowyn. If Éowyn had not brought Merry into battle, it can be argued that she most likely would have died at the hands of the Nazgûl, and the Witch King remained free to attack others.

Size often is equated with age, and the Hobbits' perceived youth is another source of feeling Other from the warriors or even the rest of the Fellowship. Théoden first seems to assume that Merry, because of his smaller stature and youthful appearance, is little more than a child and takes him under his protection. Even Éowyn, who understands Merry's desire to fight for his friends and family because she also feels the duty to protect her people, shows bias against the Hobbit as the warriors prepare for battle.

When Éowyn outfits Merry as a soldier of Rohan, she provides him the appropriately sized gear. In Jackson's version, Merry feels proud of his war garb and pulls his sword to show how "dangerous" he looks. However, he nearly catches Éowyn with the blade, and she laughingly jumps back. Merry quickly apologizes, but then ruefully notes, " 'T'isn't all that dangerous. It isn't even sharp."[10] Éowyn then clasps the blade between her hands, proving that it is indeed dull, and tells Merry to have the blade sharpened if he wants to be able to kill Orcs. In the way that Jackson's scene is filmed, there are no sexual overtones, and the interaction between the characters is playful and friendly, not flirtatious or seductive.

However, one interpretation of this scene can be that Éowyn does not seriously consider Merry as an adult male. (In Tolkien's trilogy, Merry is an adult, of-age Hobbit. Jackson's trilogy portrays him as young but of indeterminate age. He is not so young as to be "childlike.") Éowyn laughs with Merry and makes shooing motions as she hurries him toward the blacksmith. Her tone and attitude seem more like a mother humoring a beloved child than one warrior helping another prepare for battle. In essence, even Éowyn emasculates Merry in this scene by clasping the blade and then noting that it is not useful; as a potential warrior, Merry seems impotent. The symbolic gesture seems in character for all the bigger people, men or women, who encounter the Hobbits. Throughout Tolkien's and Jackson's trilogies, comments are also made about Pippin's youthful nature—which is sometimes a pleasant diversion to keep up the spirits of his comrades, but often a deterrent to effective action. Being smaller and younger are key sources of Otherness for Merry and Pippin, yet they do not hinder them in performing heroically.

Éowyn's sense of being Other is based on gender expectations. Although Éowyn has skill with a sword and is prepared to fight, she is not expected to take on the same role as men who have similar training and desire to serve their people. Her gender separates her from the other warriors. In Tolkien's *The Return of the King*, Éowyn solves the problem by dressing as a man to fit in with the rest of the army and be unnoticed at least until she is too far away to be sent back.[11] In Jackson's streamlined version, Éowyn dresses in a soldier's helmet and mail, but audiences—and Merry—always know that she retains her identity. This choice is probably more of a convenience than a feminist storyline; it is easier not to introduce the new character of Dernhelm and thus to slow the action building in the "going to war" scenes. Éowyn's gender plays the key role in slaying the Witch King. Because she and Merry are different from men, they can fulfill the prophecy that no man could kill the Witch King.

However, Éowyn also is Other from women in Rohan, not only because of her social standing as niece of the king, but also by the expectations placed on her sociopolitical role. Éowyn is expected to lead her people. In Jackson's trilogy, this is clearly shown twice. In *The Two Towers*, Éowyn is coaxed into leading the children, women, wounded, and old men to Helm's Deep while the male warriors stave off Orcs.[12] She prefers to fight, but Théoden pleads for her to take the people to safety "for me." In *The Return of the King*, Théoden tells Éowyn that he has "left instruction" that she succeed him if he dies in battle, a duty that Éowyn reluctantly accepts.[13] She prefers to serve their people directly—in action—rather than wait in safety and lead those who have been left behind. She understands the expectation for her to be able to lead and rule, which places her in a different light from other women in her land. Her duty always is to serve her people, not the more typical gender expectation for a woman to serve just her immediate family. Éowyn does that, too, especially in *The Two Towers*, but she also must meet other expectations of service.

Galadriel and Arwen also are Other from the characters with whom they interact in the story, but their Otherness is a result of their choices. Galadriel has long guided the Elves in Lothlórien, and although she also is a wife and mother (although these roles are not emphasized in *The Lord of the Rings*), she carries a ring of power. Her power and responsibility as a ringbearer separate her from other leaders and Elves. Gender is only a part of her Otherness; the ability to wield power, and the choices associated with handling power wisely, differentiate her from other powerful characters.

Galadriel's choices to accept the Fellowship in Lothlórien and provide them gifts to help them on the Quest are different from those of other powerful leaders who help or hinder the Fellowship along the way. Gandalf also struggles with the One Ring and its power, but chooses to guide the Fellowship directly and to participate in battles. Galadriel manipulates events behind the scenes, as noted especially in Jackson's trilogy. For example, Galadriel encourages Elrond to send a fighting force of archers to Helm's Deep, and Galadriel also sends Elves to the battle.[14] In the third film, she mystically encourages Frodo to continue the Quest, and she understands the challenge of his journey.[15] Her immortality gives her a great sense of history and the ebb and flow of time. Although this sense of time may be true in other Elves, Galadriel tries to influence the future through her choices and use of power, which separates her further from other Elves without her responsibilities or foresight.

Arwen also becomes separated from other Elves through her choices, most notably her decision to give up immortality to stay in Middle-earth as Aragorn's queen. She also influences the outcome of events through her guidance of and assistance to Aragorn, but her choice to remain behind, and to die eventually, make her Other from the rest of the Elves.

Gimli and Legolas, although opposites in many ways, are similar in that they choose to be Other by joining the Fellowship, eventually developing a close bond that they maintain for the rest of their lives. Legolas, especially through Orlando Bloom's portrayal in Jackson's trilogy, is much more involved in the affairs of Middle-earth than most Elves. His loyalty to Aragorn also separates him from Elves who eventually fight alongside Men but do not choose to live or work as closely with them. Legolas defends Aragorn during the Council of Elrond and eagerly agrees to assist the Fellowship when Aragorn pledges his life to help Frodo succeed in his mission.[16] Loyalty to Men is not a common trait among the Elves, although they have fought a mutual enemy in the past. Legolas does not seem disturbed to be "different" from his brethren and does not waiver in his support of Aragorn throughout the journey.

Gimli originally joins the Fellowship because he does not want the Elves to have the One Ring or to leave the Dwarves unrepresented in a Fellowship that includes an Elf. The history of the Elves and Dwarves is one of mistrust. This longstanding feud between the races, plus the former enmity between the houses of Thranduil and Glóin, make Gimli's later friendship with Legolas an important source of being Other.

Gimli's size is one other source of being Other, but his prowess as a warrior negates any long-lasting bias against him because of size. Instead,

Jackson uses humor in the latter two films to emphasize the difference in size between Gimli and both Legolas and Aragorn. When Gimli tries on mail that is obviously made for a Man, he tells Legolas and Aragorn that he wishes for time to get the shirt adjusted, as it is too snug around the chest.[17] He ignores the fact that the shirt covers his ankles. Immediately before the Battle of Helm's Deep, Gimli complains that Legolas has chosen a poor vantage point to see the battlefield.[18] Legolas teases, "Shall I describe it? Or would you like me to find you a box?" Gimli only laughs in response. These gests, along with a few dwarf-tossing jokes, point out Gimli's size difference from other warriors, but his effectiveness as a soldier is never questioned. Unlike the Hobbits' size, which often is used as a determinant of their possible usefulness, Gimli's stature is just another difference between himself and Legolas, another aspect of the "opposites attract" part of their unlikely friendship.

Through both trilogies, these characters either overcome their sense of Otherness to show the dominant group (e.g., Men, Elves, the Rohirrim, the Fellowship) that size, age, or gender do not matter, or, despite the consequences, they make choices that create Otherness. They accept their differences from others as part of their unique gifts. Because they are Other to typical male warriors, kings, and wizards, they provide a different perspective on the Quest and enrich the telling of the tale. They also show how those who are different from the rest of the group often use their uniqueness in heroic ways. When these characters are true to who they really are, they become effective heroes.

Film and the Mass Marketing of Tolkien

Comparing Tolkien's trilogy and Jackson's trilogy is often difficult, not only because of different artistic choices made by Jackson, but because of the numerous differences between print and film in the telling of a story. Each trilogy has its merits, fans and detractors, and unique strengths and weaknesses owing to each medium and artist's skill and talent. However, there is a further distinction between the two trilogies: the marketing and public awareness of the works. A discussion of heroes in Jackson's trilogy also should account for the mass marketing of the films.

The original publication of Tolkien's trilogy did not excite the public in the same way as a world premiere of a multimillion dollar project. Tolkien's original fandom also did not have the Internet to spread rumors and news from the time the film was announced and to continue this sharing of information about actors, shooting locations, and new collectible items through post-production five years later. Although Tolkien fans are frequently passionate about his works, especially *The Lord of the Rings*, nothing has compared to the vibrancy of *The Lord of the Rings* fandom in the early 2000s. Web sites from advertisers, product manufacturers, New Line Cinema, fans, fanzines, Tolkien Society members and affiliated associations, the actors, and news organizations have devoted a great deal of bandwidth to information about the cinematic trilogy and the individuals involved in its many phases of production.

During late 2003 and early 2004, the Internet, broadcast media, and print media saturated the market with images related to the final film in the trilogy. Almost every day brought a new interview with writers, producers, the director, and actors, as well as many "The Making of" broadcast specials, Internet trailers and teasers, features in magazines and newspapers, and advertisements on billboards, television, and movie screens. In many different ways, and in differing degrees of seriousness, *The Lord of the Rings* has had a large commercial and popular impact on Western cultures. Even with his imagination and creativity, Tolkien probably could not have envisioned such a marketing campaign.

Even those without interest in Tolkien or films based on his works grasped at least part of the story, because film clips, photographs, and even jokes appeared in nearly every public information medium in late 2003. During December, after the film opened in the United States, the actors appeared on *The Today Show, The Tonight Show, CBS Morning Show, Regis & Kelly, The Late Show with David Letterman,* and *Oprah* among other television programs. Footage of fans lining up to see *The Return of the King*, broadcasts of premieres, and clips from the film were broadcast by major Western news outlets, including BBC, Sky, ABC, NBC, CBS, and CNN. The tabloid television programs ran many stories about the actors, the premieres, and the films. At the international premiere of the third film, held in Wellington, New Zealand, more than 100,000 fans cheered the director, producers, and actors. Actors, producers, and the director attended at least some of the multiple premieres worldwide, notably those in Los Angeles, New York, London, Berlin, Copenhagen, and Tokyo, all to media coverage and wild fan approval.[19,20]

This type of media blitz, especially in Europe, North America, Australia, Japan, and New Zealand, made it almost impossible for anyone watching television or surfing the Internet not to notice. Although the furor died down after *The Return of the King* won eleven Oscars at the Academy Awards in February 2004 (including the most coveted Best Picture award), interest in the actors' future projects, tourism in New Zealand, Tolkien's many works, and film collectibles continues. In addition, the Internet has fueled dozens of fanfiction sites that elaborate on the characters' adventures, continuing the interest in further stories of the heroes

from the books and films. An Internet fan campaign started almost immediately for New Line Cinema, promoting Jackson again as director, to
bring *The Hobbit* to film.[21]

As is typical with such highly promoted films with a young fan base,
action figures and collectibles of all types are important money-making
ventures for multiple companies. Although Tolkien's books through the
years have inspired the creation of artwork and calendars, for example, the
marketing of images based on *The Lord of the Rings* reached epic proportions
with the release of Jackson's films. One aspect of the creation of heroes in
Western popular culture is the toys for children and teenagers and the social/
political/personal roles being enacted through role play. Action figures and
videogames in particular invited role play as *Lord of the Rings* characters.

For each film in *The Lord of the Rings* trilogy, new action figures
appeared for the major characters, and after the release of the third film, a
wider range of action figures included secondary characters, both "good
guys" and "bad guys." With the exception of toys like Arwen/Barbie and
Aragorn/Ken, which encourage children to enact a love relationship with a
bridal couple, most action figures indicate that the heroes' action involves
warfare. Although Jackson's films, especially *The Two Towers* and *The Return
of the King*, spend a great deal of time detailing warfare and use spectacular
effects to indicate the immense scope of each battle, the films are not war
films. The huge scale of the battles and the details of the slashing and bashing
do not glorify war, but instead show its overwhelming devastation. However,
that is not the image produced by most action figures.

Even Hobbit action figures come with armor and swords in their individual or group toy packs. (Two exceptions are ToyBiz's "There and
Back" collection of Hobbits in their post-War finery, with not a weapon in
sight, and Treebeard with Merry and Pippin.)[22] In the books, Tolkien's
most passive characters fight only under duress and the great necessity of
saving Middle-earth. In contrast, the action figures often show Merry and
Pippin in battle gear with swords, or at least carrying a sword. Even Frodo
and Sam, who seldom used weaponry in either the books or films, and are
not in large battle scenes, are portrayed in some toy sets as carrying swords.
Frodo's sword Sting is a toy in its own right.

Other characters are posed for battle, too. Éowyn is dressed in mail and
with a removable helmet, and she carries spear and sword. A separate action
figure shows her in a flowing dress, but she still has an arm with "sword-
slashing action." Gimli and Legolas always have weapons, and even Arwen
has a sword-wielding action figure based on one scene in Jackson's first film
in the trilogy. The emphasis of the series of action toys is more heavily on
war instead of peacetime activities or even the Quest itself. In most cases,
the character's readiness to fight puts the "action" in action figures.

What does that say about Western culture, the perception of the films, and the changing definition of heroes? Although action toys such as GI Joe, Rambo, Xena, and other battle-related characters have been successfully marketed for generations, the perception of *The Lord of the Rings* characters as most often battle driven gives a far different perception of them as heroes than either Jackson's trilogy or Tolkien's original story. Even in Jackson's action-oriented sequences, especially in the final film, there are scenes showing a fearful Pippin, regretful Aragorn, or sentimental Gimli. Tolkien's emphasis was not on warfare, but on the overcoming of evil with good, with a good deal of character development and personal growth along the way.

Children who play with action figures, not just collect them, probably are going to have the characters use their sword-slashing action to fight others. In their role play, are they overcoming evil, or just bashing another character to win? Are they emulating heroic deeds or simply killing?

Older children, teenagers, and adults turn from playing with action figures to simulated role play in videogames. During previews before *The Return of the King*, the latest *Lord of the Rings*–related game showcased battle action sequences that allow players to act as a main character to fight against the "bad guys." To survive a videogame requires overcoming enemies, usually by killing them directly or otherwise ensuring they fall. How many actions in videogames are heroic, and how many are merely violent? In videogames, as with children's play, the emphasis is more likely on violence and winning, with little thought to the meaning of hero or heroic, self-sacrificing deeds.

On the one hand, the mass marketing of Jackson's films allows more people at least to be aware of Tolkien's works and to be more likely to view their adaptation on screen or through other products. Perhaps people who like the current product will return to Tolkien's trilogy to discover his themes of friendship and loyalty in the making of heroes. On the other hand, Tolkien's original message and his perception of heroes as necessary "for a moral meaning in a world of horrors" may be lost in the marketing of special effects and action-oriented products.[23]

Jackson's trilogy does highlight, albeit in different ways, the importance of heroes and provides a whole range of heroes with whom audiences can identify. The films themselves may provide a different interpretation of the heroism of characters, including the seven discussed in this book, but they promote the *ideal* of the hero and of the development of heroic qualities across the individual quests making up the larger journey. However, the marketing of these films emphasizes a much narrower range of actions for characters and limits the types of role play for children and young adults. Children need other outlets, not only war games, to develop a mature worldview, preferably one that is not violent or overly aggressive. Whereas some toys can encourage role play of heroic activities, completed without weapons, other toys encourage violent solutions to problems. Weaponed action figures do not have to involve violent role play, but unfortunately, they often do. This type of role play does not match Tolkien's themes for the books, including one that violence is not the only solution to problems.

The Fine Line between Fiction and Reality

Actors in such a popular series of films are given a great deal of publicity during the course of the promotion of the films. In the case of *The Lord of the Rings*, the publicity machine rolled out in three consecutive years, with other bursts of promotional appearances, photo opportunities, and interviews as the extended DVD versions of each film were released. Through interviews and public appearances, the actors' social, political, environmental, and other concerns were discussed in addition to their work on the respective films. That brings up an important issue of celebrity when the actors from Jackson's hugely popular trilogy took an interest in a political, environment, or social cause.

For example, did Viggo Mortensen's political viewpoint not only gain more media attention because of Aragorn's, and thus the actor's, popularity?—and then did fans of either Mortensen or Aragorn begin to think differently in terms of politics, or to question their own political views? When Dominic Monaghan supported the saving of an old-growth forest, did fans who want to be associated with that cause really begin to value trees—or did they simply want to be linked in whatever small way to Monaghan? When Sean Astin participated in a local right-to-read program as part of Project Elanor, a community-based reading project, did fans create similar programs in their own communities? The power of celebrity can be used to get the audience, in the case of Jackson's trilogy a huge worldwide audience, to become aware of issues. However, the lasting power of celebrity remains to be seen.

Does it matter if a fan's onscreen hero takes a stand that will improve some aspect of humanity? In other words, if the result is a positive action, and it takes the endorsement of an actor who played a hero in a movie to bring public attention to something that needs to be changed, does it matter that the line between onscreen hero and actor activism is blurred? If, for example, more children value books because adults organize a volunteer program to read to them, does it matter how the program came about? If an actor raises money for a good cause, does it matter that people give money because of the actor, not because of the cause?

The line between reality and fantasy often is unclear in a celebrity-driven culture where actors seem like the people next door (if with more money and better looks) because audiences know so many personal details about them and tend to link real people with their character counterparts. Fans performing good deeds because they relate to a beloved actor or character is a strangely late twentieth-, early twenty-first- century phenomenon in Western cultures, and it will be interesting to see if film fans continue to support the actors' pet projects long after the films are part of cinematic history.

To further cloud the issue of celebrity, some actors who play heroes on screen end up acting heroically in real life. In his role as private pilot, Harrison Ford (Indiana Jones, Han Solo) flew to a remote mountain location near his home to save an injured hiker.[24] During the New York City blackout in summer 2003, Sean Astin (Samwise Gamgee) worked with local firefighters and police officers to save people trapped in an elevator; he later directed traffic on a busy Manhattan street, all while waylaid between flights in the city.[25] Instances such as these build the image of the everyperson hero—people, no matter from which social strata, who pitch in to help and end up saving others. Although Ford or Astin may not have been in much personal danger during these heroic ventures, they did face some risk and obviously did not have to step forward to help others.

The power of celebrity often builds the definition of a modern hero, even if *everyperson* may be only in the perception of fans. When actors act heroically like their fictional characters, the value of both the character and the actor increases for fans of either. The actor shows that it is possible to act heroically in real life, not just in the Hollywood version of life, and therefore can serve as a role model as much as his or her onscreen alterego.

The Lasting Influence of the Trilogies

During an interview broadcast in early 2004, a journalist asked a group of actors from the films why the trilogy is so popular now, what it offers modern audiences who obviously do not live in a time of "medieval" upheaval. Dominic Monaghan (Merry) replied that we "want to find the person that we most believe in, the person that will save the day as being the everyday guy . . . because that's us. We think . . . 'Maybe I can do that' . . . It's the normal folk that you empathize with." Billy Boyd (Pippin) concurred: "Somewhere in our subconscious we all understand . . . that the greatest heroes are not Hollywood heroes [that] you know are going to be heroes because they look like heroes."[26]

Film audiences, including readers of Tolkien's trilogy, want to relate to one or more of these heroes, who do not look like the noble, high-born heroes described in classic literature or who do not fit the Hollywood ideal of youth, perfect features, and strong physique. The everyperson hero, which a reader or filmgoer may someday become, looks and acts like one of the "normal folk," stepping forward when needed to intercede on behalf of others. Everyperson heroes stand for, and stand up for, a society's core values and best show what that culture represents.

According to Tolkien, values, not just battle heroics, make heroes. Without some inner strength or core belief on which to act, an individual is not likely to step forward in a crisis and act heroically. A true hero may act impulsively or spontaneously, but there is an inner sense of what is right or why someone or something should be saved—there is something for which to risk one's life.

In the film *The Two Towers*, Sam tells a weary Frodo that there is something worth fighting for, even when their journey is unbelievably difficult.[27] "What are we fighting for, Sam?" Frodo asks. "That there's some good in this world worth saving," Sam replies. Heroes fight for what they value—to save what is good in the world, but they do more than that. They do not always *fight*. They *live* their values and show through their deeds the best that a culture represents. As one scholar notes, "the real danger is not that the free world might be defeated; it is that we might be corrupted, brutalized and degraded by the conflict itself, and in particular by the means we employ to secure victory."[28] The end does not justify the means if the means requires people to act so abominably that they lose sight of the good they are trying to accomplish. Ideally, this "good" is not more money or power, but, for lack of a better word, moral values—decency, kindness, friendship, loyalty, love.

One strength of Tolkien's trilogy is its ability to reach readers at many levels. The heroes show "love, courage, justice, mercy, kindness, integrity, and ... other virtues," and readers' exposure to such virtues, or values, can have a "purifying effect."[29] Of course, some readers may find only an adventure or a mythic history, but many may find something worth emulating from the heroes' struggles and growth. For the many complaints that some readers voice about Jackson's films, his trilogy does show these values in a cinematically valid way, and it introduces to the story many more people who might otherwise never have become familiar with any form of Tolkien's work. As one member of the Tolkien Society writes about the hoopla over the films, "How many copies of the book have been sold—and how many millions of readers does that make? Let's relish the good things the films have given us.... The book is unassailable."[30]

For those who return again and again to the cinemas to see the films, and who purchase the videotapes and DVDs to watch scenes multiple times at home, the films not only bring entertainment but something more as well. No matter how much audiences like a film, they can only watch it so many times without becoming a bit bored with the action alone. Jackson's trilogy also shows characters about whom audiences can care and from whom they can learn. The values of mercy, friendship, loyalty, and love are also portrayed on film.

The unsung heroes discussed in this book have inner strengths and values, although these characters do not realize their depth or power until they are called on in times of crisis. Until Pippin is faced with the loss of his cousins, he may not realize the depth of his love for or commitment to them enough to ensure that he not only survives the battlefront but actually overcomes his fears and natural passivity in order to fight. Until he faces the imminent death of a friend such as Faramir, or Gandalf in the theatrical version of *The Return of the King*, he may not know that love of others will overcome the need for self-preservation. Until Gimli spends nearly every waking moment in the presence of Legolas, he does not know that he can overcome racial prejudice and would willingly die for or alongside an Elf he considers a close friend. At the beginning of each character's story, he or she does not know that the Quest to destroy the One Ring and overthrow its evil power will instead turn into a personal quest to realize some inner strength or to challenge a belief, and eventually to become transformed into a spiritually better, more pragmatically effective member of the larger world.

What do these characters value, and how do their values affect their postwar life, according to Tolkien? Merry values loyalty and knowledge. He eventually spends time conducting research for the books he writes. His wartime experiences give him contacts outside the Shire, and he travels to Rohan, Rivendell, and Gondor as he gathers and shares information and ideas. His codified knowledge shows how the Shire fits agriculturally and linguistically with other cultures in Middle-earth. Although Merry initially likes to wear his livery in public, it is more a matter of pride in connection with and service to his lord, Éomer, than a display of power. Even as a Shire leader, he does not become a warlord or a tyrant but a representative of the Shire in King Elessar's council during more peaceful times. He remains loyal to his friends and continues to visit them, and he works closely with the remnants of the Fellowship during their remaining time in Middle-earth.

Pippin values love, especially that of family and friends, and most especially for Merry. At a much younger age than Merry, Pippin settles into family life with a wife and child. Pippin also serves the Shire and Middle-earth much as Merry does, although as Thain he has more potential power to advise and guide changes in the Shire during peacetime. Pippin creates libraries, perhaps as a reflection of his affection for Frodo and Merry, who write books. His relationships and later-life activities indicate his love of family and homeland.

Éowyn values self-fulfillment and, through that, the best way to serve her people. After the Ring has been destroyed, Éowyn vows to become a healer. She sees self-fulfillment in the future through her role as a leader and nurturer. This is not a rejection of her assertive self and therefore a retreat into a passive role as wife. Éowyn chooses the post-war role for herself and finds in Faramir an equal, not a master. She knows herself and how she can best use her skills—in peacetime, when her skills as a warrior are not needed, she becomes a builder for the future.

Galadriel values the balance of power and sense of history. She recognizes the shift in power away from the Elves and toward humans (listed as "Men" in the book). Now that power is not to be wielded by an evil tyrant, but rather a king she trusts with the future of Middle-earth, Galadriel returns to Valinor from exile. She does not abandon Middle-earth but knows that her work there is completed. She changes location but does not give up. She understands the larger picture of Middle-earth and her place within it, gracefully returning to Valinor at the completion of her tasks.

Arwen values her relationship with Aragorn and puts it above all other relationships. She trades her immortality to become a partner in marriage and in the future direction of Middle-earth. She has achieved what she wanted, not only for Aragorn and Middle-earth, but for herself. Arwen values her role in Aragorn's ascension as the king in a time of peace, but she also receives the personal satisfaction of a love match. She fulfills the destiny she set for herself, even when it has pitted her against Aragorn's and Elrond's wishes for her in the past. Arwen stays focused on her relationship with Aragorn and is true to her vision, even at the price of immortality.

Gimli and Legolas value friendship and loyalty to their friends. Legolas remains in Middle-earth throughout Aragorn's lifetime and travels with Gimli to learn more of the Dwarves. Gimli spends more time with the Elves and learns of their race. Legolas and Gimli honor their continuing friendship, and Gimli even accompanies Legolas when he finally travels to Valinor.

These characters' core values motivate them to acts greater than their self-interest. All are outsiders in at least one way early in the larger story, but they are transformed throughout the Quest into characters who value how they are different from others but who use their unique abilities in ways that better serve others. By the end of the story, they not only have achieved heroic status for one or more specific acts, but more importantly, they value their unique contributions—they understand who they truly are and can use this self-knowledge to improve the world at large.

Tested by war, these characters move into an age of peace. They know how to protect their lands, friends, and families, but they are not defensive or proactive in their protection. Tolkien does not write that they completely isolate themselves or plan to go to war against their neighbors. They are not territorial to try to conquer others, but they do respect their neighbors' boundaries. Although the Shire is placed off limits to Men, who cannot enter without the permission of Shire leaders, and the boundaries marking the Shire from other lands are clarified, the Hobbits do not become isolated from others.

As previously mentioned, Sam, Pippin, and Merry at least continue their association with the outside world and play a part in the larger politics outside the Shire. Knowledge gained from other cultures becomes part of Shirelore through the books created and collected in the years after the war. Armies are kept for protection, and King Elessar makes the effort to create a council in which members of many lands participate. For Tolkien, war is not the answer to conflict, and the time of peace is the desired end to the Quest. Those who displayed heroism during the many crises of the War now can turn their attention to the higher matters of living well in peace; their heroism takes the form of peaceful activism to change, and improve, the lives of those back in their respective communities.

Tolkien's heroes also illustrate the value of collective action, not just individual courage and self-sacrifice. Individual effort can sway the course of great events, but it takes working together for the Quest to be successful. Even the Fellowship required nine members, representing the different races of Middle-earth, to begin the Quest. Throughout the War of the Ring, several races draw together to defeat a common enemy. Leaders in the postwar era meet to keep the peace and discuss issues. Successful endeavors require such cooperative action.

This aspect of heroism in Tolkien's trilogy is also emphasized, although to a lesser degree, in Jackson's trilogy. In the early 2000s, especially in the United States, reality television programs encourage the concept of only one "winner" in any competition. The objective in winning—whether the prize be a million dollars, a job, a fiancé, or a recording contract—is to beat out all others. On U.S. television series like *Survivor*, alliances and cooperation are only important in the short term to help one group eliminate another from the competition. Once the number of competitors dwindles, the former alliances are abandoned, and each player performs all manner of tricks not only to win the prize, but to wipe out all other competitors. Individual, not collective, action is praised, and the strongest—or most devious—player ends up with the prize.

That reality does not operate in Tolkien's or Jackson's trilogy. In fact, just the opposite strategy is needed for success. The characters who act alone or use others only to further personal gain (e.g., Saruman, Sauron, Gollum) are the characters who lose their lives or fortunes because of their greed for power. Although both Tolkien and Jackson showcase heroic individuals' actions, the heroic characters do not act to gain power for themselves. Some, like Galadriel, refuse ultimate power, as she does when she rejects Frodo's offer of the One Ring. Many, such as Merry, Pippin, Gimli, and Legolas, seem immune to the lure of the Ring. Individual heroics ultimately serve the greater cause, and collective action creates positive change in Middle-earth.

This difference highlights a schism in popular culture between interest in money and power—as shown in the popularity of reality television programs—and the interest in a simple, family- and friend-oriented life— as shown in *The Lord of the Rings*. Many U.S. communities drew together after September 11, 2001, and the spirit of togetherness is still strong in many nations. It will be interesting to see if the trend in reality television programming is truly representative of a shift in values, or if the values espoused in Tolkien's work will be the ones that endure. The "winners" of these reality-show competitions seem to have fleeting celebrity; Tolkien's influence has already survived for fifty years.

The themes in book and film illustrate the best that men and women can offer, and the characters illustrate both the heroism of past generations and the relevance of trying to do one's best, often against incredible odds, in modern life. Groups as divergent as veterans of World Wars I and II, U.S. hippies during the 1960s, videogame players in the early 2000s, and female fanfiction writers on the Internet have read their own culture- and time-specific meanings into this tale of good versus evil and the survival of hope and love in the face of destruction. Undoubtedly, future generations will latch onto some aspect of the story as a metaphor for their world.

As the definitions of hero change for future readers and filmgoers, so too will the characters and events in *The Lord of the Rings* take on new meanings. Tolkien's books and Jackson's films create a heroic myth, but it is up to the readers and audiences of these works to follow their favorite hero(es) and make the myth anew for themselves.

Notes

Preface

1. Graham Fuller, "Kingdom Come," *Film Comment* Jan.–Feb. 2004: 24–29.

Introduction

1. Ken Gelder, "Epic Fantasy and Global Terrorism," *Overland* Summer 2003: 21–27.

2. Chris Lavigne, "Weapons Inspectors in Mordor?" *The Republic* 9 Jan. 2003: 1, 7.

3. James Bell, "Viggo (Strider/Aragorn) & Elijah (Frodo) Speak Out Against a War in Iraq," Transcript from the *Charlie Rose Show*, 21 Dec. 2003, 14 April 2004, http://www.lastwizards.com/pages/modules.php?name=News&file=articl&sid=40.

Chapter 1

1. Cath Filmer-Davies, "King Arthur in the Marketplace, King Arthur in the Myth," *Mythlore* Summer 1996: 12. The quotation as well as information about tourism involving Arthurian sites can be found in this article.

2. Imogen Tilden, "*Lord of the Rings* Musical Planned for London Stage." *Guardian Unlimited* 23 May 2003, 24 Jan. 2004, http://www.guardian.co.uk/arts/news/story/ 0,11711,965572, 00.html.

3. TheOneRingNet (TORN). "ROTK Play in Cincinnati." 3 Oct. 2003, 24 Jan. 2004, http://www.theonering.net/perl/newsview/8/1065188752.

4. Ian Brodie, The Lord of the Rings *Guidebook*. Rev. ed. (Auckland, N.Z.: HarperCollins, 2003). Books like Brodie's encourage fans to visit New Zealand. Tour operators within the country indicate that the film locations may intrigue visitors and prompt them to come to New Zealand, but the country itself attracts repeat visitors or makes first-time visitors want to return. This seems particularly true of guests who have been brought up in urban areas. Melissa Heath, the owner of and guide for Wanaka Sightseeing in the Otago region, where many of the films' scenes were shot, notes that visitors often are surprised they "can travel all day without seeing another soul other than in passing cars" (p. 137). She also believes that New Zealanders, on the whole, are less stressed than visitors from other countries. Heath believes that interest in Jackson's trilogy will continue for years to come (Amanda Cropp, "Ringleader," *Next, 240* (July 2004), 132–134, 137).

5. Lord Raglan (Baron FitzRoy Richard Somerset Raglan), *The Hero*. Reprint. (New York: Dover, 2003). The book first was published in 1936. A list of the twenty-two characteristics of a classic literary hero can be found in this book, but the list also has been included in Leslie Ellen Jones's *Myth and Middle-Earth*.

6. Leslie Ellen Jones, "Chapter 9. Kings and Heroes," *Myth and Middle-earth* (Cold Spring Harbor, N.H.: Cold Spring Press, 2001), 114.

7. Northrop Frye, *Anatomy of Criticism: Four Essays* (Princeton, N.J.: Princeton University Press, 1957).

8. *The Lord of the Rings: The Fellowship of the Ring*, Dir. Peter Jackson, Prods. Barrie M. Osborne, Peter Jackson, and Fran Walsh, New Line Cinema, 2001; Scenes 18. "The Spoiling of Isengard" and 22. "Rivendell" show, respectively, Gandalf's communication and his escape.

9. *Fellowship of the Ring*, 2001, Scene 33. "Moria."

10. *The Lord of the Rings: The Two Towers*, Dir. Peter Jackson, Prods. Barrie M. Osborne, Peter Jackson, and Fran Walsh, New Line Cinema, 2002, Scene 15. "The White Rider."

11. *The Lord of the Rings: The Return of the King*, Dir. Peter Jackson, Prods. Barrie M. Osborne, Peter Jackson, and Fran Walsh, New Line Cinema, 2003, Scene 57. "The Return of the King."

12. Joseph Campbell, *The Hero with a Thousand Faces*, 2nd ed. (Princeton, N.J.: University of Princeton Press, 1968).

13. Almira F. Poudrier, "The Virtue of the Weaponed Hero," *The Humanist* July–Aug. 2001: 35.

14. Poudrier, Ibid.

15. Patrick Curry, *Defending Middle-earth: Tolkien, Myth, and Modernity* (New York: St. Martin's Press, 1997), 164.

16. Ibid., 165.

17. Colin Duriez, *Tolkien and* The Lord of the Rings: *A Guide to Middle-earth* (London: HiddenSpring, 2001), 194–195.

18. *Return of the King*, 2003, Scene 14. "The Lighting of the Beacons."

19. Ibid., Scene 35. "The Ride of the Rohirrim."

20. Ibid., Scene 37. "The Battle of the Pelennor Fields."

21. Simon Gray, "The Fate of Middle-earth," *American Cinematographer* Jan. 2004: 56.

22. Ibid., 66.

23. Ian Spelling, "The Middle-earth Years," *Starlog* Feb. 2004: 50.

24. *The Lord of the Rings: The Return of the King*, CD soundtrack, Composer Howard Shore, Exec. Album Prods. Peter Jackson, Fran Walsh, and Paul Broucek, 2003, Cut 2. "Hope and Memory."

25. *Return of the King*, 2003, Scene 6. "The Palantír."

26. *Fellowship of the Ring*, 2001, Scene 6. "Farewell Dear Bilbo."

27. Ibid., Scene 17. "The Midgewater Marshes."

28. *Return of the King*, 2003, Scene. 57. "The Return of the King."

29. *Two Towers*, 2002, Scene 21. "The Funeral of Théodred."

30. *Fellowship of the Ring*, 2001, Scene 38. "Caras Galadhon."

31. Ibid., Scene 9. "At the Green Dragon."

32. *Return of the King*, 2003, Scene 4. "Return to Edoras."

33. Ibid., Scene 20. "The Sacrifice of Faramir."

34. Ibid., Scene 58. "Homeward Bound."

35. Ian Nathan, "Peter Jackson. Part 1," *Empire* Jan. 2004: 90.

36. Paul Watson, "Fellowship of the Script: An Adaptation of *The Two Towers*," *Screentalk* Nov.–Dec. 2002: 42.

37. Ibid., 45.

38. *Return of the King*, 2003, Scene 40. "The Black Ships."

39. Ibid., Scene 50. "The Last Move."

40. George Clark, "J. R. R. Tolkien and the True Hero," *J. R. R. Tolkien and His Literary Resonances* (George Clark and Daniel Timmons, Eds., Westport, Conn.: Greenwood Press, 2000), 44.

41. Roger Kaufman, "Lord of the Rings Taps a Gay Archetype," *The Gay and Lesbian Review Worldwide* July–Aug. 2003, 20 May 2004, http://gateway.proquest. com/openurl? url_ver=Z3988–2004&res_dat=xri:pqd&rft_val_fmt=info:of/journal& genre=article&rft_dat=xri:pqd:didi000000621098771&svc_dat=xri:pqil:fmt=text& req_dat=xri:pqil:pq_clntid=17916

42. *Two Towers*, 2002, Scene 51. "The Breach of the Deeping Wall."

43. *Return of the King*, 2003, Scene 40. "The Black Ships."

44. *Two Towers*, 2002, Scene 48. "The Host of the Eldar."

45. Clark, "J. R. R. Tolkien and the True Hero." An excellent analysis of Sam's role as ultimate hero is found in this chapter, especially pages 47–49.

46. Petty, *Tolkien in the Land of Heroes*, 259–260.

47. J. R. R. Tolkien, *The Lord of the Rings: The Return of the King* (New York: Ballantine, 1965), 54, is one example of this sentiment, when Merry feels like baggage, as written in the chapter "The Passing of the Grey Company." Another example is Pippin's lament that he is luggage, as written in J. R. R. Tolkien, *The Lord of the Rings: The Two Towers* (New York: Ballantine, 1965), 59, in the chapter "The Uruk-hai."

48. *Two Towers*, 2002, Scene 26. "A Daughter of Kings."

Chapter 2

1. J. R. R. Tolkien, *The Lord of the Rings: The Fellowship of the Ring* (New York: Ballantine, 1965), 19.

2. Ibid., 20.

3. Roger Ebert, "Review. *Lord of the Rings: The Fellowship of the Ring*," *Chicago Sun-Times* 19 Dec. 2001, 26 April 2004, http://www.suntimes.com/ebert/ebert_reviews/ 2001/12/121901.html.

4. Roger Ebert, "Review. *Lord of the Rings: The Two Towers*," *Chicago Sun-Times* 18 Dec. 2002, 26 April 2004, http://www.suntimes.com/ebert/ebert_reviews/2002/12/121801.html.

5. Deborah C. Rogers, "Everyclod and Everyhero: The Image of Man in Tolkien," *A Tolkien Compass* (Jared Lobdell, Ed., Chicago: Open Court, 2003), 69–70.

6. Tolkien, *Fellowship of the Ring*, 31.

7. Tolkien, *The Return of the King*, appendix C, 476–477.

8. Campbell, *The Hero with a Thousand Faces*.

9. Tolkien, 37–39. In the "Note on the Shire Records," Tolkien describes how histories of the Hobbits, as well as lore from the Shire, Gondor, and Rohan, become part of the great libraries at the Great Smials and Brandy Hall. Merry's role in the creation and collection of information is explained.

10. Marion Zimmer Bradley, "Men, Halflings, and Hero Worship," *Tolkien and the Critics: Essays on J. R. R. Tolkien's* The Lord of the Rings (N. D. Isaacs and R. A. Zimbardo, Eds., Notre Dame, Ind.: University of Notre Dame Press, 1968), 112.

11. Joe Kraus, "Tolkien, Modernism, and the Importance of Tradition," The Lord of the Rings and Philosophy: One Book to Rule Them All (Gregory Bassham and Eric Bronson, Eds., Chicago: Open Court Press, 2003), 145.

12. Tolkien, *Fellowship of the Ring*, 38–39.

13. Tolkien, *Fellowship of the Ring*, summarized from the chapters, "Three Is Company" (99–124), "A Short Cut to Mushrooms" (124–140), and "A Conspiracy Unmasked" (141–154).

14. Tolkien, *Fellowship of the Ring*, summarized from the chapter "Many Meetings" (289–313).

15. Tolkien, *The Two Towers*, 77.

16. Tolkien, *Fellowship of the Ring*, 37–39.

17. Kathryn W. Crabbe, "The Quest as Legend: *The Lord of the Rings*," *Modern Critical Interpretations: J. R. R. Tolkien's* The Lord of the Rings (Harold Bloom, Ed., Philadelphia: Chelsea House, 2000), 141–170.

18. Tolkien, *Fellowship of the Ring*, 142.

19. Tolkien, *Fellowship of the Ring*, summarized from the chapter "The Old Forest" (155–171).

20. Petty, *Tolkien in the Land of Heroes*, 237.

21. Tolkien, *Two Towers*, 208.

22. Tolkien, *Return of the King*, summarized from the chapter "The Muster of Rohan" (76–94).

23. Tolkien, *Fellowship of the Ring*, 38.

24. Ibid., 150.

25. Tolkien, *Return of the King*, 128.

26. Ibid., 177–179.

27. Ibid., 196.

28. Tolkien, *Return of the King*, summarized from the chapter "The Scouring of the Shire" (342–371). The description of Merry's actions through the Battle of Bywater are found in this chapter.

29. Ibid., 353.

30. Bradley, "Men, Halflings, and Hero Worship," 115.

31. Randel Helms, *Tolkien's World* (Boston: Houghton Mifflin, 1974), 106.

32. Anne C. Petty, *One Ring to Bind Them All: Tolkien's Mythology* (University: University of Alabama Press, 1979), 90.

33. Tolkien, *Return of the King*, 364.

34. Ibid., 373.

35. Ibid., 377.

36. Guy Haley, "*The Lord of the Rings: The Return of the King*. Review," *SFX* Feb. 2004: 24.

37. Bob Longino, "Hobbits Loom Large on Heroism Scale," *The Age* 9 Jan. 2004, 15 Jan. 2004, http://theage.com.au.

38. Ian Spelling, "Merry Man," *Dreamwatch* Dec. 2003: 42.

39. Stephen Eramo, "Frodo's Friend," *British Heritage* Sept. 2004: 22.

40. *The Fellowship of the Ring*, "Scene 13. A Short Cut to Mushrooms."

41. Ibid., Scene 14. "Bucklebury Ferry."

42. Ibid., Scene 16. "The Nazgûl."

43. Ibid., Scene 27. "The Council of Elrond."

44. Ibid., Scene 44. "The Breaking of the Fellowship."

45. Brian Sibley, The Lord of the Rings *Official Movie Guide* (Boston: Houghton Mifflin, 2001), 55.

46. Steven Eramo, "A Very Merry Man," *Xposé Special 24* 2003: 23–24.

47. Ibid., 20.

48. *Fellowship of the Ring*, Scene 5. "A Long-Expected Party."

49. Ibid., Scene 13. "A Short Cut to Mushrooms."

50. Ibid., Scene 16. "The Nazgûl."

51. Ibid., Scene 31. "The Ring Goes South."

52. Ibid., Scene 34. "A Journey in the Dark."

53. Ibid., Scene 36. "The Bridge of Khazad-Dûm."

54. *The Two Towers*, Scene 10. "Night Camp at Fangorn."

55. Ibid., Scene 4. "The Uruk-hai."

56. Ibid., Scene 10. "Night Camp at Fangorn."

57. Ibid., Scene 13. "Treebeard."

58. Ibid., Scene 19. "Ent Draft."

59. Ibid., Scene 63. "Flotsam and Jetsam."

60. Ibid., Scene 47. " 'Don't Be Hasty, Master Meriadoc!' "

61. Nick Joy, "Force of Hobbit: Billy Boyd & Dominic Monaghan," *Film Review* Dec. 2003: 39.

62. *Return of the King*, Scene 6. "The Palantír."

63. Ibid.

64. Ibid., Scene 44. "Oaths Fulfilled." Although the title of this scene refers to the Army of the Dead's oath, which is fulfilled to the King of Gondor (currently Aragorn), the title also is appropriate for Pippin. He shares an unspoken promise of loyalty and care with Merry and in this scene begins to fulfill this promise to his elder cousin. The scene also indicates Pippin's future oath to Merry, as he solemnly speaks this line.

65. Ibid., Scene 59. "The Grey Havens."

66. *Fellowship of the Ring*, Scene 19. "A Knife in the Dark."

67. Ibid., Scene 31. "The Ring Goes South."

68. Ibid., Scene 35. "Balin's Tomb."

69. Ibid., Scene 36. "The Bridge of Khazad-Dûm."

70. *The Lord of the Rings: The Two Towers*, Theatrical Version DVD, Dir. Peter Jackson, Prods. Barrie M. Osborne, Peter Jackson, and Fran Walsh, New Line Cinema, 2002, Special Features, "Behind the Scenes Preview 'The Return of the King.'"

71. *Return of the King*, Scene 26. "The Muster of Rohan."

72. Ibid., Scene 35. "The Ride of the Rohirrim."

73. Tolkien, *Return of the King*, 142–143.

74. *Return of the King*, Scene 21. "Marshalling at Dunharrow."

75. Ibid., Scene 26. "The Muster of Rohan."

76. Lawrence French, "All Hail the King, Part 1," *Cinefantastique* Dec. 2003–Jan. 2004: 33.

77. *Return of the King*, Scene 50. "The Last Move."

78. Ibid., Scene 58. "Homeward Bound."

79. Ian Spelling, "Standing Small," *Starlog* Jan. 2004: 57.

80. *Return of the King*, Scene 58. "Homeward Bound."

81. Ibid., Scene 59. "The Grey Havens."

82. Tolkien, *Fellowship of the Ring*, 20.

83. Bob Longino, "Hobbits Loom Large on Heroism Scale." *The Age* 9 Jan. 2004, 15. Jan. 2004 <http://theage.com.au>.

84. Greg Harvey, *The Origins of Tolkien's Middle-earth for Dummies* (Hoboken, N.J.: Wiley, 2003), 126–127.

85. *Fellowship of the Ring*, Scene 29. "Bilbo's Gifts."

86. *Two Towers*, Scene 63. "Flotsam and Jetsam."

87. *Return of the King*, Scene 3. "The Road to Isengard."

88. *Fellowship of the Ring*, Scene 41. "Farewell to Lorien."

89. Ibid., Scene 33. "Moria."

90. Haley, *"The Return of the King.* Review," 73.

91. Brian Roseburg, *Tolkien: A Cultural Phenomenon* (New York: Palgrave Macmillan, 2003), 48.

92. Tolkien, *Return of the King*, appendix C, 474–477.

93. Ibid., summarized from the chapter "Homeward Bound" (331–341).

94. Ibid., 179.

95. *Return of the King*, Scene 35. "The Ride of the Rohirrim."

96. Ibid., Scene 37. "The Battle of the Pelennor Fields."

97. Ibid., Scene 41. "Shieldmaiden of Rohan."

98. Ibid., Scene 44. "Oaths Fulfilled."

99. Tolkien, *Return of the King*, 163–165.

100. *Return of the King*, Scene 56. "The Fellowship Reunited."

101. Ibid., Scene 58. "Homeward Bound."

102. Ibid., Scene 59. "The Grey Havens."

103. Nick Joy, "Small Soldier," *Starburst* Oct. 2003: 34.

104. A&E *Breakfast with the Arts*, "The Making of *The Lord of the Rings*," 11 Jan. 2004, A&E network.

105. Grand Maiden, "Dominic Monaghan: Merry the Hobbit," *Pavement* Dec. 2002–Jan. 2003: 106.

106. Tolkien, *Return of the King*, 165.

107. Ibid., 195.

108. Ibid., 316.

109. *Return of the King*, Scene 57. The Return of the King.

110. Joe Kraus, "Tolkien, Modernism, and the Importance of Tradition," Gregory Bassham and Eric Bronson (Eds.). The Lord of the Rings *and Philosophy: One Book to Rule Them All*. Chicago: Open Court Press, 2003, 145.

111. Tolkien, *Fellowship of the Ring*, 37–39.

112. *Two Towers*, Scene 52. "The Entmoot Decides."

113. Jane Chance Nitzsche, "*The Lord of the Rings:* Tolkien's Epic," *Modern Critical Interpretations: J. R. R. Tolkien's* The Lord of the Rings (Harold Bloom, Ed., Philadelphia: Chelsea House, 2000), 100.

114. Helms, *Tolkien's World*, 102.

115. Petty, *One Ring to Bind Them All*, 90.

116. *Two Towers*, Scene 11. "The Riders of Rohan."

117. *Return of the King*, Scene 26. "The Muster of Rohan."

118. *Two Towers*, Scene 13. "Treebeard."

Chapter 3

1. Shanti Fader, "A Fool's Hope," *Parabola* Fall 2001: 51.

2. Tolkien, *The Return of the King*, 203.

3. *The Return of the King*, Scene 9. "Minas Tirith."

4. Joy, "Force of Hobbit: Billy Boyd & Dominic Monaghan," 39.

5. Tolkien, *Return of the King*, 153.

6. Ibid., 207–208.

7. Ibid., 357, 363–365.

8. *The Fellowship of the Ring*, Scene 13. "A Short Cut to Mushrooms."

9. *Return of the King*, Scene 6. "The Palantír."

10. Tolkien, *The Two Towers*, 73–74.

11. *The Two Towers*, Scene 52. "The Entmoot Decides."

12. Tolkien, *Return of the King*, 61.

13. Alan K. Wheatley, "Can We Have Our Book Back?" *Amon Hen* March 2004: 17.

14. Ibid., 15.

15. J. E. A. Tyler, *The Tolkien Companion* (New York: St. Martin's Press, 1976), 38.

16. Tolkien, *Return of the King*, 47.

17. Harvey, *The Origins of Tolkien's Middle-earth for Dummies*, 119.

18. Tyler, *The Tolkien Companion*, 466.

19. Tolkien, *Return of the King*, 97.

20. Tolkien, *The Fellowship of the Ring*, 30.

21. Ibid., 71.

22. Ibid., summarized from the chapter "A Shortcut to Mushrooms" (125–140).

23. Ibid., 233.

24. Ibid., summarized from the chapters "A Knife in the Dark" (238–263) and "Flight to the Ford" (264–286)

25. Ibid., 275–276.

26. Ibid., 361–362.

27. Ibid., 362.

28. Ibid., 408. The further description of this scene is summarized from the chapter "A Journey in the Dark" (385–416).

29. Tolkien, *The Two Towers*, 65.

30. Ibid.

31. Ibid., *Two Towers*, 73.

32. Tolkien, *Return of the King*, 153–154.

33. Ibid., 207–208.

34. Ibid., 287–288.

35. Ibid., 357, 364–365.

36. Ibid., 373.

37. Ibid., 340.

38. Ibid., 384–385.

39. *Fellowship of the Ring*, Scene 5. "A Long-Expected Party."

40. Ibid., Scene 13. "A Short Cut to Mushrooms."

41. Ibid., Scene 15. "At the Sign of the Prancing Pony."

42. Ibid., Scene 16. "The Nazgûl."

43. *Two Towers*, Scene 63. "Flotsam and Jetsam."

44. *Fellowship of the Ring*, Scene 19. "A Knife in the Dark."

45. Ibid., Scene 27. "The Council of Elrond."

46. *Two Towers*, Scene 19. "Ent Draft."

47. Ibid., Scene 63. "Flotsam and Jetsam."

48. *Return of the King*, Scene 3. "The Road to Isengard."

49. Ibid., Scene 10. "The Deep Breath Before the Plunge."

50. Ibid., Scene 58. "Homeward Bound."

51. Derek Robinson, "The Hasty Stroke Goes Oft Astray: Tolkien and Humor," *J. R. R. Tolkien: The Far Land* (Robert Giddings, Ed., London: Vision Press, 1983), 119.

52. *Fellowship of the Ring*, Scene 35. "Balin's Tomb."

53. Carla Atkinson, "The Artful Dodger," *The Lord of the Rings Fan Club Official Movie Magazine* April–May 2003: 39.

54. *Fellowship of the Ring*, Scene 35. "Balin's Tomb."

55. Ibid.

56. Ibid., Scene 36. "The Bridge of Khazad-dûm."

57. Ibid., Scene 44. "The Breaking of the Fellowship."

58. Ibid., Scene 45. "The Departure of Boromir."

59. *Return of the King*, Scene 9. "Minas Tirith."

60. *Two Towers*, Scene 4. "The Uruk-hai."

61. Ibid., Scene 10. "Night Camp at Fangorn."

62. Ibid., Scene 54. "Master Peregrin's Plan."

63. Ian Spelling, "Middle-shipman," *Starlog* Dec. 2003: 62.

64. *Two Towers*, Scene 54. "Master Peregrin's Plan."

65. *Return of the King*, Scene 3. "The Road to Isengard."

66. Ibid., Scene 6. "The Palantír."

67. Ibid.

68. Ibid., Scene 9. "Minas Tirith."

69. Ibid.

70. Ibid., Scene 10. "The Deep Breath Before the Plunge."

71. A&E *Breakfast with the Arts*, "The Making of *The Lord of the Rings*."

72. Tyler, *The Tolkien Compass*, 304.

73. *Return of the King*, Scene 10. "The Deep Breath Before the Plunge." Pippin is shown looking over his uniform, complete with sword, as he speaks with Gandalf. Throughout this scene, however, he wears the white shirt of his civilian clothing.

74. Roseburg, *Tolkien: A Cultural Phenomenon*, 164.

75. *Return of the King*, Scene 12. "The Board is Set. . . ."

76. Ibid., Scene 14. "The Lighting of the Beacons."

77. Ibid., Scene 34. "Denethor's Madness."

78. Ibid., Scene 35. "The Ride of the Rohirrim."

79. Ibid., Scene 36. "The Pyre of Denethor."

80. Ibid., Scene 28. "The Siege of Gondor."

81. Ibid., Scene 50. "The Last Move."

82. *Fellowship of the Ring*, Scene 16. "The Nazgûl."

83. Ibid., Scene 35. "Balin's Tomb."

84. Ibid., Scene 17. "The Midgewater Marshes."

85. Ibid., Scene 34. "A Journey in the Dark."

86. Ibid., Scene 31. "The Ring Goes South."

87. *Two Towers*, Scene 4. "The Uruk-hai."

88. Ibid., Scene 10. "Night Camp at Fangorn."

89. *Return of the King*, Scene 14. "The Lighting of the Beacons."

90. Ibid., Scene 36. "The Pyre of Denethor."

91. Ibid., Scene 44. "Oaths Fulfilled."

92. Tolkien, *Return of the King*, 207–208.

93. Ibid., 289.

94. *Fellowship of the Ring*, Scene 41. "Farewell to Lórien."

95. Ibid., Scene 20. "The Sacrifice of Faramir."

96. *Return of the King*, Scene 28. "The Siege of Gondor."

97. Ibid., Scene 44. "Oaths Fulfilled."

98. Ibid., Scene 38. "A Far Green Country."

99. Ibid., Scene 44. "Oaths Fulfilled."

100. Tolkien, *Return of the King*, 203.

101. Ibid., 207.

102. Ibid., 208.

103. Tom Shippey, "From Page to Screen," *World Literature Today* July–Sept. 2003. ProQuest. 20 May 2004, http://gateway.proquest.com/openurl?url_ver= Z39.88–2004&res_dat= xri:pqd&rft_val_fmt=info:ofi/fmt:kev:mtx:journal&genre= article&rft_dat=xri:pqd:did=000000454795721&svc_dat=xri:pqil:fmt=text&req_ dat=xri:pqil:pq_cintid=17916.

104. *Return of the King*, Scene 38. "A Far Green Country."

105. Damian Christie, "Billy Boyd: Pippin the Hobbit," *Pavement* Dec. 2002– Jan. 2003: 110.

106. Tolkien, *Return of the King*, 30–31.

107. Ibid., 59.

108. Ibid., 95–98.

109. Ibid., 58–59, 93.

110. Ibid., 83–88.

111. Ibid., 90.

112. Ibid., 120.

113. Ibid., 93.

114. Ibid., 150–159.

115. Ibid., 93.

116. Ibid., 142–143.

117. Ibid., 143–144.

118. Michael N. Stanton, *Hobbits, Elves, and Wizards: Exploring the Wonders and Worlds of J. R. R. Tolkien's* The Lord of the Rings (New York: Palgrave, 2001), 75.

119. Tolkien, *Fellowship of the Ring*, 38, and *Return of the King*, appendix B 472.

120. Petty, *Tolkien in the Land of Heroes*, 208.

121. *Return of the King*, Scene 20. "The Sacrifice of Faramir."

122. Ibid., Scene 10. "The Deep Breath Before the Plunge."

Chapter 4

1. Cover, *Xposé* January 2003 (Issue 75).

2. *Return of the King*, Scene 41. "Shieldmaiden of Rohan."

3. Richard Alleva, "Peter Jackson's Sorcery: *The Lord of the Rings* Trilogy," *Commonweal* 30 Jan. 2004, 5 May 2004, http://www.commonwealmagazine.org/ 2004/january302004/013004_mv.htm.

4. *Return of the King*, Scene 57. "The Return of the King." Reports from Comic Con 2004, held in San Diego, California, in July, indicate that Faramir's and Éowyn's relationship is developed more fully in scenes added to the extended version DVD (Xoanon, "Comic-Con: ROTK EE DVD Panel Review!" TheOne Ring.net, 24 July 2004, 24 July 2004, http://www.theonering.net/perl/newsview/8/1090681214). The theatrical version only brings the two characters together in the final "group" scene, and they appear to have developed a bond by that time.

5. *Two Towers*, Scene 20. "The King of the Golden Hall."

6. Ibid., Scene 8. "The Banishment of Éomer."

7. Ibid. Éowyn tends the wounded Théodred during part of this scene; she also tries to talk with Théoden. By Scene 20, Théodred has died, and Éowyn mourns him at his bedside. She also tells Théoden of his son's death.

8. Ibid., Scene 23. "The King's Decision."

9. Tyler, *The Tolkien Compass*, 157.

10. Tolkien, *Return of the* King, 314.

11. Ibid., 93.

12. Ibid., 291–294.

13. Claire E. White, "Talking Tolkien with Thomas Shippey," March 2002, 8 May 2004, http://www.writerswrite.com/journal/mar02/shippey.htm.

14. Humphrey Carpenter, "Letter 214. From a draft to a reader of *The Lord of the Rings*," *The Letters of J. R. R. Tolkien* (Boston: Houghton Mifflin, 1981), 323.

15. Ibid.

16. Tolkien, *Return of the King*, 292–293.

17. Ibid., 315–316.

18. Ibid., 276.

19. *Two Towers*, Scene 20. "The King of the Golden Hall."

20. Tolkien, *Two Towers*, 152.

21. Ian Spelling, "Sword of Éowyn," *Fantasy Worlds* Feb. 2004: 31.

22. Helen Barlow, "The Warrior Woman," *The Lord of the Rings: The Two Towers, Souvenir Edition, The New Zealand Herald*, 10 Dec. 2002, 11.

23. *Two Towers*, Scene 8. "The Banishment of Éomer."

24. Ibid., Scene 20. "The King of the Golden Hall."

25. Ibid.

26. Ibid., Scene 8. "The Banishment of Éomer."

27. Ibid., Scene 20. "The King of the Golden Hall."

28. Ibid.

29. Ibid.

30. *Return of the King*, Scene 43. "The Passing of Théoden."

31. *Two Towers*, Scene 26. "A Daughter of Kings."

32. *Return of the King*, Scene 15. "Théoden's Decision."

33. Ibid., Scene 23. "Aragorn Takes the Paths of the Dead."

34. Ibid., Scene 24. "No More Despair."

35. Dan Madsen, "Thwarted Heroine," *The Lord of the Rings Fan Club Official Movie Magazine* Feb.–March 2003: 40.

36. *Return of the King*, Scene 26. "The Muster of Rohan."

37. Ibid., Scene 15. "Théoden's Decision."

38. Catherine O'Donnell, "The Women of Middle-Earth," *Catholic Exchange* 18 Dec. 2003, 5 May 2004, http://www.catholicexchange.com/VM/Pfarticle.asp? vm_id=2&art_id=21650 &sec_id=41243.

39. *Return of the King*, Scene 35. "The Ride of the Rohirrim."

40. Ibid., Scene 37. "The Battle of the Pelennor Fields."

41. Ibid., Scene 39. "The Nazgûl and His Prey."

42. Ibid., Scene 43. "The Passing of Théoden."

43. Nitzsche, "*The Lord of the Rings*: Tolkien's Epic," 99.

44. *Return of the King*, Scene 37. "The Battle of the Pelennor Fields."

45. Ibid., Scene 39. "The Nazgûl and His Prey."

46. Ibid., Scene 57. "The Return of the King."

47. *Two Towers*, Scene 20. "The King of the Golden Hall."

48. *Return of the King*, Scene 57. "The Return of the King."

49. *Two Towers*, Scene 45. "The Glittering Caves."

50. *Return of the King*, Scene 23. "Aragorn Takes the Paths of the Dead."

51. *Two Towers*, Scene 33. "The Evenstar."

52. *Return of the King*, Scene 4. "Return to Edoras."

53. Tolkien, *Return of the King*, 66–68.

54. Ibid., 68.

55. Ibid.

56. Tolkien, *Return of the King*, 69.

57. *Two Towers*, Scene 26. "A Daughter of Kings."

58. Ibid., Scene 61. "Fangorn Comes to Helm's Deep." In the extended version, this brief snippet of Éowyn greeting Aragorn was added at the end of Scene 61. It occurred earlier in the theatrical version.

59. *Return of the King*, Scene 4. "Return to Edoras."

60. Ibid., Scene 23. "Aragorn Takes the Paths of the Dead."

61. Tolkien, *Return of the King*, 300.

62. Harvey, *The Origins of Tolkien's Middle-earth for Dummies*, 300.

63. *Two Towers*, Scene 32. "One of the Dúnedain."

64. "Let Slip the Dogs of War," *Xposé* Jan. 2003: 18.

65. *Two Towers*, Scene 31. "Dwarf Women."

66. Ibid., Scene 21. "The Funeral of Théodred."

67. Ian Spelling, "Warrior Princess," *Starlog* March 2004: 35.

68. Tolkien, *Return of the King*, 291–300.

69. Catherine O'Donnell, "The Women of Middle-Earth."*Catholic Exchange* 18 Dec. 2003, 5 May 2004 <http://www.catholicexchange.com/vm/Pfarticle.asp? vm_id=2&art_id=21650&sec_id=41243>.

70. Tolkien, *Return of the King*, 373–375.

71. W. A. Senior, "Loss Eternal in J. R. R. Tolkien's Middle-earth," *J. R. R. Tolkien and His Literary Resonances* (George Clark and Daniel Timmons, Eds., Westport, Conn.: Greenwood Press, 2000), 179.

72. *Return of the King*, Scene 26. "The Muster of Rohan."

73. *Two Towers*, Scene 34. "The Wolves of Isengard."

74. *Return of the King*, Scene 26. "The Muster of Rohan."

75. *Two Towers*, Scene 20. "The King of the Golden Hall."

76. *Return of the King*, Scene 43. "The Passing of Théoden."

77. Spelling, "Warrior Princess," 36.

Chapter 5

1. Tolkien, *Fellowship of the Ring*, 486, 490.

2. Tolkien, *Return of the King*, 312–313.

3. J. R. R. Tolkien, *The Silmarillion* (Boston: Houghton Mifflin, 1977), 61.

4. Humphrey Carpenter (Ed.), "Letter 354 to Priscilla Tolkien," *The Letters of J. R. R. Tolkien* (Boston: Houghton Mifflin, 1981), 431.

5. Tyler, *The Tolkien Companion*, 189–190.

6. Paul H. Kocher, *Master of Middle-earth: The Fiction of J. R. R. Tolkien* (Boston: Houghton Mifflin, 1972), 43.

7. Carpenter, "Letter 210. From a Letter to Forrest J. Ackerman," *Letters of J. R. R. Tolkien*, 274.

8. Carpenter, "Letter 320. From a Letter to Mrs. Ruth Austin," *Letters of J. R. R. Tolkien*, 407.

9. Tolkien, *Fellowship of the Ring*, 473–474.

10. Lisa Hopkins, "Female Authority Figures in the Works of Tolkien, C. S. Lewis and Charles Williams," *Mythlore* Winter 1995: 365.

11. *Fellowship of the Ring*, Scene 39. "The Mirror of Galadriel."

12. Tyler, *Tolkien Companion*, 30.

13. Tolkien, *Return of the King*, appendix A, 425–428.

14. Tolkien, *Fellowship of the Ring*, 300.

15. Ibid., 303, 313.

16. Ibid., 368.

17. Tyler, *Tolkien Companion*, 330.

18. Tolkien, *Return of the King*, 309–130.

19. Ibid., 311–312.

20. Ibid., 312.

21. Ibid., appendix A, 420–428.

22. Tolkien, *Silmarillion*, 162–187.

23. Tolkien, *Fellowship of the Ring*, 300.

24. Ibid., 362.

25. Tolkien, *Return of the King*, 312.

26. Ibid., appendix A, 421.

27. *Fellowship of the Ring*, Scene 17. "The Midgewater Marshes."

28. Carpenter, "Letter 181. To Michael Straight [drafts]," *Letters to J. R. R. Tolkien*, 237.

29. Michael Martinez, "Much Ado about Arwen: Elven Princess," 3 March 2000, 9 June 2004, http://www.suite101.com/article.cfm/4786/34740.

30. Tolkien, *Return of the King*, appendix A, 422–423.

31. Ibid., 425.

32. Tolkien, *Fellowship of the Ring*, 485–486.

33. *Fellowship of the Ring*, Scene 21. "Flight to the Ford."

34. Ibid., Scene 25. "The Sword That Was Broken."

35. *Return of the King*, Scene 7. "Arwen's Vision."

36. Ibid.

37. Helen Armstrong, "There Are Two People in this Marriage," *Mallorn 36* (Nov. 1998): 9.

38. *Fellowship of the Ring*, Scene 21. "Flight to the Ford."

39. *Two Towers*, Scene 43. "The Grace of the Valor."

40. *Return of the King*, Scene 7. "Arwen's Vision"; Scene 22. "Andúril—Flame of the West."

41. Tolkien, *Silmarillion*, summarized from the chapter "Of Beren and Luthien" (162–187).

42. Tolkien, *Return of the King*, appendix A, 424.

43. *Two Towers*, Scene 39. "The Story Foreseen from Lórien."

44. Ibid., Scene 48. "The Host of the Eldar."

45. Ibid., Scene 39. "The Story Foreseen from Lórien."

46. *Fellowship of the Ring*, Scene 38. "Caras Galadhon."

47. Ibid., Scene 41. "Farewell to Lórien."

48. Tolkien, *Two Towers*, 42.

49. *Fellowship of the Ring*, Scene 37. "Lothlórien."

50. Ibid., Scene 55. "The Mirror of Galadriel."

51. Tolkien, *Fellowship of the Ring*, 469–472.

52. *Return of the King*, Scene 29. "Shelob's Lair."

53. Ibid., Scene 7. "Arwen's Vision."

54. *Two Towers*, Scene 43. "The Grace of the Valor."

55. *Return of the King*, Scene 22. "Andúril—Flame of the West."

56. *Two Towers*, Scene 24. "Brego."

57. Ian Spelling, "Evenstar Farewell," *Starlog 320* (March 2004): 39.

58. *Return of the King*, Scene 22. "Andúril—Flame of the West."

59. *Fellowship of the Ring*, Scene 25. "The Sword That Was Broken."

60. Ibid., Scene 26. "Evenstar."

61. *Return of the King*, Scene 22. "Andúril—Flame of the West."

62. Ibid., Scene 6. "The Palantír."

63. *Fellowship of the Ring*, Scene 41. "Farewell to Lórien."

64. Tolkien, *Fellowship of the Ring*, 200–201.

65. *Two Towers*, Scene 3. "The Taming of Sméagol."

66. Ibid., Scene 2. "Elven Rope."

67. *Return of the King*, Scene 29. "Shelob's Lair."

68. *Fellowship of the Ring*, Scene 41. "Farewell to Lórien."

69. Tolkien, *Fellowship of the Ring*, 486.

70. Ibid.

71. *Two Towers*, Scene 4. "The Uruk-hai."

72. Tolkien, *Fellowship of the Ring*, 479.

73. Jane Chance Nitzsche, *Tolkien's Art: A 'Mythology for England'* (New York: St. Martin's Press, 1979), 108–109.

74. Mac Fenwick, "Breastplates of Silk: Homeric Women in *The Lord of the Rings*," *Mythlore* (Summer 1996): 18.

75. Ibid., 20.

76. *Fellowship of the Ring*, Scene 26. "Evenstar."

77. Tolkien, *Return of the King*, 312.

78. *Fellowship of the Ring*, Scene 41. "Farewell to Lórien."

79. *Two Towers*, Scene 34. "The Wolves of Isengard."

80. Ibid., Scene 43. "Aragorn's Return."

81. *Return of the King*, Scene 22. "Andúril—Flame of the West."

82. *Fellowship of the Ring*, Scene 1. "Prologue: One Ring to Rule Them All. . . ."

83. Ibid., Scene 41. "Farewell to Lórien."

84. Jessica Yates, "Arwen the Elf-Warrior?" *Amon Hen 165* (Sept. 2000): 12.

85. Spelling, "Evenstar Farewell." Liv Tyler also mentions an early script version of Arwen as a warrior.

86. Michael Fleming, "LiVing It Up!" *Movieline's Hollywood Life* (March/April 2004): 58.

87. *Fellowship of the Ring*, Scene 21. "Flight to the Ford."

88. Ibid., Scene 30. "The Departure of the Fellowship."

89. *Two Towers*, Scene 38. "Arwen's Fate."

90. *Return of the King*, Scene 7. "Arwen's Vision."

91. Ibid., Scene 8. "The Reforging of Narsil."

92. Tom Shippey, "Another Road to Middle-earth: Jackson's Movie Trilogy," *Understanding* The Lord of the Rings: *The Best of Tolkien Criticism* (Eds. Rose A. Zimbardo and Neil D. Isaacs). Boston: Houghton Mifflin, 2004, 237.

Chapter 6

1. Kocher, *Master of Middle-Earth*, 107.

2. Tolkien, *The Silmarillion*, summarized from the chapter "Of the Coming of the Elves and the Captivity of Melkor" (47–54).

3. Ibid., 44.

4. Dwayne Thorpe, "Tolkien's Elvish Craft," *Mythlore* Winter 1996: 318.

5. Ibid.

6. David A. Funk, "Explorations into the Psyche of Dwarves," *Mythology* Winter 1996: 330.

7. Tolkien, *The Silmarillion*, 44.

8. Tolkien, *Fellowship of the Ring*, 413–414.

9. Ibid., 444, 446.

10. *Two Towers*, Scene 5. "The Three Hunters."

11. Funk, "Explorations into the Psyche of Dwarves," 333.

12. Tolkien, *Fellowship of the Ring*, 490.

13. Ibid., 319–322.

14. J. R. R. Tolkien, *The Hobbit* (New York: Ballantine, 1965), summarized from the chapters "Flies and Spiders" and "Barrels Out of Bonds." In these chapters, the treatment of Thorin is detailed more than that of the other Dwarves, but Glóin is also among the captured Dwarves, and the entire party's captivity is discussed.

15. Tom Shippey, *J. R. R. Tolkien: Author of the Century* (Boston: Houghton Mifflin, 2000), 71.

16. Tolkien, *Fellowship of the Rings*, 314–355.

17. Shippey, *J. R. R. Tolkien: Author of the Century*, 70.

18. *Fellowship of the Ring*, Scene 27. "The Council of Elrond."

19. Tolkien, *Fellowship of the Ring*, 397.

20. *Fellowship of the Ring*, Scene 33. "Moria."

21. Tolkien, *Fellowship of the Ring*, 395.

22. Ibid., 445, 450–451.

23. Petty, *Tolkien in the Land of Heroes*, 121.

24. Jones, *Myth and Middle-earth*, 88.

25. Ibid., 100.

26. Tolkien, *Two Towers*, 42.

27. *Two Towers*, Scene 11. "The Riders of Rohan."

28. Tolkien, *The Two Towers*, 193.

29. Ibid., 194.

30. *Return of the King*, Scene 25. "Dwimorberg—The Haunted Mountain."

31. Dan Madsen, "Standing Tall: An Interview with John Rhys-Davies," *The Lord of the Rings Fan Club Official Movie Magazine* Aug.–Sept. 2002: 33.

32. Michael Martinez, "Speaking of Legolas," 31 March 2000, 20 May 2004, http://www.suite101.com/article.cfm/4786/36517.

33. Tolkien, *Two Towers*, 188.

34. *Two Towers*, Scene 62. "The Final Tally."

35. *Return of the King*, Scene 40. "The Black Ships."

36. Ibid., Scene 48. "The Black Gate Opens."

37. Tolkien, *Return of the King*, 312–313.

38. Tolkien, *Fellowship of the Ring*, 487.

39. Sibley, The Lord of the Rings *Official Movie Guide*, 44.

40. *Fellowship of the Ring*, Scene 35. "Balin's Tomb."

41. *Two Towers*, Scene 51. "The Breach of the Deeping Wall."

42. *Return of the King*, Scene 43. "Victory at Minas Tirith."

43. *Two Towers*, Scene 20. "The King of the Golden Hall."

44. *Return of the King*, Scene 42. "Victory at Minas Tirith."

45. *Fellowship of the Ring*, Scene 35. "Balin's Tomb."

46. Tolkien, *Fellowship of the Ring*, 416.

47. *Two Towers*, Scene 11. "The Riders of Rohan."

48. *Two Towers*, Scene 43. "Aragorn's Return."

49. *Return of the King*, Scene 56. "The Fellowship Reunited."

50. *Fellowship of the Ring*, Scene 36. "The Bridge of Khazad-dûm."

51. *Two Towers*, Scene 53. "The Retreat to the Hornburg."

52. Tolkien, *Return of the King*, 289.

53. *Return of the King*, Scene 57. "The Return of the King."

54. Tolkien, *Return of the King*, 303–304.

55. *Return of the King*, Scene 57. "The Return of the King."

56. Harvey, *The Origins of Middle-earth for Dummies*, 70–71.

57. Tolkien, *Return of the King*, 317.

58. Ibid., appendix A, 451.

59. Christine Davidson, "Coming of Age: Changes of Heart," *Mallorn* *39*(Sept. 2001), 17.

60. Michael Martinez, "Do Elves Dream of Eclectic Sheep?" 30 Nov. 2001, 20 May 2004, http://www.suite101.com/article.cfm/4788/88105.

61. Tolkien, *Fellowship of the Ring*, 488.

62. Michael Swanwick, "A Changeling Returns," *Meditations on Middle-Earth* (Karen Haber, Ed., New York: St. Martin's Griffin, 2001), 36.

63. Ibid., 36–37.

64. Davidson, "Coming of Age," 18.

65. Sibley, The Lord of the Rings *Official Movie Guide*, 44.

66. Nick Joy, "Axe Lyrical: John Rhys-Davies," *Film Review* Dec. 2003: 38.

67. *Two Towers*, Scene 51. "The Breach of the Deeping Wall."

68. Ibid., Scene 53. "The Retreat to the Hornburg."

69. *Return of the King*, Scene 27. "The King of the Dead."

70. Ibid., Scene 53. "The Crack of Doom."

71. Ibid., Scene 23. "Aragorn Takes the Paths of the Dead."

72. Madsen, "Standing Tall: An Interview with John Rhys-Davies," 33.

Chapter 7

1. TheOneRing.Net (TORN), "Tehanu's Note 22. Where To From Here?" 29 April 2004, 1 May 2004, http://www.theonering.net/features/notes/note22.html.

2. Holli Weiss, "Rewarded by Reading," *Herald Journal*, Logan, Utah, 6 May 2004, 15 May 2004, http://hjnews.townnews.com/articles/2004/05/06/news/news02.txt.

3. Nathan Hunt, "The Importance of Trivia: Ownership, Exclusion, and Authority in Science Fiction Fandom," *Defining Cult Movies: The Cultural Politics of Oppositional Taste* (Mark Jankovich, Antonio Lázaro Reboll, Julian Stringer, and Andy Willis, Eds., Manchester, U.K.: Manchester University Press, 2003), 198.

4. Philip W. Helms, "The Evolution of Tolkien Fandom," *Tolkien's Peaceful War: A History and Explanation of Tolkien Fandom and War*, Rev. ed. (Paul S. Ritz, Ed., Highland, Mich.: The American Tolkien Society, 1994), 7.

5. Ibid., 7–8.

6. Jeff Giles, "Secrets of 'The King,'" *Newsweek* (1 Dec. 2003): 61.

7. White, "Talking Tolkien with Thomas Shippey."

8. *Return of the King*, Scene 14. "The Lighting of the Beacons."

9. Ibid., Scene 21. "Marshalling at Dunharrow."

10. Ibid.

11. Ibid., Scene 26. "The Muster of Rohan."

12. *Two Towers*, Scene 34. "The Wolves of Isengard."

13. *Return of the King*, Scene 24. "No More Despair."

14. *Two Towers*, Scene 39. "The Story Foreseen from Lórien."

15. *Return of the King*, Scene 29. "Shelob's Lair."

16. *Fellowship of the Ring*, Scene 27. "The Council of Elrond."

17. *Two Towers*, Scene 48. "The Host of the Eldar."

18. Ibid., Scene 49. "The Battle of the Hornburg."

19. TORN, "*Return of the King* Premiere Live on Sky," 1 Dec. 2003, 14 May 2004, http://www.theonering.net/perl/newsview/1/1071152724.

20. Cathy Aronson, "Red Carpet Commentary: Wellington Celebrates the World Premiere," *New Zealand Herald*, 1 Dec. 2003, 14 May 2004, http://nzherald. co.nz/storydisplay.cfm?storyID=3537021&thesection=entertainment&thesubsection= film&thesecondsubsection=general.

21. Hobbit Film, "Let the Hobbit Happen," April 2004, 14 May 2004, http:// www.thehobbitfilm.com/partners.

22. ToyBiz, *Online Catalog*, 2004. 14 May 2004, http://www.marvel.com/ toybiz/lotr/index.htm.

23. Clark, "J. R. R. Tolkien and the True Hero," 39.

24. CNN, "Harrison Ford Credited with Helicopter Rescue of Sick Hiker in Idaho," 7 Aug. 2000, 14 May 2004, http://edition.cnn.com/2003/SHOWBIZ/ Movies/08/07/harrisonford.rescue.ap.

25. TORN, "Sean Astin to the Rescue," 15 Aug. 2003, 12 May 2004, http:// www.theonering.net/archives/main_news/8.15.03–8.21.03.

26. A&E, "Journey to Middle Earth: *The Lord of the Rings: The Return of the King*," *Inside the Lord of the Rings*. Prod. Catharine Harrington. 11 Jan. 2004. A&E Network.

27. *Two Towers*, Scene 60. "The Tales That Really Mattered...."

28. Stratford Caldecott, "The Horns of Hope: J. R. R. Tolkien and the Heroism of Hobbits," *Chesterton Review: The Journal of the G. K. Chesterton Institute*, Feb.–May 2002: 31.

29. Ibid., 32–33.

30. Marion Kershaw, "So What Has PJ Done For Us?" *Amon Hen*, March 2004: 18.

Online Resources For
Tolkien Studies

In late 2004, I conducted online searches through several engines, including Google, Yahoo!, Dogpile, and Ask Jeeves, to determine how many Web sites would be listed under a general search for "Tolkien" or "J. R. R. Tolkien." As might be imagined, the resulting list in each search engine would be unusable without narrowing. Online Tolkien sites number in the hundreds of thousands. They are produced by fans of books or films or both, companies producing or marketing Tolkien- or film-related products, students or teachers showcasing course-related information, artists, writers, gamers, and others not in any of these categories but in some way interested in promoting Tolkien or his works.

To provide such an exhaustive list of sources would be meaningless. Nevertheless, some sites stand out because of their "official" nature, their direct link to either the films or the books, well-documented and easily navigable information about Tolkien, or news archives that can provide a searchable history of the development of Jackson's films and their relationship to Tolkien's works. Although other sites may provide similar information, the following annotated list is a good starting point for more research about the scholarly or popular aspects of J. R. R. Tolkien's *The Lord of the Rings*, *The Hobbit*, and/or *The Silmarillion* and Peter Jackson's cinematic adaptation of *The Lord of the Rings*. These are well-established sites, and even though they are online resources and therefore not permanent, they are more likely than many other sites to continue to be available. In alphabetical order, these are the site names, URLs, and brief comments about the content.

Beyond Bree (www.cep.unt.edu/bree.html)

The American Mensa society sponsors a special-interest group about Tolkien. Although the special-interest group's newsletter requires a subscription (which can be made online), a sample article and a sample review not only provide some information about Tolkien but indicate the type of information available through the newsletter. For those who like the samples and want to learn more through the newsletter, the subscription is not expensive.

El Señor de los Anillos—La Trilogia (www.elfenomeno.com)

This Spanish site provides information about Tolkien as well as Jackson's films. Games, news, pictures, and other types of information, especially related to the films, are highlighted.

Elvish Linguistic Fellowship (ELF) (www.elvish.org/)

This international organization provides links to journals with articles about the languages Tolkien created. One journal is by subscription, but a separate journal is available online. The site also provides links to articles and other sites. There is also a mailing list.

The Grey Havens (tolkien.cro.net/)

This Croation site provides a discussion forum, articles, and links to sites with more information about Tolkien. Although the site was not frequently updated in 2004, the forum seems active, and previously posted or linked information may be useful.

J.R.R. Tolkien and Middle-earth (www.suite101.com/welcome.cfm/tolkien)

Michael Martinez edits this section of Suite 101 and frequently contributes articles about Tolkien's characters and works. Articles about Jackson's adaptation also are common on this site, which includes thought-provoking topics and encourages readers to discuss the articles.

J.R.R. Tolkien by Barahir (www.tolkien.art.pl)

This Polish site covers the books and films. Artwork and an encyclopedia related to Tolkien's world are high points of this site, although another strong feature is the number of downloadable "extras," such as fonts.

Lalaith's Middle-earth Science Pages (rover.wiesbaden.netsurf.de/~lalaith/M-earth.html)

Backgound texts and information helpful to understanding Middle-earth are listed at this site. Articles include various areas of science, including ethnography, geography, and astronomy. Other articles provide background about linguistics and history. Only a few articles are written specifically for German readers; the majority of texts are accessible for all readers.

The Lord of the Rings Trilogy (www.lordoftherings.net)

New Line Cinema's official *The Lord of the Rings* site still includes information about Jackson's trilogy as well as new links to video games and merchandise affiliated with the trilogy. Information specific to the films may be found here, either in current or archived news and links.

The Mythopoeic Society (www.mythsoc.org/)

This nonprofit educational and literary organization produces three periodicals (e.g., *Mythlore*), which are available by subscription and described at the site. Tolkien is one of three authors discussed; the others are C. S. Lewis and Charles Williams. A table of contents to the latest issues is provided, but there is no online index to previous issues. However, back issues can be ordered online, and the site provides e-mail links for readers who need more information.

New Line Cinema (www.newline.com)

Although this corporate site features information from the most recent films coming from the studio, in 2004 it maintained links to information and products related to its three *Lord of the Rings* films in the Movies-Archive section.

One Ring: The Complete Guide to Tolkien Online (onering.virbius.com/)

Although the site also sells products, it includes a great deal of information about the books and films. The resource is useful for popular culture aspects of Tolkien studies.

Planet Tolkien (www.planet-tolkien.com/)

The U.K.-based site links visitors to journals, news, updates, and polls. Chats and forums encourage discussion of anything related to Tolkien.

The Thain's Book (www.tuckborough.net/)

The site provides an ever-growing encyclopedia of information about Middle-earth in the Third Age. An important feature is a series of indexes to people, places, creatures, things, and events found in Tolkien's works.

The Tolkien Timeline (gollum.usask.ca/tolkien)

This chronology highlights events in Tolkien's life, in addition to important dates in history that may have influenced Tolkien. The timeline is broken into sections: Pre-Tolkien Era, The Early Years (of Tolkien's life), The Lord of the Rings, The Post-Oxford Years, and After the King.

The Valaquenta: The Account of the Valar (www.valaquenta.com/)

Information specific to *The Silmarillion* is discussed at this site. A discussion board and essays provide information about the Valar. Links to sites with Tolkien's biography and other works are provided.

TheOneRingNet (www.theonering.net/)

This international fan-based and -supported site in 2004 provided an archive of news articles from 1999 to the present related to Jackson's trilogy, actors and artists involved in the production, Tolkien's works, and Tolkien-related events. Links to many other types of online resources are also provided.

There and Back Again (www.thereandbackagain.net/)

The site provides character information and a Tolkien biography. This resource is a useful primer to works.

The Tolkien Meta-FAQ (tolkien.slimy.com/)

The title is self-descriptive; the lists at this site provide links to other FAQs. The information is easy to navigate, so that readers' questions can be found easily and responses located. Lists of articles, books, and essays are parts of these FAQs.

Tolkien Online (www.tolkienonline.com/)

The news updates were being continued in 2004, with the latest information about films and gaming, as well as news articles related to Tolkien's works in general.

Tolkien Society (www.tolkiensociety.org/)

This nonprofit educational society based in the United Kingdom furthers interest in Tolkien and his works. Links to other sites' resources, as well as on-site information about the author, his books, and the film adaptations, should be useful to readers at any stage of familiarity with Tolkien's writing. The Society also sponsors conferences and other events and produces a members-only publication, *Amon Hen*.

Tolkien.co.uk (www.tolkien.co.uk/)

The site allows product ordering, but it also provides information and links to information about Tolkien, as well as Tolkien's own works. Artwork (by John Howe, Alan Lee, and Michael Nasmith), interviews, Tolkien's biography, and a FAQ about Tolkien's books provide multiple resources for further study.

Selected Bibliography

These sources were used either as direct references within the preceding chapters or as consulted works in the preparation of this book.

Television Broadcasts

A&E. "Journey to Middle Earth: *The Lord of the Rings: The Return of the King.*" *Inside* The Lord of the Rings. Producer Catharine Harrington. Exec. Producer David Doss. 11 Jan. 2004. A&E Network.

A&E. "The Making of *The Lord of the Rings.*" *Break fast with the Arts.* 11 Jan. 2004. A&E Network.

Films and DVDs of Films

The Lord of the Rings: The Fellowship of the Ring. Director. Peter Jackson. Producer Barrie M. Osborne. New Line Cinema. 2001.

The Lord of the Rings: The Fellowship of the Ring. Extended DVD. Director Peter Jackson. Producers Barrie M. Osborne, Peter Jackson, and Fran Walsh. New Line Cinema. 2001.

The Lord of the Rings: The Return of the King. Director Peter Jackson. Producers Barrie M. Osborne, Peter Jackson, and Fran Walsh. New Line Cinema. 2003.

The Lord of the Rings: The Two Towers. Director Peter Jackson. Prodducers Barrie M. Osborne, Peter Jackson, and Fran Walsh. New Line Cinema. 2002.

The Lord of the Rings: The Two Towers. Extended DVD. Director Peter Jackson. Producers. Barrie M. Osborne, Peter Jackson, and Fran Walsh. New Line Cinema. 2002.

Articles

Alleva, Richard. "Peter Jackson's Sorcery: *The Lord of the Rings* Trilogy." *Commonweal, 81*(2). 30 Jan. 2004, 5 May 2004. http://www.commonwealmagazine.org/2004/january302004/013004_mv.htm.

Anderson, Neil S. "Dior—Mortal or Elven?" *Amon Hen, 129*(Nov. 1994), 8–9.

Anderson, Neil S. "The Durable Durins." *Amon Hen, 126*(March 1994), 10–12.

Armstrong, Helen. "There are Two People in This Marriage." *Mallorn, 36*(Nov. 1998), 5–12.

Aronson, Cathy. "Red Carpet Commentary: Wellington Celebrates the World Premiere." *New Zealand Herald.* 1 Dec. 2003, 14 May 2004. http://nzherald.co.nz/storydisplay.cfm?storyID=3537021&thesection=entertainment&thesubsection=film&thesecondsubsection=general.

Associated Press. "Harrison Ford: Real American Hero. Harrison Ford Credited with Helicopter Rescue of Sick Hiker in Idaho." 7 Aug. 2000, 12 May 2004. http://www.allstarz.org/harrisonford/hero.htm#.

Atkinson, Carla. "The Artful Dodger." *The Lord of the Rings Fan Club Official Movie Magazine, 8*(April–May 2003), 32–41.

Barlow, Helen. "The Warrior Woman. The Lord of the Rings: The Two Towers. Souvenir Edition." *The New Zealand Herald,* 10 Dec. 2002, 11.

Bell, James. "Viggo (Strider/Aragorn) & Elijah (Frodo) Speak Out Against a War in Iraq." Transcript from the *Charlie Rose Show.* 21 Dec. 2003, 14 April 2004. http://www.lastwizards.com/pages/modules.php?name=News&file=articl&sid=40.

Caldecott, Stratford. "The Horns of Hope: J. R. R. Tolkien and the Heroism of Hobbits." *The Chesterton Review: The Journal of the G. K. Chesterton Institute, 28*(1–2, Feb.–May 2002), 29–55.

Chance, Jane. "Is There a Text in this Hobbit? Peter Jackson's *Fellowship of the Ring*." *Literature/Film Quarterly, 30*(2), 79–86.

Christie, Damian. "Billy Boyd: Pippin the Hobbit." *Pavement, 36*(Dec. 2002–Jan. 2003), 110–111.

CNN. "Harrison Ford Credited with Helicopter Rescue of Sick Hiker in Idaho." 7 Aug. 2000, 15 May 2004. http://www.cnn.com/2000/SHOWBIZ/Movies/08/07/harrisonford.rescue.ap/.

CNN. "*Rings*' Gets Rousing New Zealand Premiere." 1 Dec. 2003, 14 May 2004. http://edition.cnn.com/2003/SHOWBIZ/movies/12/01/rings.premiere.reut/index.html.

Cropp, Amanda. "Ringleader." *Next, 240*(July 2004), 132–134, 137.

Davidson, Christine. "Coming of Age: Changes of Heart." *Mallorn, 39,* 15–22.

Ebert, Roger. (December 19, 2001). "Review. *Lord of the Rings: The Fellowship of the Ring*." *Chicago Sun-Times.* 19 Dec. 2001, 26 April 2004. http://www.suntimes.com/ebert/ebert_reviews/2001/12/121901.html.

Ebert, Roger. (December 18, 2002). "Review. *Lord of the Rings: The Two Towers*." *Chicago Sun-Times.* 18 Dec. 2002, 26 April 2004. http://www.suntimes.com/ebert/ebert_reviews/2002/12/121801.html.

Eramo, Stephen. "Frodo's Friend." *British Heritage*, Sept. 2004, 20–25.

Eramo, Steven. "A Very Merry Man." *Xposé Special #24,* 18–24.

Fader, Shanti. "A Fool's Hope." *Parabola, 26*(3) (Fall 2001), 48–52.

Fenwick, Mac. "Breastplates of Silk: Homeric Women in *The Lord of the Rings,*" *Mythlore,* Summer 1996, 17–23, 50.

Filmer-Davies, Cath. "King Arthur in the Marketplace, King Arthur in the Myth." *Mythlore,* Summer 1996, 12–16.

Fleming, Michael. "LiVing It Up!" *Movieline's Hollywood Life,* March/April 2004, 56–61, 105.

French, Lawrence. "All Hail the King, Part 1." *Cinefantastique,* Dec. 2003–Jan. 2004, 30–36, 39, 43, 49.

Fuller, Graham. "Kingdom Come." *Film Comment, 40*(1) (Jan.–Feb. 2004), 24–29.

Funk, David A. "Explorations into the Psyche of Dwarves." *Mythlore,* Winter 1996, 330–333.

Gelder, Ken. "Epic Fantasy and Global Terrorism." *Overland,* Summer 2003, 21–27.

Giles, Jeff. "Secrets of 'The King.'" *Newsweek* (1 Dec. 2003), 50–58, 60–62.

Gray, Simon. "The Fate of Middle-earth." *American Cinematographer, 85*(1) (Jan. 2004), 54–58, 60–67.

Haley, Guy. "*The Lord of the Rings: The Return of the King.* Review." *SFX* (Feb. 2004), 70–73.

Hopkins, Lisa. "Female Authority Figures in the Works of Tolkien, C. S. Lewis and Charles Williams." *Mythlore,* Winter 1995, 364–366.

Joy, Nick. "Axe Lyrical: John Rhys-Davies." *Film Review, 638*(Dec. 2003), 38.

Joy, Nick. "Force of Hobbit: Billy Boyd and Dominic Monaghan." *Film Review, 638*(Dec. 2003), 39.

Joy, Nick. "Small Soldier." *Starburst, 28*(4), 32–36, 38–39.

Kaufman, Roger. "*Lord of the Rings* Taps a Gay Archetype." *The Gay & Lesbian Review Worldwide,* 10, 4: 31. Proquest. July–Aug. 2003, 20 May 2004. http://gateway.proquest.com/openurl?url_ver=Z3988–2004&res_dat=xri:pqd&rft_val_fmt=info:of/journal&genre=article&rft_dat=xri:pqd:didi000000621098771&svc_dat=xri:pqil:fmt=text&req_dat=xri:pqil:pq_clntid=17916.

Kershaw, Marion. "So What Has PJ Done for Us?" *Amon Hen, 186*(March 2004), 18–19.

Lavigne, Chris. "Weapons Inspectors in Mordor?" *The Republic,* 9 Jan. 2003, 1, 7.

"Let Slip the Dogs of War." *Xposé, 75,* Jan. 2003, 17–22.

"Let the Hobbit Happen." April 2004, 14 May 2004. http://www.thehobbitfilm.com/partners.html.

Libling, Margie. "An Extremely Random Interview with a Mischievous Hobbit." *Ink 19.* 2003, 2 May 2004. http://www.ink19.com/issues/december2003/interviews/billyBoyd.html.

Madsen, Dan. "Standing Tall: An Interview with John Rhys-Davies." The Lord of the Rings *Fan Club Official Movie Magazine,* Aug.–Sept. 2003, 28–37.

Madsen, Dan. "Thwarted Heroine." The Lord of the Rings *Fan Club Official Movie Magazine,* Feb.–March 2003, 34–43.

Maiden, Grant. "Dominic Monaghan: Merry the Hobbit." *Pavement,* 56, 106–107.

Martinez, Michael. "Do Elves Dream of Eclectic Sheep?" 30 Nov. 2001, 20 May 2004. http://www.suite101.com/article.cfm/4788/88105.

Martinez, Michael. "Much Ado about Arwen: Elven Princess." 3 March 2000, 9 June 2004. http://www.suite101.com/article.cfm/4786/34740.

Martinez, Michael. "Speaking of Legolas." 31 March 2000, 20 May 2004. http://www.suite101.com/article.cfm/4786/6517.

Nathan, Ian. (Ed.). *The Lord of the Rings:* A Celebration. Special Insert." *Empire,* Jan. 2004.

Nathan, Ian. "Peter Jackson, Part 1." *Empire,* Jan. 2004, 86–90.

O'Donnell, Catherine. "The Women of Middle Earth." *Catholic Exchange.* 18 Dec. 2003, 5 May 2004. http://www.catholicexchange.com/VM/Pfarticle.asp?vm_id=2&art_id=21650& sec_id=41243.

Poudrier, Almira F. "The Virtue of the Weaponed Hero." *The Humanist,* July–Aug. 2001, 35–37.

Shippey, Tom. "From Page to Screen." *World Literature Today,* 77, 2: 69. Proquest. July–Sept. 2003. 20 May 2004. http://gateway.proquest.com/openurl?url_ver=Z39.88–2004&res_dat=xri:pqd&rft_val_fmt=info:ofi/fmt:kev:mtx:journal&genre=article&rft_dat=xri:pqd:did=000000454795721&svc_dat=xri:pqil:fmt=text&req_dat=xri:pqil:pq_cintid=17916.

Spelling, Ian. "Evenstar Farewell." *Starlog, 320*(March 2004), 38–41.

Spelling, Ian. "Merry Man." *Dreamwatch, 110*(Dec. 2003), 42–43.

Spelling, Ian. "Middle-shipman." *Starlog, 317*(Dec. 2003), 60–63.

Spelling, Ian. "Standing Small." *Starlog, 318*(Jan. 2004), 54–57.

Spelling, Ian. "Sword of Eowyn." *Fantasy Worlds, 3*(Feb. 2004), 30–33.

Spelling, Ian. "Warrior Princess." *Starlog, 320*(March 2004), 34–37.

Talbot, Norman. "Where Do Elves Go To? Tolkien and a Fantasy Tradition." *Mythlore,* Winter 1996, 94–106.

TheOneRingNet (TORN). "Hall of Fire Discussion: 09/22/09. Discerning the Hero and the Heroic in *Lord of the Rings.*" 22 Sept. 2003, 11 Jan. 2004. http://www.theonering.net/barlimans/hall_logs/092202_p.html.

TheOneRingNet (TORN). "ROTK Play in Cincinnati." 3 Oct. 2003, 24 Jan. 2004. http://www.theonering.net/perl/newsview/8/1065188752.

TheOneRing.Net. *Return of the King* Premiere Live on Sky." 1 Dec. 2003, 14 May 2004. http://www.theonering.net/perl/newsview/1/1071152724.

TheOneRing.Net. "Sean Astin to the Rescue." 15 Aug. 2003, 12 May 2004. http://www.theonering.net/archives/main_news/8.15.03–8.21.03.

TheOneRing.Net. "Tehanu's Note 22. Where to from Here?" 29 April 2004, 1 May 2004. http://www.theonering.net/features/notes/note22.html.

Thorpe, Dwayne. "Tolkien's Elvish Craft." *Mythlore,* Winter 1996, 315–321.

Tilden, Imogen. "Lord of the Rings Musical Planned for London Stage." *Guardian Unlimited.* 23 May 2003, 24 January 2004. http://www.guardian.co.uk/arts/news/story/0,11711,965572,00.html.

Watson, Paul. "Fellowship of the Script: An Adaptation of *The Two Towers.*" *Screentalk, 3*(Nov.–Dec. 2002), 1, 40–45.

Weiss, Holli. "Rewarded by Reading." *Herald Journal.* Logan, Utah. 6 May 2004, 15 May 2004. http://hjnews.townnews.com/articles/2004/05/06/news/news02.txt.

Wheatley, Alan K. "Can We Have Our Book Back?" *Amon Hen, 186,* March 2004, 15–17.

White, Claire E. "Talking Tolkien with Thomas Shippey." March 2002, 8 May 2004, http://www.writerswrite.com/journal/mar02/shippey.htm.

Xposé. Cover, 75(Jan. 2003).

Yates, Jessica. "Arwen the Elf-Warrior?" *Amon Hen, 165*(Sept. 2000), 11–15.

Books or Chapters within Books

Bassham, Gregory, and Eric Bronson (Eds.). The Lord of the Rings *and Philosophy: One Book to Rule Them All.* Chicago: Open Court Press, 2003.

Bloom, Harold (Ed.). *Modern Critical Interpretations: J. R. R. Tolkien's* The Lord of the Rings. Philadelphia: Chelsea House, 2000.

Bradley, Marion Zimmer. "Men, Halflings, and Hero Worship." N. D. Isaacs & R. A. Zimbardo (Eds.), *Tolkien and the Critics: Essays on J. R. R. Tolkien's* The Lord of the Rings. 109–127. Notre Dame, Ind.: University of Notre Dame Press, 1968.

Brodie, Ian. *The Lord of the Rings Location Guidebook.* Rev. ed. Auckland, N.Z.: HarperCollins, 2003.

Campbell, Joseph. *The Hero with a Thousand Faces.* 2nd ed. Princeton, N.J.: University of Princeton Press, 1968.

Clark, George. "J. R. R. Tolkien and the True Hero." George Clark and Daniel Timmons (Eds.), *J. R. R. Tolkien and His Literary Resonances: Views of Middle-earth.* 39–51. Westport, Conn.: Greenwood Press, 2000.

Clark, George, and Daniel Timmons. (Eds.). *J. R. R. Tolkien and His Literary Resonances.* Westport, Conn.: Greenwood Press, 2000.

Crabbe, K. W. "The Quest as Legend: *The Lord of the Rings.*" Harold Bloom (Ed.), *Modern Critical Interpretations: J. R. R. Tolkien's* The Lord of the Rings. 141–170. Philadelphia: Chelsea House, 2000.

Curry, Patrick. *Defending Middle-earth: Tolkien, Myth, and Modernity.* New York: St. Martin's Press, 1997.

Day, David. *Guide to Tolkien's World: A Bestiary.* San Diego, Calif.: Thunder Bay Press, 1979.

Duriez, Colin. *Tolkien and* The Lord of the Rings: *A Guide to Middle-earth.* London: Hidden Spring, 2001.

Frye, Northrop. *Anatomy of Criticism: Four Essays.* Princeton, N.J.: Princeton University Press, 1957.

Giddings, Robert. (Ed.). *J. R. R. Tolkien: The Far Land.* London: Vision Press, Ltd., 1983.

Harvey, Greg. *The Origins of Tolkien's Middle-earth for Dummies.* Hoboken, N.J.: Wiley, 2003.

Helms, Philip W. "The Evolution of Tolkien Fandom." Paul S. Ritz (Ed.), *Tolkien's Peaceful War: A History and Explanation of Tolkien Fandom and War.* 7–10. Rev. ed. Highland, Mich.: The American Tolkien Society, 1994.

Helms, Randel. *Tolkien's World.* Boston: Houghton Mifflin, 1974.

Hunt, Nathan. "The Importance of Trivia: Ownership, Exclusion, and Authority in Science Fiction Fandom." Mark Jancovich, Antonio Lazaro Reboll, Julian Stringer, and Andy Willis (Eds.), *Defining Cult Movies: The Cultural Politics of Oppositional Taste.* 185–201. Manchester, U.K.: Manchester University Press, 2003.

Jones, Leslie Ellen. *Myth & Middle-earth.* Cold Spring Harbor, N.H.: Cold Spring Press, 2002.

Kocher, Paul H. *Master of Middle-Earth: The Fiction of J. R. R. Tolkien.* Boston: Houghton Mifflin, 1972.

Kraus, Joe. "Tolkien, Modernism, and the Importance of Tradition." Gregory Bassham and Eric Bronson (Eds.), The Lord of the Rings *and Philosophy: One Book to Rule Them All.* 137–149. Chicago: Open Court Press, 2003.

Lobdell, Jared. (Ed.). *A Tolkien Compass.* Chicago: Open Court, 2003.

Nitzsche, Jane Chance. "*The Lord of the Rings:* Tolkien's Epic." Harold Bloom (Ed.), *Modern Critical Interpretations: J. R. R. Tolkien's* The Lord of the Rings. 79–106. Philadelphia: Chelsea House, 2000.

Petty, Anne C. *One Ring to Bind Them All: Tolkien's Mythology.* University: University of Alabama Press, 1979.

Petty, Anne C. *Tolkien in the Land of Heroes: Discovering the Human Spirit.* Cold Spring Harbor, NY: Cold Spring Press, 2003.

Raglan, FitzRoy Richard Somerset, Baron. *The Hero.* Reprint. New York: Dover, 2003.

Robinson, Derek. "The Hasty Stroke Goes Oft Astray: Tolkien and Humour." Robert Giddings (Ed.), *J. R. R. Tolkien: The Far Land.* 108–124. London: Vision Press, Ltd., 1983.

Rogers, Deborah C. "Everyclod and Everyhero: The Image of Man in Tolkien." Jared Lobdell (Ed.), *A Tolkien Compass.* 67–73. Chicago: Open Court, 2003.

Roseburg, Brian. *Tolkien: A Cultural Phenomenon.* New York: Palgrave Macmillan, 2002.

Senior, W. A. "Loss Eternal in J. R. R. Tolkien's Middle-earth." George Clark and Daniel Timmons (Eds.), *J. R. R. Tolkien and His Literary Resonances.* 173–182. Westport, Conn.: Greenwood Press, 2000.

Shippey, Tom. "Another Road to Middle-earth: Jackson's Movie Trilogy." Rose A. Zimbardo and Neil D. Isaacs (Eds.), *Understanding* The Lord of the Rings: *The Best of Tolkien Criticism.* 233–254. Boston: Houghton Mifflin, 2004.

Shippey, Tom. *J. R. R. Tolkien: Author of the Century.* Boston: Houghton Mifflin, 2000.

Shippey, Tom. *The Road to Middle-earth.* Rev. and expanded ed. Boston: Houghton Mifflin, 2003.

Sibley, Brian. The Lord of the Rings *Official Movie Guide.* Boston: Houghton Mifflin, 2001.

Stanton, Michael N. *Hobbits, Elves, and Wizards: Exploring the Wonders and Worlds of J. R. R. Tolkien's* The Lord of the Rings. New York: Palgrave, 2001.

Swanwick, Michael. "A Changeling Returns." Karen Haber (Ed.), *Meditations on Middle-Earth.* New York: St. Martin's Griffin, 2001.

Tolkien, J. R. R. "Letter 246. From a letter to Mrs. Eileen Elgar (drafts). September 1963." Humphrey Carpenter (Ed.), *The Letters of J. R. R. Tolkien.* 325–333. Boston: Houghton Mifflin, 1981.

Tolkien, J. R. R. "Letter 181. To Michael Straight (drafts)." Humphrey Carpenter (Ed.), *The Letters of J. R. R. Tolkien.* pp. 232–237. Boston: Houghton Mifflin, 1981.

Tolkien, J. R. R. "Letter 153. To Peter Hastings (draft). September 1954." Humphrey Carpenter (Ed.), *The Letters of J. R. R. Tolkien.* pp. 187–196. Boston: Houghton Mifflin, 1981.

Tolkien, J. R. R. *The Lord of the Rings: The Fellowship of the Ring.* New York: Ballantine, 1965.

Tolkien, J. R. R. *The Lord of the Rings: The Return of the King.* New York: Ballantine, 1965.

Tolkien, J. R. R. *The Lord of the Rings: The Two Towers.* New York: Ballantine, 1965.

Tolkien, J. R. R. *Poems from* The Lord of the Rings. London: HarperCollins, 2002.

ToyBiz. *Online catalog.* 2004, 14 May 2004. http://www.marvel.com/toybiz/lotr/index.htm.

Tyler, J. E. A. *The Tolkien Companion.* New York: St. Martin's Press, 1976.

Zimbardo, Rose A., and Neil D. Isaacs. (Eds.). *Understanding* The Lord of the Rings: *The Best of Tolkien Criticism.* Boston: Houghton Mifflin, 2004.

Index

About the Author

LYNNETTE R. PORTER is Professor at Embry-Riddle Aeronautical University, where she teaches Honors Literature and Humanities. She is the author of three other books.